PHILOSOPHERS AND THESPIANS

Cultural Memory
in
the
Present

Mieke Bal and Hent de Vries, Editors

PHILOSOPHERS AND THESPIANS
Thinking Performance

Freddie Rokem

STANFORD UNIVERSITY PRESS

STANFORD, CALIFORNIA

Stanford University Press
Stanford, California

© 2010 by the Board of Trustees of the Leland Stanford Junior University. All rights reserved.

No part of this book may be reproduced or transmitted in any form or by any means, electronic or mechanical, including photocopying and recording, or in any information storage or retrieval system without the prior written permission of Stanford University Press.

Printed in the United States of America on acid-free, archival-quality paper

Library of Congress Cataloging-in-Publication Data

Rokem, Freddie, 1945–
　Philosophers and thespians: thinking performance / Freddie Rokem.
　　p. cm. — (Cultural memory in the present)
　Includes bibliographical references and index.
　　ISBN 978-0-8047-6349-3 (cloth : alk. paper)—ISBN 978-0-8047-6350-9 (pbk. : alk. paper)
　　1. Theater and philosophy. 2. Drama—Technique. I. Title. II. Series: Cultural memory in the present.
PN2039.R65 2010
792.01—dc22

2009015734

Typeset by Motto Publishing Services in 11/13.5 Adobe Garamond

To Alma

Engel und Puppe: dann ist endlich Schauspiel
Dann kommt zusammen, was wir immerfort
entzwein, indem wir da sind.
—RAINER MARIA RILKE, *Duineser Elegien*, #4

Angel and puppet: a real play, finally.
Then what we separate by our very presence
Can come together.
—TRANSLATED BY STEPHEN MITCHELL

Contents

Preface   xi

Introduction   1

PART I. ENCOUNTERS

1. The First Encounter: Plato's *Symposium* and the Ancient Quarrel between Philosophy and Poetry   21
2. "Who's There?" Hamlet as Philosopher and Thespian   59
3. Stagings of the Self: The Nietzsche-Strindberg Correspondence   87
4. Walter Benjamin and Bertolt Brecht Discuss Franz Kafka: Exilic Journeys   118

PART II. CONSTELLATIONS

5. Accidents and Catastrophic Constellations: Performative Agendas   141
6. Wishes, Promises, and Threats: The Performative Storytelling of Walter Benjamin   177

Notes   199

Index   219

Preface

> Poetry, therefore, is a more philosophical and a higher thing than history: for poetry tends to express the universal, history the particular.
> —Aristotle, *The Poetics*

This book explores the relationships between the discursive practices of theatre and philosophy by focusing on four concrete and specific encounters between philosophers and thespians. By "thespians," I mean those who in different ways are connected to or actually create theatre and performance. My previous study, *Performing History: Representations of the Past in Contemporary Theatre* (University of Iowa Press, Iowa City, 2000), focused on post–World War II stage productions depicting historical events. In that work I explored the discursive practices of historiography and theatre performances. In this book I address another discursive interaction, between philosophy and theatre/performance, examining and analyzing a much broader range of texts than only performances as such—except for an analysis of Brecht's own production of *Mother Courage and Her Children*.

My sources in this book stem from before the Second World War, beginning with an encounter from the Greek classical period and ending with a dialogue in which Walter Benjamin and Bertolt Brecht discuss a short text by Franz Kafka. The direct encounters I present over the course of the book in turn lead, in the latter part of the book, to a series of reflections on the constellations of philosophy of the theatre as seen from Brecht's perspective and on the performative nature of philosophy as seen from Benjamin's.

As this preface's epigraph shows, Aristotle recognized that poetry is aligned both with philosophy and history, reaching out in two directions to the universal and the particular. I say more about this later. I want to begin by situating this book within discursive frameworks in which I have had the privilege to be and to work during its inception and gradual development. Looking back, it has been an exciting adventure to research and write this book, in particular because of the encouraging remarks and comments from friends, colleagues, and students with whom I have had the opportunity to share my gradually emerging ideas.

First I want to thank my students at Tel Aviv University as well as at the following institutions, where I have had the privilege to teach during this time: Mainz University in Mainz, Germany; Stanford University in Stanford, California; the University of California at Berkeley; the University of Helsinki in Finland; and Freie Universität in Berlin. I also want to thank my many dialogue partners during the various preparation stages of this book. In different ways they all have provided encouragement, assistance, and inspiration: Sharon Aronson-Lehavi, Dafna Ben-Shaul, Linda Ben-Zvi, Herbert Blau, Mateusz Borowski, Daniel Boyarin, Gabriele Brandstetter, Tracy Davis, Harry Elam, Erika Fischer-Lichte, Heidi Gilpin, Richard Gough, Stephen Greenblatt, Kristina Hagström-Ståhl, Dror Harari, Jerry Hewitt, Shannon Jackson, Gad Kaynar, Pirkko Koski, Friedemann Kreuder, Shimon Levy, Jerzy Limon, Jeanette Malkin, Peter Marx, Bruce McConachie, Paul Mendes-Flohr, Hatty Myers, Matthias Naumann, David Nirenberg, Catalin Partenie, Tom Postlewait, Martin Puchner, Alan Read, Janelle Reinelt, Joe Roach, Yvonne Rock, Linda Rugg, Karin Sanders, Helmar Schramm, Ludger Schwarte, David Shulman, Inger Stinnerbom, Leif Stinnerbom, Malgorzata Sugiera, Carl Weber, Christel Weiler, Stephen Wilmer, Brandon Woolf, Bill Worthen, and Nurit Yaari. Thank you all. Stephanie Schulze and Russell Bucher have also been of great assistance. During the years 2006 to 2009, a grant from the Israel Science Foundation partly supported this research, for which I am very grateful.

I also want to express my special thanks to Hent de Vries, the editor of this series, for his deep engagement in the project as well as for his friendship and trust. And to Emily-Jane Cohen at Stanford University Press for her extremely supportive encouragement.

This book is dedicated to Alma, the daughter of Na'ama Rokem and Itamar Francez, niece of Ariel Rokem, and granddaughter of Galit Hasan-Rokem and me. It has been a wonderful experience to see how she is gradually becoming a fully integrated member of our family, the network most intimately and intensively based on encounters, not only between the performative and thinking capacities but of much more. I thank each of you for your individual talents and for your inspiration and support.

PHILOSOPHERS AND THESPIANS

Introduction

> It is characteristic of philosophical writing that it must continually confront the question of representation.
> —Walter Benjamin, *The Origin of German Tragic Drama*

> My grandfather used to say: "Life is astoundingly short. As I look back over it, life seems so foreshortened to me that I can hardly understand, for instance, how a young man can decide to ride over to the next village without being afraid that, quite apart from accidents, even the span of a normal life that passes happily may be totally insufficient for such a ride."
> —Franz Kafka, "The Next Village"

This study examines the interactions between the two discursive practices of philosophy and theatre / performance. I could have set out by raising general issues, on a wide-ranging theoretical level, concerning the multifaceted and extremely complex relationships, sometimes even competition and confrontation, between these discursive practices. Instead I have made a "dramaturgical" decision to focus on four direct encounters between individual representatives of these two fields. These exchanges involve some form of direct contact between the philosophers and individuals engaged in theatrical activities, the "thespians" of my title. The encounters consist of meetings, correspondences, cooperations—even parties—or any other form of direct exchange and dialogue between representatives of these two disciplines, and in one case an interior "dialogue" within a dramatic character. The first section of this book presents the four "Encounters," which besides being examined in the greatest possible detail are also contextualized with the aim of raising more general issues concerning the relations between the two discursive practices as represented by these individuals. The second section, "Constellations," widens the theoretical perspectives at the same time as it focuses more directly on a specific historical context, the years leading up to the Second World War and its beginning. During these years of a gradually intensified crisis, conflict, and destruction, the interactions between philosophy and performance were reformulated in terms that I believe need to be carefully examined so that we might grasp more fully what the stakes are, also today, in the interaction between philosophical and thespian discourses.

In general terms philosophers are concerned with questions of how one should live to achieve happiness. They also ask what sorts of things exist and what their essential nature is, in particular which things are beautiful, what counts as genuine knowledge, and what are the correct principles of reasoning. Thespians—or people working toward the creation of stage performances, for want of a generally accepted, inclusive term—come from a number of different fields and professions, such as playwrights and stage directors; scenographers and designers of costumes; light and sound technicians; as well as the actors who actually "do" the performing by appearing onstage in front of a live audience. The term "thespian" derives from Thespis, the sixth century B.C. poet often credited with inventing Greek tragedy by introducing actors performing the roles of individual characters and spoken dialogue into the traditional choral structure, also legendarily claimed to be the first to appear as an actor. In most cases the thespians I focus on, however, are playwrights and directors, sometimes even both, though some were also involved in other aspects of creative work for the theatre. Discussion of these thespians however would not be complete without touching upon the theories of acting and how they relate to the philosophical ideas developed just before the Second World War.

Encounters between philosophers and thespians have been profoundly informed by different kinds of competition and even outright struggles between their respective modes of discourse. The four examples examined here are no exception. Both partners in these dialogues frequently give vent to a general interest, even a direct desire, to include central aspects of the other's discursive practices within the creative and intellectual endeavors of his own field. Therefore, one of the central aims of this book is to explore how philosophers have tried to embrace thespian modes of expression, appropriating theatrical practices, within their own discursive fields. The book also seeks to explore how the philosophers' thespian partners have frequently applied philosophical tools and modes of thinking in their own work.

The wide range of possibilities for the mobility of and even oscillation between the discursive practices of philosophy and theatre/performance—in both directions—reveals an interesting border landscape, a liminal discursive space situated somewhere "between" the discursive practices of both philosophers and thespians. But as in all fields, any vacuum is always filled by either side of the discursive divide. Therefore this book tries to map this liminal, sometimes even ludic, space in which each partner in the dialogical encounter desires to take over the other's practices. Such encounters are frequently transformed into a competition, even an outright struggle. Some of the examples examined are quite well known and have long and complex histories of reception. Nevertheless this liminal space—as well as the repeated desire of each of the partners to transgress and even invade the more strictly defined borderlines between the philosophical and thespian discursive practices—has remained an almost totally unexplored field of research.[1] My own aim is to shed new light on what has traditionally been perceived as an arena for competition and strife—or for what Plato on several occasions referred to as "the ancient quarrel between philosophy and poetry"[2]—that has been a site not just for expressions of envy and jealousy but for mutual inspiration and productive cross-fertilization as well. This radical ambivalence concerning the communication between the discursive practices of these two fields and their representatives is the first of many reasons that this topic is both abundant and complex.

The discursive practices of each of these professions cannot always be clearly defined or sharply delineated. Alexander Nehamas has claimed that "the boundaries of philosophy have never been absolutely clear: just as at one end, philosophy comes close to mathematics, psychology, and even physics, it slides into literature at the other. But differences still remain."[3] I would also include theatre and performance in Nehamas's notion of "literature." In any case because of their respective and distinct modes of expression, in particular in the case of theatre, which as a rule can be easily and even intuitively apprehended, we are able to make some basic, even ad hoc, distinctions between philosophers and thespians. But at the same time, exactly how (and where) the boundary between their respective discursive practices is situated and how the strife becomes a source of inspiration vary widely in the four cases I examine.

Furthermore some philosophers, having embraced thespian practices within their own discursive regimes, have also confronted—also in the sense of directly challenging—the thespian practices and forms of expression of the professional thespians. Thus while "theatricalizing" their own modes of expression, some philosophers have at the same time argued that the theatre, and its representational practices, is not as inclusive or as "true" as the philosophical modes of discourse. And according to the worst-case scenario, for the thespians as well as for other artists, some philosophers have censored or even banned the theatre and other forms of art, as Plato did, from the ideal society. Yet there are philosophers like Nietzsche for whom classical tragedy represented the most perfect and ideal form of expression, from which, after the demise of this "perfect" form of expression, philosophical thinking was born. In short, because there are many extreme positions, it is impossible to make any sweeping generalizations about the respective positions of philosophical and thespian discourses in their complex relationship to each other. And that is, of course, what finally makes each of the four encounters completely unique but at the same time part of a mosaic of discursive encounters and interactions. The total picture is more complex than the simple sum of the individual encounters.

From the thespian perspective, more conventional forms of theatre, as well as the many other forms of the scripted and embodied practices we generally term "performance art," have made philosophical claims. Thus the thespians in principle also frequently move beyond their own, supposedly more strictly defined, discursive boundaries. Scripted embodiments, in which actors or performers present some form of preconceived or set script for an audience, are a necessary constituent feature of theatre and performance. In certain cases, however, the thespians have attempted to present alternatives to the traditional forms of philosophical discourses. *Oedipus Tyrannus* and *Hamlet*, scripts composed with the intention of performative embodiments on a stage, are my primary examples of thespian discourses that in different ways have critiqued and even "invaded" the discursive space traditionally assigned to philosophical thinking. These dramatic texts have in turn been appropriated and even "used" by generations of philosophers and theoreticians to make claims that go far beyond their "original" status as thespian discourses.

Plato wanted to ban theatrical activities from his ideal state and with them the thespians, who he claimed were not searching for truth because they lacked the tools for such an endeavor. But I do not think there has ever been a thespian who has tried to restrict any form of discourse, including philosophy. On the contrary the theatre has relied on philosophical arguments to alleviate the restrictions and bans that it has suffered from by using philosophical argumentation. An interesting example of this strategy can even be found in some of Plato's own dialogues, which, while they radically critique the theatre, are also theatrical in the deepest sense of this term. Plato's *Symposium* is one of the prime examples of this paradoxical form of discourse, and my first chapter is devoted to a detailed examination of this fascinating text as well as some of its hitherto unrecognized intertexts.

Although the four specific encounters between philosophers and thespians examined in detail set the stage for my central arguments, this book also has an implicit agenda, motivated by the recent debates within the humanities and the arts concerning interdisciplinary border crossings and multidisciplinary dialogues. The relationship between the academic disciplines that focus on the arts, on the one hand, and the forms of thinking and reflection produced by practicing artists, on the other, both within as well as outside of the universities, are of utmost importance. In the more institutional contexts, this issue is directly related to two questions: how can artistic practice be considered a form of research? and what kind of thinking is produced by such artistic and creative practices? These are some of the most urgent issues on the agenda of today's institutions of higher education, in particular in those where the humanities and the arts still play an important role. The institutions in which the arts are given a high priority however seem to be constantly diminishing as new ways to define these relationships are explored. This study therefore examines some of the ways in which performance and theatre "think," as well as how philosophy, in particular as practiced by Walter Benjamin, develops intricate performative strategies. But, as this book points out, it is possible to distinguish performative strategies in the writings of other philosophers as well.

From my own, more academic perspective, cultural studies and critical theory, with their many subdivisions within existing university departments or newly created academic programs, have as a rule been based on the notion that philosophy—in particular what in the United States has been termed "continental philosophy"—constitutes a necessary point of departure for a deepened understanding of cultural processes as well as artistic creativity. But the academic disciplines based on this assumption, including the discipline that, with slightly different variations, calls itself "theatre and performance studies"—to which I am most closely affiliated myself—have not paid sufficient attention to their own disciplinary borders and specificities. Therefore the role of the theories informed by these philosophical systems and ideas often remains unclear.[4] I will however not engage directly in this debate of theories, even if they are an important part of my agenda.

And as I worked on the final version of this book, Harvard University published its *Report of the Task Force on the Arts*. It contains the following telling opening statements:

> To make the arts an integral part of the cognitive life of the university will mean finding new places for art-making—a term which includes performance as well as the fashioning of material and textual objects—within the undergraduate and graduate curricula. It will mean forging new, productive relations between artistic creativity and the creative work of the sciences and engineering. It will mean making contemporary art a subject of vital attention and intellectual interest. It will mean new adventurous spaces where art can be exhibited, made, and performed.[5]

In the context of this book, these issues serve as the backdrop; but they must not be neglected if we want our examination of the two fields of research and creativity to make a significant difference within broader academic and social contexts.

Thus, while also hoping to shed some indirect light on these quite urgent and perhaps more political as well as economic issues—which are also highly charged ideologically—this study examines the four specific encounters between philosophers and thespians from a broad historical perspective, beginning in classical times and ending with the beginning of the Second World War. No claim is made for completeness regarding either of these complex fields of study or the encounters between philosophers and thespians. The first encounter, among Socrates, Agathon, and Aristophanes, which takes place within the semifictional context of Plato's *Symposium*, is no doubt the first meeting among representatives of these two disciplines to have been recorded in detail. Plato's dialogue, depicting the celebration of Agathon's victory at the Lenaean theatre festival in 416 B.C., during which the celebrants present their eulogies of Eros, is both a literary-dramatic masterpiece and an important philosophical tractate. Even though the dialogue relates to a historical event, its literary qualities, in combination with its sophisticated treatment of philosophical ideas, have been the subject of admiration—frequently, even awe—from generations of readers across a number of disciplines.

The reading of the *Symposium* will focus on the two moments in the text in which Plato has explicitly focused our attention on the potential and actual direct communication between Socrates and the two playwrights, and in particular on the different forms of competition between them. The first of these moments takes place immediately after Socrates' own speech eulogizing Eros, in which Socrates presents his intimate dialogues with Diotima about Eros. When Socrates is done, Aristophanes wants to protest against something that Socrates has just said. But because of the dramatic entry of Alcibiades, we never learn what Aristophanes wanted to say. The second exchange, between Socrates and the two playwrights, which I examine in detail, takes place at the very end of the dialogue, when the day is already breaking and Socrates is lecturing to the two exhausted playwrights, arguing that "authors should be able to write both comedy and tragedy: the skillful tragic dramatist should also be a comic poet" (505, 223d).[6]

In both these instances, Plato has excluded certain crucial details from his text concerning the communication between the philosopher and the two playwrights. In the first chapter I present an interpretative approach in which I attempt to explain why this is the case and why Plato, no doubt intentionally, has excluded some crucial information from his own text. To broaden the scope of the interdisciplinary discussion that is the core of this study, I also present a detailed intertextual reading of Plato's dialogue and Sophocles' play *Oedipus Tyrannus*. I emphasize the relationship between the riddle of the Sphinx and Aristophanes' speech in the *Symposium*, both of which are texts that present the number of legs as one of the defining characteristics of the most philosophical of all questions: What is a human? In this case, intertextuality is also a form of encounter.

My second example, Shakespeare's *Hamlet*, is even more emphatically fictional than the *Symposium*. This play has led to a mass of philosophical readings. My own reading argues that, instead of presenting a competition between individual representatives of the two fields as Plato did in the *Symposium*, Shakespeare's play presents an internal strife within the character of Hamlet himself, who aspires to be both a philosopher and a thespian. "Who's There?"—the title of my chapter on *Hamlet*—quotes the first line of the play and serves as the point of departure for my thesis, specifically, that the protagonist of this play is both a philosopher and a thespian, in one person. This desire to be "both" constitutes an integral aspect of Hamlet's individual tragedy, although the play's "authorial" voices (intentionally in the plural, because the ghost is also such a voice) repeat, reinforce, and frequently even subvert the encounters between the philosophical and thespian discourses that the protagonist of this play attempts to create and develop. Hamlet, I argue, becomes a victim of this desire.

No other play, except perhaps *Oedipus Tyrannus*, has been so frequently discussed by a broad range of thinkers who have philosophized about the theatre and its representational apparatus as has *Hamlet*. The paradoxical situation I examine in this study is that the protagonists of these plays, Oedipus and Hamlet, are heroes who philosophize, although in quite different ways, and yet the two plays they appear in can simultaneously be interpreted as a serious critique and as a sophisticated appropriation of philosophical discourses. In the chapter on the *Symposium*, I treat Oedipus as an aspiring philosopher who fails in knowing himself. And in the chapter on *Hamlet*, I examine the philosophical tradition that has appropriated this play for its own purposes. I then present a brief critical examination of the ghost of Hamlet's father as prefiguring a Utopian state of affairs.

After presenting the two "authored" encounters between philosophers and thespians that take place in the *Symposium* and in *Hamlet*, as well as in some of their intertexts, the next two chapters closely examine two encounters that actually took place and have been documented, of Nietzsche and Strindberg, and of Benjamin and Brecht. The short but extremely intense correspondence between Friedrich Nietzsche and August Strindberg began in the fall of 1888 and ended with the onset of Nietzsche's final illness in January 1889. This correspondence can be read as part of a complex performance-dialogue in which both correspondents, in diverse ways, dramatize the elusive borderlines between sanity and madness in their epistolary "stagings" of themselves for the other. The theme of insanity in relation to the communication between the discursive practices of philosophers and thespians can also be seen in both of my previous examples: in particular, in Hamlet's supposedly feigned madness (while Ophelia actually becomes insane) and also in Oedipus's hubris, as well as in the catastrophic consequences of the discovery of his own identity. In the Nietzsche/Strindberg chapter, I connect their respective "stagings" of themselves to other aspects of their oeuvre; in Strindberg's case, to a letter he wrote to Siri von Essen, the actress who was to become his first wife. This letter can be seen as an early blueprint for *A Dream Play*, which Strindberg wrote for his third wife, Harriet Bosse, also an actress. My reading of Nietzsche's *The Birth of Tragedy from the Spirit of Music* as a self-dramatization distills from this formative text a counter-narrative, which I argue has not been sufficiently recognized and which could be characterized as "the birth of the philosopher from the ruins of tragedy."

The last encounter I examine presents certain aspects of the long and multifaceted friendship between Walter Benjamin and Bertolt Brecht. I focus on a particular day in August 1934, during Benjamin's first visit to Skovsbostrand, the small village on the southern shore of the small Danish island of Fyn, where Brecht was living in exile for several years. On this particular day they discussed the short text by Kafka called "The Next Village," or *"Das Nächste Dorf"* (which I quote in this introduction's second epigraph), about the rider who most probably will never reach "the next village." Their respective interpretations, as penned by Benjamin in his diary, present in a remarkably concentrated form the respective positions of Benjamin and Brecht as philosopher and thespian in relation to their perceptions of the state of exile that they were subjected to at the time. Their respective interpretations of Kafka's short text also each serves as a key to Benjamin's philosophy of history as well as to Brecht's theory and practice of the theatre.

The close examination of the Benjamin-Brecht discussion of Kafka's text leads to the second section of the book and its two final chapters, where the discursive border crossings in the work of Brecht and Benjamin are explored in further detail. Brecht's unfinished *Messingkauf Dialogues* were an attempt to cross the border between the two discursive practices by theatricalizing philosophical thinking. Benjamin's likewise unfinished *Arcades Project* (*Das Passagen-Werk*) contains a similar desire, but was conceived from the opposite direction, exploring the performative dimensions of philosophical thinking. The aspects of these monumental projects I examine in detail are Brecht's notion of the "Street Scene," which he developed in an essay of the same name, subtitled, "A Basic Model for an Epic Theatre," as well as his poem "On Everyday Theatre" that was planned to be included in the larger *Messingkauf Dialogues*. These texts focus on the street accident as a primal scene (even in the Freudian sense) for Brecht's model of the theatre. To understand the larger cultural implications of this option, I take a closer look at different aspects of the street accident as it was perceived by writers and thinkers during this time, and in particular how it was appropriated in theories of acting. I also present some quite extraordinary materials connected to a car accident in May 1929, in which Brecht himself was involved.

The second section of this chapter explores Benjamin's notion of the "constellation" in connection with the man-made catastrophes leading up to the Second World War. In particular, I examine the bombings of Guernica and the performative strategies employed to represent them by aesthetic means, through, for example, Picasso's well-known mural *Guernica* as well as through Benjamin's meditation on the Klee painting *Angelus Novus*.

Finally, the last chapter discusses the rhetorical strategies developed by Benjamin in his short prose writings published in various contexts called *Denkbilder*, a genre of writing usually bringing out an abstract, philosophical idea through a short narrative or description. In many of his *Denkbilder* Benjamin created a performativity in a philosophical mode—"performances of the mind" that are "staged" in collaboration with the reader through the interpretation of these texts. This was a time when the world was drawing closer to the catastrophe we now call the Second World War. Benjamin himself was fleeing from place to place until he committed suicide in Port Bou on the Franco-Spanish border in September 1940. In this context, the *Denkbilder* became a form of experimentation, in which the competition between the discursive practices of philosophy and theatre were transformed into a form of expression through which the philosopher becomes a thespian, while at the same time keeping his initial philosophical identity. My study ends at this moment of crisis, recognizing that even if the "performative" as well as "performativity" constituted an important aspect of Benjamin's philosophical practice, he did not have an opportunity to elaborate these ideas more systematically.

The postwar developments in the understanding of the relationship between the discursive practices of philosophy and performance are quite a different story and are not examined in detail. Rather my aim is to present some of the prehistories of these more current debates. However, it is important to draw attention to the fact that when, in the 1950s, the notions of the "performative" and "performativity" enter the philosophical discourses, fictional practices were not embraced. The group of philosophers of language who began to examine the idea that speech (language) is in itself a form of action, speech acts, at least initially rejected fictional discourses, just as Plato had done. J. L. Austin's groundbreaking study *How to Do Things with Words*, which originated as the William James Lectures at Harvard University in 1955, thus expresses a strong suspicion, even animosity, toward the theatre. In this lecture series Austin examined how certain modes of speech "do" things under certain conditions, performing certain actions in and by themselves. But because of the parameters of sincerity that he introduced, the performative usage of speech was restricted to nonfictional discourses. Austin even went so far as to claim that "a performative utterance will, for example, be *in a peculiar way* hollow or void if said by an actor on the stage, or if introduced in a poem, or spoken in soliloquy"[7] (italics added).

This means that the theatre was excluded from being "performative." This line of thinking basically reiterates Plato's critique of the theatre, but from a nonessentialist, pragmatic perspective. In this study I argue that the forms of performativity Austin illuminates and examines by focusing on linguistic expressions, the so-called speech acts, are limiting and in some cases even misleading. My own aim is to reexamine performativity in a broader historical context. I argue that the four encounters between philosophers and thespians presented reveal aspects of the performative and performativity that Austin, as well as his followers, because of their exclusive linguistic interests, obviously did not include in their discussions. It is actually only with the connections between performativity and embodiment made by Judith Butler, in particular in *Antigone's Claim*, that this impasse has been at least partly resolved. In this book Butler has made a great effort to bridge the paradoxical gap between saying and doing within the legal contexts on which Sophocles' play is based, focusing on the question of what it means to make a "claim" both in language as well as in action. Words, Butler argues, are not a substitute for action but "become indissociable from deeds."[8]

In my own study I try to take an additional step toward understanding the interaction and juxtaposition of language and action by examining Benjamin's storytelling practices, and in particular how he relates to the performativity of wishes, promises, and threats. In Benjamin's *Denkbilder* the philosophical and the thespian discourses are not clashing or competing with each other but serve a common purpose, incorporating the reader in a performative scenario that navigates between the constantly recurring catastrophes of history and an imagined Utopia.

In the opening paragraphs of this introduction I defined performance as a form of "scripted embodiment." This means that verbal discourses "activate" the human body in different ways, creating a broad range of activities of "doing," which in classical Greek is the original meaning of the word *drama*: "to do, to act, and to perform." This study attempts to qualify this general claim by drawing attention to additional aspects of performativity and performance, which as a rule have not received attention in discussions of these notions. Besides the Benjaminian wishes, promises, and threats, the competition (the *agon*) also serves as a source for the performative and performativity.[9] Plato's *Symposium* emphasizes the interaction between the human body and a broad range of "scripts" activated by many different forms of competition. Finally, Plato's dialogue "performs" a competition between philosophy—literally embodied by Socrates—and the theatre as represented by the two playwrights, Agathon and Aristophanes. The many layers of competition that come into being and are activated in the discursive border landscapes between philosophy and performance are an expression of the heightened performativity the exchanges between them give rise to. The performativity of the *agon* can even be compared to a play within a play, embedded in a discursive interaction between the philosophical and the performative fields. This in turn draws attention both to the boundaries as well as to the frequent transgressions of these discursive practices.

The idea of positioning theatre and philosophy in relation to each other, creating different forms of competition between them, originated in the classical period. On several occasions Plato referred to "the ancient quarrel between philosophy and poetry." Plato's basic approach is based on a dichotomy that is examined at length in the first chapter of this book. Aristotle on the other hand developed a model of relationships between philosophy and poetry that also included history and historiography. In a well-known passage in Chapter 9 of his *Poetics*, Aristotle argued that the difference between the poet and the historian is not whether one or the other is writing in verse or in prose, but rather that "one relates what has happened, the other what may happen." From this Aristotle draws the following conclusion: "Poetry, therefore, is a more philosophical and a higher thing than history: for poetry tends to express the universal, history the particular."[10] Because they are more closely aligned, this makes the competition between poetry and philosophy much fiercer than the competition between poetry and history. Aristotle presents a broader discursive field because poetry is situated on a spectrum with philosophy and historiography on either side, whereas Plato sets up a direct clash between poetry and philosophy.

Aristotle goes on arguing that the particulars of history are "what Alcibiades did or suffered." In the passage immediately following this mention of Alcibiades, Aristotle makes a detailed comparison between comedy and tragedy with regard to the relationship between the particular and the universal, arguing that in comedy,

the poet first constructs the plot on the lines of probability, and then inserts characteristic names—unlike the lampooners who write about particular individuals. But tragedians still keep to real names, the reason being that what is possible is credible: what has not happened we do not at once feel sure to be possible; but what has happened is manifestly possible: otherwise it would not have happened. Still there are even some tragedies in which there are only one or two well-known names, the rest being fictitious. In others, none are well known—as in Agathon's Antheus, where incidents and names alike are fictitious, and yet they give none the less pleasure. We must not, therefore, at all costs keep to the received legends, which are the usual subjects of Tragedy.[11]

This complex passage has received numerous interpretations as readers have attempted to comprehend what Aristotle meant by claiming that tragedians stick to real names, while writers of comedy first construct their plots and only then insert the names. What interests me in this passage is Aristotle's own mention of names to exemplify his point about philosophy, poetry, and history. According to Gerald F. Else, in spite of seeming like a totally random choice, the mention of Alcibiades is interesting for two reasons: first because according to Aristotle character determines action, but also because Alcibiades appeared as a character in two of Aristophanes' comedies.[12]

I also want to consider the possibility that the issues dealt with in this passage can be read intertextually as a discussion about, or even as Aristotle's polemic response to, Plato's *Symposium*. From his general claim that poetry is more philosophical than is history, Aristotle enters into a brief discussion of the complex relationship between comedy and tragedy with regard to the use of characteristic or real names. As I show in detail later, this double constellation—poetry/philosophy and tragedy/comedy—also figures prominently in the *Symposium*, in which Plato included two playwrights—Aristophanes, the writer of comedies, and Agathon, the writer of tragedies—as Socrates' thespian dialogue partners. But he also includes Alcibiades, the representative of historical action, who arrives after the speeches and in a gesture of deep disappointment and even fury "eulogizes" Socrates. Both in Plato's *Symposium* and in Aristotle's *Poetics*—two foundational texts—the dramatic genres of comedy and tragedy are played out against each other in a discussion that is directly related to the relationship between philosophy and poetry, and directly and indirectly related to exactly the same individuals, with Aristophanes (not mentioned directly by Aristotle) as the playwright who had included not only Alcibiades but also Socrates in his plays.

Whereas Plato focuses on the dichotomous "quarrel" between poetry and philosophy, Aristotle introduces a model for examining discursive practices that also includes history. This is also the crucial difference between Socrates' and Benjamin's appropriation of performative strategies in their philosophical thinking. Socrates tellingly rejects Alcibiades while Benjamin transformed Paul Klee's painting *Angelus Novus* into the angel of history. And Shakespeare's *Hamlet*, with its own complex incorporations of philosophical thinking, marginalizes Fortinbras, the representative of history. These are crucial differences that are not immediately perceived as attention is focused on the interactions between the discursive practices of philosophy and performance. But they are part of my conclusions concerning Benjamin's *Denkbilder* in relation to the tradition to which he belongs, just as they are representative of the intertextualities situated at the crossroads between encounters and constellations, including both philosophy and history.

The journey is another expression of performance and performativity as scripted embodiment that is repeatedly activated in the encounters between philosophers and thespians. It is the journey from one place to another, and in some cases even the exilic, unending journey without a defined goal, except for the need to escape to somewhere else. In all of the four encounters presented, the travelers become inscribed by the road, at the same time as the road becomes an inscription, or a text, announcing both dangers and accidents on the uncertain journey to a desired or fortuitous goal. Benjamin and Brecht discussed Kafka's *The Next Village* ("*Das Nächste Dorf*"), about the rider setting out on a journey from one village to the next who will probably never arrive. Kafka's text reflects the exile they were forced to take on after Hitler's rise to power. And these journeys—the one in Kafka's story as well as those in the plays of Benjamin and Brecht—are then repeated in Brecht's *Mother Courage and Her Children* as well as in Benjamin's *Denkbilder*.

There is a profound relationship between theatre and exile that deserves to be examined in depth. "Exile" is based on the Latin *exilium*, meaning "wanderer"; *diaspora*, with its Greek root for "dispersion," tends toward the idea of "scattering," as do the Hebrew terms *galut* and *gola*. The terms all convey the sense of forced separation of an individual or a collective from "home." Despite important historical and contextual differences among these concepts, they all raise questions about the effect of memories of home and the longing to return.

Thus, for example, the "affliction" called nostalgia—the uncontrollable desire to return home from which soldiers in the battlefield stationed far away from home suffered—was originally a pathological state that frequently led to sudden death. Today nostalgia has rather become a kind of indulgence over things past, but something of the pain, the *algos*, still remains active. Situations of longing for "home" (such as the longing for Moscow, despite the city's closeness to the small town in which Anton Chekhov's *Three Sisters* is set) create a powerful point of departure for dramatic situations and conflicts. Una Chaudhuri has even argued that in Chekhov's drama "the discourse of home is deconstructed to produce the image of a static exilic consciousness," where the characters, as she so pointedly has formulated it, "are not exiled from where they belong but exiled to where they belong."[13]

On the more abstract, spiritual side of the spectrum, the ascent of the soul described by Socrates in the *Symposium* is a spiritual journey, in which the goal is reached by becoming a philosopher. In the intertextual reading presented, this spiritual ascent is shadowed by Oedipus's journey and his unsuccessful quest for his true identity on the roads between Corinth, Delphi, and Thebes, in particular in the quest that takes him to the place where the three roads meet, where he killed Laius, and to Mount Cithaeron, where he was left by his parents in order to be killed by the wild animals. Oedipus is the failed philosopher who does not know himself until it is already too late.

Eros is another recurring bodily inscription in these encounters. Plato's *Symposium* is of course the most obvious example, consisting of six eulogies in praise of Eros. But the encounters presented also contain other kinds of desire and sexual attraction, like the two intimate relationships in *Hamlet*, between Hamlet and Ophelia and between Claudius and Gertrude, which are only examined in passing. And the correspondence between Nietzsche and Strindberg raises a number of issues connected both to homoerotic and heterosexual relationships. In view of the fact that Nietzsche's *The Birth of Tragedy from the Spirit of Music* literally begins with a homoerotic relationship between two gods—Dionysus and Apollo—from which a dramatic genre, tragedy, is born, Eros plays a central role in this text as well. Also we need to pay attention to the fact that in *Die Geburt der Tragödie aus dem Geiste der Musik* (the German title of his book), Nietzsche described an unprecedented birth (*Geburt*), while Benjamin, in *The Origin of German Tragic Drama* (*Ursprung des deutschen Trauerspiels*) depicts a story of origin (*Ursprung*) that is not based on a direct erotic union, but rather consists of a reconstruction of the distant past from which the first leap, or jump—in German the *Sprung*, the *Ur-Sprung*, literally "the first leap"—was made. The eroticism of that moment is melancholic, representing an initial abyssal distance and separation.

That moment is also when the search for what has been lost begins. This is what Aristophanes' story about the missing half in the *Symposium* depicts, reflecting the possibility that the philosopher and the thespian can reunite in one person, as an ideal conceptual construction of the mythical origins of the two discursive practices. Plato even tries to reproduce this construction by writing a text about such a reunification. And, argues Benjamin, we need the spiritual-intellectual instrument of memory to gain access to such a point of origin, where it supposedly began, and to which we can hopefully find our way back again. Or as Benjamin formulated this process in one of the texts he wrote before his suicide, "by appropriating memory as it flashes up in a moment of danger."[14] The journey to the present from that past, and the memory that will make it possible to find the way back, is of course a narrative construction, just like Benjamin's own stories (and this book). But it is my hope that by making such a journey, it is possible to enhance the understanding of where we are now and what the dangers of our own moment in history are. Or as my own mother has repeatedly reminded me by using the proverb that—as I discovered much later—also appears in Benjamin's "The Storyteller," published in 1936: "Wenn jemand eine Reise tut, dann kann er was erzählen" (When someone makes a journey, he has a story to tell).

The inevitable caesura between making the journey and the moment of telling the story is the magnifying glass and the nexus through which the encounters between the philosophers and thespians are examined. These encounters enable us to raise the issues of if and in what sense the respective discursive practices are the lost half of each other, without any claims of hierarchy and primacy, just as Aristophanes' tale about Eros does, telling about the constant search for the missing half. And after discussing the four encounters, I make my own caesura, moving from the notion of the encounter to that of the constellation. This caesura is not based on a dichotomy between two discursive practices but on multileveled and intertextual juxtapositions of cultural practices and critical discourses. The cultural practices of the encounters gradually progress into the constellations of the critical discourses, reflecting the gradually accelerating sense of crisis and the violence leading up to the Second World War. This "state of emergency" or "exception" makes it necessary for Benjamin to reformulate and, even in a sense, reinvent the discursive practices of the philosopher and the performer by actually becoming a storyteller. And because Benjamin himself never told us the story from his own last journey, as the proverb he quotes proposes, what I finally wish to present is a firmer grasp of these changes. And only then can we go on to talk about the postwar era.

PART ONE

ENCOUNTERS

1

The First Encounter

PLATO'S *Symposium* AND THE ANCIENT QUARREL
BETWEEN PHILOSOPHY AND POETRY

> And then I came to the place where three roads meet.
> —Sophocles, *Oedipus Tyrannus*
>
> Crito, we ought to offer a cock to Asclepius. See to it, and don't forget.
> —Socrates' last words as reported in the *Phaedo*

The earliest encounter between a philosopher and thespians that has been recorded in detail is Socrates' meeting with the playwrights Agathon and Aristophanes. It takes place in Plato's dialogue the *Symposium*, where the banquet celebrating Agathon's victory at the Lenaean theatre festival in 416 B.C. is depicted. Plato portrayed in vivid detail the select group of Athenians gathered in Agathon's house during the second night after his triumph. Through this portrayal, in particular he drew attention not only to the speeches eulogizing Eros presented on this occasion but also to the setting and the interactions among the participants at the event. The *Symposium* is an outstanding example of Plato's abilities as a dramatic writer. Diogenes Laërtius even claimed that before turning to philosophy, Plato had been both a wrestler and a writer of tragedies: "He wrestled in the Isthmian Games—this is stated by Dicaearchus in his first book *On Lives*—and that he applied himself to painting and wrote poems, first dithyrambs, afterwards lyric poems and tragedies."[1] In the *Symposium* Plato has employed sophisticated narrative techniques and dramatic devices to promote Socrates' philosophical ideas. However, at the same time, he has distanced himself from his admired teacher, and even severely criticized him.

Among Plato's dialogues the *Symposium* clearly stands out as an excellent example of literary sophistication. Highlighted are the philosophical and ideological contents of the eulogies praising Eros and what they represent within the framework of the dialogue as well as within classical Greek culture (including examples from its rich corpus of dramatic literature). In addition the complex relationships between the speakers themselves and their behavior have been sharply placed in focus. These minute details are an integral aspect of Plato's text, tightly weaving philosophical arguments and human behavior together, making them reflect and comment on each other simultaneously on many levels. The depiction of the encounter between philosophical and theatrical practices in the *Symposium* presents a showdown or a competition between the two practices, directly exemplified by the interactions between Socrates and the two playwrights Agathon and Aristophanes. Furthermore attention is drawn to the characteristics of their respective discursive practices as well as to their complex personal relationships. Plato's dialogue weaves philosophical and literary issues together in complex juxtapositions that this chapter highlights from several vantage points.

Finally, however, I hope to show that the *Symposium* contains contradictory tensions that can probably never be fully resolved. At the same time as the *Symposium* (as an instance of Plato's more comprehensive anti-aesthetic stance) directs a sophisticated attack against the two playwrights and the practices of theatre in general, by using sophisticated literary and dramatic techniques, it creates a comprehensive discursive universe, evoking intra- and intertextual intersections where the competitors become integrated within the constantly expanding dialogical encounter examined in this book. Plato ends the *Symposium* with a direct confrontation between Socrates, his philosopher-hero, on the one hand, and both Agathon, who wrote tragedies (though none of them have been preserved), and Aristophanes, who wrote comedies, on the other. This fact has major implications for the interactions between the philosophical and the thespian discourses, not only within the dialogue itself, but also within the more comprehensive philosophical and performative contexts highlighted. Finally, though in a very sophisticated and implicit manner, Plato also raises some serious doubts concerning Socrates' philosophical authority as well as the integrity of his character. In order to untangle these complex contradictions, I begin by examining the ways in which the narrative techniques of the *Symposium* serve as a reflection of Plato's philosophical ideas.

Philosophy and Narrative Technique

The *Symposium* is a brilliant poetic demonstration of Plato's philosophy, showing that narratives are nothing but faint shadows of the events they depict (or are about), just as the objects in this world—like for example the chairs and the tables in our homes and classrooms, according to Plato's theory of Ideas—are nothing but faded copies of the eternal Ideas of these objects. The narrative techniques of the *Symposium* mirror this philosophical argument, showing in effect that not even Plato's own philosophical dialogue can fully represent the truth. The narrative presented in the dialogue is a report given by Apollodorus to an unknown interlocutor about the celebration in honor of Agathon. Apollodorus's report is based on what Aristodemus, who was present at the party, has previously reported to Apollodorus. And since Apollodorus had just given an account of this celebration to another interlocutor called Glaucon a few days earlier, he says that "your question does not find me unprepared" (458, 172a)[2] to tell what happened at the "gathering at Agathon's when Socrates, Alcibiades, and their friends had dinner together [and tell] about the speeches they made on Love" (458, 172 b).

In the opening section of the *Symposium*, Apollodorus carefully informs his interlocutor (and us) that he had heard about these events from Aristodemus, one of Socrates' ardent admirers, who had accompanied Socrates to the celebration (in Apollodorus's careful formulation) "because, I think, he was obsessed with Socrates—one of the worst cases at that time" (459, 173b). Through its narrative technique—having one narrator present a report he has heard from another narrator—the dialogue is actually twice removed from the banquet that took place in Agathon's house during the second night after his victory, which is the actual event, the "source" depicted in the dialogue. This corresponds to how Plato relates to works of art as being twice removed (just like the second night) from the truth, being copies of copies. This, he argues—for example, in book 10 of the *Republic*—is their essential flaw.

If Plato, on the other hand, had chosen to portray the events of the banquet in a purely dramatic form, which he did in many of his other dialogues, the narrative would of course not have reflected the Platonic theory of Ideas in this particular way. In its present form, the dialogue presents Apollodorus's knowledge about the events of the banquet after Agathon's victory as an epistemological investigation in literary form based on a complex chain of testimonies, transmitting knowledge about some "primal" truth. Such knowledge has to rely on earlier sources, which in some cases and for different reasons cannot be fully trusted. The narrators in Plato's text (and indirectly Plato himself) openly admit that their memory is not always completely reliable. Before the first speech eulogizing Eros, presented by Phaedrus, Apollodorus even says: "Of course Aristodemus couldn't remember exactly what everyone said, and I myself don't remember everything he told me. But I'll tell you what he remembered best, and what I consider the most important points" (463, 178a). After presenting what Phaedrus had said in his speech, Apollodorus adds: "There followed several other speeches which he couldn't remember very well. So he skipped them and went directly to the speech of Pausanias" (465, 180c). Plato thus openly admits that there were participants and speakers at the banquet that the dialogue, as he himself has composed it, does not account for at all.

Plato has thus composed a dialogue wherein Apollodorus, the narrator, can give only a partial account of what happened at the banquet, based on the already partial report given by Aristodemus. Furthermore, as many critics have already pointed out, Socrates repeats this basic narrative gesture of relying on an earlier source by quoting Diotima's explanations about Eros and thus transmitting her knowledge about Eros to the men assembled around the table. This creates an important gender shift in the dialogue, because after the women had been sent away in the beginning of the evening to enable the men to talk about Eros, Socrates reintroduces Diotima, a woman, as his own ultimate authority with regard to Eros. But since this report is contained within Apollodorus's report, it potentially suffers from the same incompleteness that the report as a whole (namely, the dialogue as Plato composed it) intentionally is subjected to by Plato himself, as the ultimate author(ity) of this text. And as I will show later, there is an additional detail in Socrates' report, from his conversations with Diotima, that even undermines his reliability and the philosophical core of the whole dialogue.

In both these cases—in Apollodorus's as well as in Socrates' account of what they have heard from others—Plato, by drawing detailed attention to the technicalities of the transmission of knowledge, radically problematized the ways in which oral reports and oral wisdom serve as a source of knowledge. The issue of Plato's written representation of Socratic philosophy is far too extensive to be examined in detail, but it is noteworthy that when Eryximachus proposes that the participants at the celebration should each praise Eros, he significantly adds, "If you agree, we can spend the whole evening in discussion, because I propose that each of us give as good a speech in praise of Love as he is capable of giving" (462, 177c–d). Thus what Plato has penned is not only the oral philosophy of Socrates, but an event focusing on the spoken word—the "discussion"—that is transmitted through an intricate narrative chain.

Plato has reconstructed a situation in which, besides basing the narrative on Aristodemus's partial report, he emphasizes that Apollodorus has also checked the details with Socrates himself to see if he has gotten them right (and this raises an interesting issue that I return to later). Furthermore Apollodorus mentions that only a few days before he tells his anonymous interlocutor about the banquet, he had told Glaucon about it. As it happens, Glaucon had already heard about it from another person, who in his turn had heard about it from someone called Phoenix. And Phoenix had mistakenly conveyed to this unnamed person that Apollodorus was also present at the banquet celebrating Agathon. This Apollodorus quickly refutes because, as he says, he was very young when the banquet itself took place. Plato has repeatedly interspersed small details drawing attention to the fact that the reports are unreliable approximations. And this is just as he claims in several other contexts that the copies of Ideas are unreliable with regard to the true nature of the Ideas themselves. In this respect the *Symposium* is quite radical because it indirectly questions Socrates' philosophical practices by drawing attention to the unreliability of oral reports as they are presented in the *Symposium*.

In the *Symposium* Plato presents a radical critique of mimetic representation by pointing at its limitations, not by providing a direct philosophical critique as was done in many other contexts, most notably in the *Republic*. Instead Plato has gone to great pains to point out that all of the narrators / reporters—including Socrates himself—are only able to present a partial or slanted report of what really happened at the banquet, or in Socrates' case during his meetings with Diotima. Thus this shows through the narrative technique itself that not only do narratives and dramatic representations fail to fully reveal or represent the truth, but philosophical ideas are subject to such limitations as well. Following Plato's own philosophical ideas about art and mimesis, the narrative told by Apollodorus as it is presented in the dialogue—and to be exact, this report is actually what the dialogue consists of—is a faded, twice-removed copy of the real events of the banquet. Thus what Plato actually shows in the *Symposium* is how the acquisition, the reproduction, and the transmission of knowledge depend on a complex narrative genealogy, a chain reaching backward to a source or an origin, just as, according to Plato, the objects in the world as we know them have their source or origin in the eternal Ideas, but without these objects being able to fully represent this origin.

The notions of genealogy and origin as problematized by Plato in the *Symposium* have several important implications for this study. Nietzsche and Benjamin, as well as Brecht, have in different ways formulated how tragedy, performance, and even philosophy were to be established as discursive practices. In *The Birth of Tragedy from the Spirit of Music*, Friedrich Nietzsche's tragedy was conceived as a biological birth (*Geburt*). Walter Benjamin mobilized Plato's *Symposium* as his template for the epistemological foundations, on the basis of which he investigates the German Tragic Drama and reconstructs its origin (*Ursprung*) in *The Origin of German Tragic Drama*. Bertolt Brecht's notion of the Epic theatre as presented, in 1938, in his essay "The Street Scene: Towards a Basic Model for an Epic Theatre" comes closest to the notion of a chain of transmission of reports or testimonies like that depicted in the *Symposium*. According to Brecht, the Epic theatre originates from a situation in which "an eyewitness [is] demonstrating to a collection of people how a traffic accident took place."[3] In Plato's dialogue the events at the banquet have been passed from Aristodemus, the direct witness, to Apollodorus who, after having actively verified the events with Socrates, is seen as a secondary witness, just as the spectators, according to Brecht, learn from the eyewitness report and then pass it on to other listeners, adding their own comments and conclusions, so that, according to Brecht's formulation, the "bystanders are able to form an opinion about the accident."[4]

The carefully designed opening section of the *Symposium*, which explores and examines the genealogy of the report about the banquet, serves as a warning. Although the text is composed by Plato himself, not all of its details can be fully trusted. In this instance it is even possible to talk about a "Platonic irony" through which Plato, at the same time as he presents Socrates as the source of true philosophical knowledge, undermines his own reliability through the use of this complex narrative technique of oral transmission. As I show in detail shortly, this radical ambiguity, indeterminacy in fact, between what actually happened at the party and the consciously limited possibilities of Plato's philosophical dialogue to give a full report about it, comes to a head in the very last section of the dialogue.

After its investigatory beginning, the dialogue moves into a dramatic mode of presentation in which the speeches held at the banquet are presented as direct quotes. In this section, fully using the dialogue form in the generic sense, presenting the speeches by the individuals that were supposedly present at the party, the question of reliability is not raised with the same urgency as it was in the more directly transmitted report in the opening section. In the narrative closure of the dialogue, however, where Apollodorus returns as a narrator whose presence is apparent in the text, the issues of reliability are reiterated, this time directly confronting the relations between philosophy and theatre, not only on the structural and narrative levels but also through the direct encounter between Socrates and the two playwrights.

The Ending of the *Symposium*

The *Symposium* ends with a discussion between Socrates, Agathon, and Aristophanes about drama.[5] Like the speeches eulogizing Eros, the discussion is not reported in detail. Plato returns to the form of narration with which he opened the dialogue, but with an additional twist. As a matter of fact we hardly learn anything about this discussion except that it took place as the morning was already approaching—after the more formal part of the banquet, with the speeches praising Eros, was over; after Alcibiades had presented his ferocious attack on Socrates; and after most of the guests had already left. This discussion, in which Socrates "was trying to prove to them that authors should be able to write both comedy and tragedy: the skillful tragic dramatist should also be a comic poet" (505, 223d), served as the finale of the intensive night of discussions and speeches. And it is central both for my interpretation of Plato's dialogue and the encounters between philosophers and thespians.

Apollodorus openly admits that his report about the conversation between the philosopher and the two playwrights during these early morning hours is incomplete, as during this final conversation "he [Aristodemus, from whom Apollodorus got the report] fell asleep and slept for a long time (it was winter, and the nights were quite long). He woke up just as dawn was about to break; the roosters were crowing already" (504, 223c). And then, according to Apollodorus, Aristodemus realized that he had only heard the key point of what Socrates had told the two dramatists, and he "couldn't remember exactly what they were saying—he'd missed the first part of their discussion, and he was half-asleep anyway" (505, 223d). However Aristodemus had reported to Apollodorus that he noticed Socrates was getting Agathon and Aristophanes to agree that the same man should be capable of writing both comedy and tragedy. "He was about to clinch his argument, though, to tell the truth, sleepy as they were, they were hardly able to follow his reasoning. In fact Aristophanes fell asleep in the middle of the discussion and very soon thereafter, as day was breaking, Agathon also drifted off" (505, 223d).

This is certainly quite a remarkable passage. The discussion about the two dramatic genres between Socrates, the philosopher-hero of Plato's dialogues, and the two dramatists—Agathon, the successful and apparently very handsome tragedian, and Aristophanes, the famous author of comedies—is totally clouded in a concoction of alcohol and fatigue. Neither Aristodemus, the person on whose testimony Apollodorus's (and our) knowledge of these events finally depends, nor the two dramatists themselves, who were supposed to learn something important from Socrates' arguments, were able to hear what Socrates had actually said and what his reasons for his claims were.[6]

This lack of information from the final moments of the banquet, just before the sun rises, is sharply contrasted with the opening passages of the *Symposium*, wherein Plato very minutely has drawn our attention to the fact that the report Apollodorus has received from Aristodemus is supposedly based on his careful observation of everything that took place. Only later do we learn that Aristodemus has not been able to memorize everything that was said and that he does not even report all the speeches at the celebration. The remarkable detail we learn is that during the early morning hours, as Socrates was discussing tragedy and comedy with the two playwrights, Aristodemus fell asleep. But even if this was the case, Apollodorus could have complemented the missing information from this discussion by asking Socrates himself. Because even if Apollodorus did not get the information about the banquet directly from Socrates, he had been able to check—after initially having heard about it from Aristodemus—"part of his story with Socrates, and Socrates agreed with his account" (459, 173 b). Plato obviously went to great effort to convince his readers that Apollodorus got all the details right, checking at least part of them with Socrates, which means that the account given by Apollodorus in the dialogue itself is primarily based on what he heard directly from Aristodemus. According to the fiction Plato has created, Socrates has, for some reason, not provided any information about his discussion with the two playwrights, only confirming that what Apollodorus had heard from Aristodemus was correct.

However, if Plato had wanted Apollodorus to be able to say something about what Socrates told the two playwrights about the relationship between comedy and tragedy, while they as well as Aristodemus were sound asleep, he could have given Socrates the opportunity to provide the necessary additions when Apollodorus checked the details with him. On the one hand Plato obviously chose to prevent Apollodorus (and us) from knowing the particulars of the final discussion about comedy and tragedy, just as Aristophanes and Agathon were too tired to listen to Socrates' arguments, and fell asleep. Thus we are left with nothing but the knowledge that this important conversation took place and an understanding of its main point about writers of comedy and tragedy. Plato, as the author of the *Symposium*, has in a sense even indirectly discredited Socrates for not supplying Apollodorus with these additions.

Plato's dialogue intentionally hides something that is crucial for the understanding of some of the larger issues that it raises. What did Socrates say to the two dramatists that they as well as Aristodemus were too tired and/or too drunk to hear? And why did Plato so carefully and even artfully erase these details from the final moments of the dialogue, where supposedly Socrates' final triumph over the two dramatists took place? Since the ending of the *Symposium* is constructed as the final contest in a series of consecutive and overlapping competitions, obviously, in this case too—that is, in the discussion with the two playwrights, as in the contest of speeches eulogizing Eros—Socrates was the final victor, making a point that must have devastated the playwrights both intellectually and creatively—as well as physically. He stayed awake whereas they had obviously fallen asleep.

Socrates possesses both the intellectual capacity and the physical strength to overcome his opponents on every possible level. He gets the privilege of telling the two playwrights that each one of them should know the craft of the other, although it seems that it is actually Socrates himself who knows how to combine tragedy and comedy in one inclusive, philosophical discourse. What the *Symposium* therefore implies, even if the dialogue itself does not state this directly, is that Socrates' philosophy, both in form and content, is able to unify the elements of comedy and tragedy, whereas the work of the two playwrights, each one representing only one genre, is incomplete. This is apparently the central point in Socrates' lecture to the two playwrights. Moreover by unifying two distinct and separate parts into the full "androgyne totality" of the philosophical discourse, Socrates is also, as I show in detail below, setting up an argument with Aristophanes' speech at the party.

In the *Symposium* Socrates talks to the sleeping playwrights about a unification of comedy and tragedy. This argument, the details of which we remain ignorant, is diametrically opposed to the views about poetry and drama presented by Socrates in the *Republic*, but the possibility that Aristodemus misunderstood Socrates' main point seems out of the question. Therefore it is difficult to understand why in the *Republic*, Socrates quotes himself (because he is also the narrator of this dialogue) as having said,

> Then he'll hardly be able to pursue any worthwhile way of life while at the same time imitating many things and being an imitator. Even in the case of two kinds of imitation that are thought to be closely akin, such as tragedy and comedy, the same people aren't able to do both of them well. . . . Nor can they be both rhapsodes and actors . . . Indeed, not even the same actors are used for tragedy and comedy. . . . And human nature, Adeimantus, seems to me to be minted in even smaller coins than these, so that it can neither imitate many things well nor do the actions themselves, of which those imitations are likenesses. (1032–1033, 394e–395b)[7]

Pronouncements like this—and there are quite a few of them in the *Republic* as well as in several other Platonic dialogues—are part of an animosity toward the arts and toward the theatre and the art of acting in particular that is much more direct than the views presented in the *Symposium*, which celebrates the theatre rather than arguing against it.[8] In book 10 of the *Republic*, when Socrates is arguing that poetry should be banned from the ideal *polis*, he asks us "in case we are charged with a certain harshness and lack of sophistication" to "tell poetry that there is an ancient quarrel between it and philosophy" (1211, 607b). However, at the same time, he continues, "If the poetry that aims at pleasure and imitation has any argument to bring forward that proves it ought to have a place in a well-governed city, we at least would be glad to admit it, for we are well aware of the charm it exercises" (1211, 607c). This ambivalence toward the arts cannot be easily accommodated.[9]

Furthermore both the *Symposium* and the *Republic* depict a nightly scene of philosophizing that takes place after the main participants have attended a festival. In the case of the *Republic* they have made a journey from which they are returning. In the *Symposium* they are celebrating Agathon's victory in the Lenaean theatre festival. But even if the attitude toward the arts and, for obvious reasons, the ways in which the arts are referred to differ strongly in these dialogues, both the *Symposium* and the *Republic* combine the visit to the festival with a philosophical discussion about art, and theatre in particular. This collocation between visiting a festival and philosophizing further strengthens the semantic family relations between *theoria* and *theatron*. Andrea Wilson Nightingale has argued that in "the effort to conceptualize and legitimize theoretical philosophy, the fourth-century thinkers invoked a specific civic institution: that which the ancients called "*theoria*." In the traditional practice of *theoria*, an individual (called the *theoros*) made a journey or pilgrimage abroad for the purpose of witnessing certain events and spectacles."[10] This in effect means that philosophizing as a discursive practice developed and flourished in the wake of attending performances and of having made a journey to attend them. And this idea, that the experience of the theatre and the scene of philosophizing are connected by having made, or actually having been in the middle of, such a journey, is central for this study as a whole; it is its substratum.

Both the *Symposium* and the *Republic* are retold by a narrator, which means that the reader is not "witnessing" the events directly (as in a dramatic text). Instead a report of the events is delivered through the mediation of a narrator. As examined in detail already, Apollodorus, the narrator of the *Symposium*, was not present at the event that he is recounting to his interlocutor and to the readers of this dialogue. In the *Republic*, on the other hand, it is Socrates himself who tells "us" how a group of people had assembled in the home of Glaucon. This could even be the same Glaucon who Apollodorus in the *Symposium* had told about the banquet celebrating Agathon's victory a few days before Apollodorus tells it to his anonymous interlocutor (and to us). In the *Republic*, however, Socrates is both the narrator and the leading character of the dialogue. This means that in the *Republic* it is impossible to create situations in which the details of an important argument like "knowing how to compose comedies and knowing how to compose tragedies must combine in a single person" can be hidden behind a veil of intoxication and fatigue like in the *Symposium*.

In Plato's *Laws* there is also a direct reference to this issue. Here the Athenian, the leader of the argument in this dialogue, almost in accordance with the claim made by Socrates at the end of the *Symposium*, argues, "If we intend to acquire virtue, even on a small scale, we can't be serious and comic too, and this is precisely why we must learn to recognize buffoonery, to avoid being trampled by our ignorance of it into doing or saying anything ridiculous when there's no call for it. Such mimicry must be left to slaves and hired aliens, and no one must ever take it at all seriously."[11] The speaker emphasizes the necessity to learn or know both comedy and tragedy, but "not" to combine them, as opposed to what Socrates apparently recommended in the *Symposium*. In *Laws* the argument is that slaves and hired strangers should learn to imitate "such things" only as a reminder of their lack of virtue.

The Competitions

The Platonic dialogues integrate dramatic-theatrical modes of writing within the philosophical discourse—and in this context it is not important if they present Plato's own views or those of Socrates—at the same time as they frequently argue for a ban of the arts (and in particular the theatre) from the ideal *polis*. Therefore the pronouncements about drama and theatre do not have to be fully consistent.[12] But these ambiguities or ambivalences toward the discursive practices of philosophy and the theatre only present a partial solution to the constantly recurring dilemmas that Plato's dialogues pose. In the *Symposium* the interactions between these discursive practices are triggered by the complex network of competitions beginning with the playwriting and the competition between the guests as to who can present the most worthy praise of Eros. And this competition gradually triggers a competition between competitions, giving rise to a kind of meta-competition. While the guests are competing among themselves, Plato presents a competition between Socrates and Agathon/Aristophanes as representatives of the philosophical and thespian discursive practices.

The competition, or the *agon*—which in classical Greek culture meant the competitive demonstration of skill in everything from boxing to flute playing to the gaining of erotic favors—could also be constituted by the argumentation between the characters in a play, moving the action forward through words. The competition can also assist us in shedding light on the relations between the discursive practices of philosophy and theatre/performance. In the *Symposium* the encounter between philosophy and theatre/performance can be seen as such an *agon*, highlighting the performative aspects of philosophy and philosophical thinking. Plato's Socrates performs philosophy in a competitive spirit and he is obviously the ultimate winner in all of the competitions the dialogue presents, the intellectual as well as the physical ones. But at the same time that he is gloriously victorious, he also stumbles.

The *Symposium* consists of a tightly woven network of competitions. The public playwriting competition Agathon has won is celebrated with another, this time domestic, contest in which the participants are competing by presenting eulogies praising Eros in Agathon's home. Both the playwriting competition and the speech contest focus on the use of spoken language. They constitute the performative backbone of Plato's dialogue, reflecting an important aspect of a cultural scene in which competitions—not only of the physical prowess of sport and warfare, but of intellectual ability, and in particular the use of language for the sake of persuasion—develop into a central mode of expression and communication. To the playwriting competition and the speech contest, the *Symposium* adds a metacontest, foregrounding the "ancient dispute between philosophy and poetry," in which poetry competing with philosophy is represented by drama and playwriting. Thus Plato's dialogue actually depicts a contest, that of drama and playwriting, between two other contests—the thespian playwriting competition and the eulogies. Socrates' final philosophical arguments in his report from his conversations with Diotima lead to the ultimate "showdown," in which Socrates reproaches the two exhausted playwrights for the limitations of their own particular individual skills: they know how to write only either tragedy or comedy.

The *Symposium* can be viewed as a multileveled expression of this competitive spirit, with Plato's text in itself, both in form and content, literally "performing" the contest between philosophy and drama, crowning Socrates the philosopher, who through the philosophical discourse is apparently capable of combining the two genres. He is the ultimate winner of all the contests, including the competition between philosophy and poetry. The multileveled interactions created by these competitions, gradually building up to what I have termed the final "showdown" at the end of the dialogue—in which Socrates points out the limitations of the two playwrights—are an important, though not sufficiently recognized aspect of the notion of "performativity" itself. Competitions, in all their forms, are actually an important expression of performativity. The *Symposium*, at the same time as it is critiquing the existent forms of the dramatic *agon*, pointing out the inherent limitations in its capacity for being either tragic or comic, and not both, presents a mode of discourse competing with the drama through the philosophical discourse personified by Socrates himself. The genre of the symposium actually implies such a multileveled discourse of competitions.[13]

There is however no explicit announcement that the guests gathered around the table are to compete through their speeches praising Eros. Nobody openly declares that a competition is going to take place. But it is no doubt implied in the words of Eryximachus, who quotes Phaedrus with regard to the lack of praise for Eros, and therefore suggests that "each of us give as good a speech in praise of Love as he is capable of giving" (462, 177d). It is actually Socrates himself who first explicitly remarks that all the speeches are part of such a competition. After Aristophanes has presented his praise of Eros through the story of the three forms of the androgynes (four-legged creatures), Eryximachus, who together with Phaedrus, has taken the role of "referee," says that "if I couldn't vouch for the fact that Socrates and Agathon [the only ones yet to have made their speeches] are masters of the art of love, I'd be afraid that they'd have nothing left to say" (476, 193e). And when Eryximachus adds that he is sure they have certainly not run out of things to say, Socrates retorts "That's because *you* did beautifully in the contest,[14] Eryximachus. But if you ever get in my position, or rather the position I'll be in after Agathon's spoken so well, then you'll really be afraid. You'll be at your wit's end, as I am now" (476–477, 194a). Obviously, with this carefully measured ironic comment, Socrates aspires to become the victor of the speech contest.

Agathon responds that Socrates' words are no doubt aimed at making him even more nervous. And responding to this remark, Socrates makes an explicit comparison between the competition of speeches in praise of Eros that they are involved in and the playwriting competition that took place a few days earlier, in which Agathon was the winner: "How forgetful do you think I am? I saw how brave and dignified you were when you walked right up to the theatre platform along with the actors and looked straight out at that enormous audience" (477, 194b). To this Agathon retorts, "You must think that I have nothing but theatre audiences on my mind! So you suppose I don't realize that, if you're intelligent, you find a few sensible men much more frightening than a senseless crowd?" (477, 194b). Because this exchange between Socrates and Agathon is actually also part of the *agon*, Socrates quickly responds to Agathon's flattery, asking him ironically if he does not include Socrates himself among the ordinary people, because, as Socrates says, "we were at the theatre too, you know, part of the ordinary crowd." At that point Phaedrus intervenes, asking Agathon to begin his speech, because "if you answer Socrates, he'll no longer care whether we get anywhere with what we're doing here, so long as he has a partner for discussion. Especially, if he's handsome" (477, 194c–d). This comment, even if it supposedly was Phaedrus who intervened, implicitly expresses a criticism of Socrates by Plato for manipulating the speech competition by his repeated remarks and interventions. These manipulations are an integral aspect of the competition itself.

Alcibiades, who only arrives after Socrates has presented his speech and who therefore was not present during this short conversation, is also deeply aware of Socrates' competitive personality. Because Alcibiades was quite drunk when he arrived and because the garland he is wearing "slipped over his eyes" (495, 213a) before he placed it on Agathon's head, he did not notice Socrates' presence among the guests. However a while after his dramatic entry, realizing that Socrates was also present at the party and actually sitting next to him, Alcibiades asks Agathon to return the garland he had given him for his victory in the playwriting competition. "I'd better make a wreath for him [that is, for Socrates] as well—look at that magnificent head! Otherwise"—Alcibiades continues—"he'll make a scene. He'll be grumbling that, though I crowned you for your first victory, I didn't honor him even though he has never lost an argument in his life" (495, 213e). Alcibiades implies that Socrates wins philosophical arguments through everyday battles of words rather than through the more confined tragic competitions. In this way he directs attention to the contest between the playwriting and the speech competitions that constitute the performative backbone of Plato's dialogue.

All of this, Alcibiades says, is motivated by jealousy. Socrates "hasn't allowed me to say two words to anybody else . . . I can't so much as look at an attractive man but he flies into a fit of jealous rage" (495, 213d). And before beginning his own speech, Alcibiades asks if "it's fair to put my drunken ramblings next to your sober orations?" (496, 214c). The solution to this problem, Eryximachus suggests, is that Alcibiades will "offer an encomium to Socrates" (496, 214e). Alcibiades, in his theatrical, "Dionysian" state promises to tell the truth, thereby at the same time transforming Socrates into a divine figure, the supreme exemplar of Eros himself. Socrates not only stands out as the winner of all the verbal competitions, he becomes transformed into the divine figure all the others have already been praising, implicitly personifying his own quest, assisted by Diotima, as the realization of himself as philosophical Eros.

All the competitions are also tightly woven together with the competition between Agathon and Alcibiades for the erotic attention of Socrates, a competition Socrates distances himself from. After his dramatic entry and the discovery that Agathon is actually lying beside Socrates, Alcibiades even accuses Socrates of playing one of his usual tricks, saying that "you always do this to me—all of a sudden you'll turn up out of anywhere where I least expect you!" (495, 213c). In Plato's dialogue it is actually Alcibiades who turns up unexpectedly, asking, "Why aren't you with Aristophanes or anyone else we would tease you about? But no, you figured out a way to find a place next to the most handsome man in the room!" (495, 213c). Alcibiades' ensuing speech is a litany of accusations against Socrates for not having responded to his continuous efforts to seduce him. Seduction and the speeches praising Eros are two sides of the same coin, but with diametrically opposed goals.

With regard to the expressions and practices of erotic relations between men, Pausanias's speech, earlier in the *Symposium*, lays this groundwork:

> We can now see the point of our customs [that is, the complex conventions, common in Athens, for the relations existing between men], they are designed to separate the wheat from the chaff, the proper from the vile. That's why we do everything we can to make it as easy as possible for lovers to press their suits and as difficult as possible for young men to comply; it is like a competition,[15] a kind of test to determine to which sort each belongs. (468, 184a)

It therefore does not come as a surprise that Socrates is constantly testing his "co-competitors" around the table, ending with the competition he himself has set up against the two playwrights in which he argues that a playwright who writes only either comedy or tragedy has insufficient skills.

The argument Socrates presented to the two playwrights in the last section of the *Symposium* is crucial for our understanding of this series of competitions. As I have already pointed out, Plato creates a narrative in which the detailed arguments leading to Socrates' final victory have been suppressed by the complex techniques of reporting in the dialogue. Therefore it is possible only to conjecture what Socrates' point actually was. It seems to me—and I have already presented this solution—what Socrates said is that only the philosopher, searching for the full and complete "truth" (whatever this implies), can encompass both tragedy and comedy.

Plato has obviously set up his dialogue so that Socrates, the philosopher, has the ability to unify the tragic and the comic modes of expression. And this makes him superior to both of the dramatists, who represent only half of this complete totality because they write in one of the genres only. As I will clarify in connection with Aristophanes' speech, this argument is based on the notion of finding the missing half. Philosophy is the discursive practice in which tragedy and comedy become reunified into an original totality. But poets, generally without being aware of this—Socrates probably told the two drowsy playwrights—are apparently not able to find the missing half of the discourses they practice. Socrates, on the other hand, has obviously found his missing half, through Diotima, who is the source of his understanding of Eros and who, through her female voice, complements his knowledge (or rather his ability to ask questions) about its mysteries. Furthermore—as the ending of Plato's dialogue implies—Socrates has found the key to discursive fullness, because the philosophical discourse, personified by Socrates himself (as Eros), unifies tragedy and comedy in a higher, more inclusive sense. Therefore philosophy wins the ultimate competition in the "ancient quarrel" with poetry, being able to bring back its discursive practices to their original state of fullness and unity. This desire for fullness, searching for a missing half, is actually what both Aristophanes, in his speech about the three kinds of four-legged creatures, as well as Socrates, in his presentation of his dialogues with Diotima, sought to convey. This is also the reason why the competition between Aristophanes and Socrates constitutes the core of the *Symposium*.

Four-Legged and Two-Legged Creatures

The remarkable complexities of the *Symposium* now bring us to Aristophanes' speech eulogizing Eros. He begins by describing the three kinds of spherical four-legged creatures who "in strength and power . . . were terrible, and they had great ambitions. They made an attempt on the gods" (473, 190b). Because of their rebelliousness they were punished. This is how Aristophanes describes their punishment:

> Then Zeus and the other gods met in council to discuss what to do, and they were sore perplexed. They couldn't wipe out the human race with thunderbolts and kill them all off, as they had the giants, because that would wipe out the worship they receive, along with the sacrifices we humans give them. On the other hand, they couldn't let them run riot. At last, after great effort, Zeus had an idea. "I think I have a plan," he said, "that would allow human beings to exist and stop their misbehaving: they will give up being wicked when they lose their strength. So I shall now cut each of them in two. At one stroke they will lose their strength and also become more profitable to us, owing to the increase in their number. They shall walk upright on two legs. But if I find they still run riot and do not keep the peace," he said, "I will cut them in two again, and they'll have to make their way on one leg, hopping." (473–474, 190c–d)

And, continues Aristophanes, "since their natural form had been cut in two, each one longed for its own other half, and so they could throw their arms about each other, weaving themselves together, wanting to grow together" (474, 191a).

Aristophanes does not personify Eros as many of the other speakers have done but depicts her/him/it in terms of the energies and desires that aspire to reconstitute an original, mythical wholeness that has been cut in half. The aim of Eros, as such a force, is to bring about the reunification of these two halves, not necessarily to bring about any offspring from the union between them. This becomes even more evident a little further on in Aristophanes' speech, when he says:

> Love is born into every human being; it calls back the halves of our original nature together; it tries to make one out of two and heal the wound of human nature. Each of us, then, is a "matching-half" of a human whole, because each was sliced like a flatfish, two out of one, and each of us is always seeking the half that matches him. (474, 191d)

Aristophanes goes on to explain that the search for these counterparts depends on the mix of genders of the original four-legged creature, expressing three distinct possibilities of union between humans: man and woman (the androgynes), woman and woman, and man and man. Besides being the source of the sexual preference of every two-legged individual, the desire for the missing half also serves as a metaphor for the reunification and ultimate unity of tragedy and comedy through philosophy for which Socrates is supposedly advocating in his discussion with the two drowsy playwrights.

It is important to point out that the narrative dynamics of the *Symposium*, constantly moving between the states of fullness and union, on the one hand, and the states of separation and the desire for the missing half, on the other, foreshadow the historical dynamics (which is of course also a narrative construction) depicted by Nietzsche in *The Birth of Tragedy from the Spirit of Music*. Here too, two forces—the Dionysian and the Apollonian—are brought together, creating the fullness that Nietzsche considers as the irreplaceable starting point for Attic tragedy, and which are separated by the introduction of the Socratic, rational discourse. But as I argue in a later chapter, this separation created a new form of discourse about which Nietzsche is critical, but which he also integrates within his own philosophical discourse through a complex, ambivalent, and daring gesture.

Plato's *Symposium* implies that the philosophical discourse has to align and integrate the performative practices of both the tragic and the comic—represented by Agathon and Aristophanes—in order to reach totality and fullness. This implies that philosophy, just like the four-legged creatures before they were cut in two halves, is perceived as a rebellious, even subversive, form of discourse. The four-legged creatures in Aristophanes' myth were so rebellious that Zeus cut them in half, just as philosophy—at least potentially—can be subversive, as it encompasses a total, composite discourse, including both the tragic and the comic modes. And Socrates, as every reader of the *Symposium* must be aware, finally had to pay with his life for being a philosopher. Therefore, the arguments that Socrates probably presented to the two playwrights—which they as well as Aristodemus were too tired to hear or grasp, but which signaled his final victory in Plato's dialogue—must, I believe, have drawn attention to the subversive potentials of philosophy, and this was obviously an aspect that Plato could not openly acknowledge in his dialogue. This was apparently also something Aristophanes was aware of, mentioning that Zeus had warned the two-legged creatures that if they continued to be rebellious he would cut them in half again so they would end up hopping on one leg (quoted above, 474, 190d).

One Voice and Many Legs

But there is also another aspect of Aristophanes' speech about the four-legged creatures that are cut in half in order to become human beings as we know them. This aspect is directly relevant to "the ancient quarrel between philosophy and poetry." Aristophanes' speech can be seen as an answer not only to what Eros is, but also to the more inclusive question about what a human being is. And these two questions are of course profoundly related. According to Aristophanes, a human being is defined as a two-legged creature searching for her/his missing half and who realizes her/his human potential through the reunification with this missing half. In what follows I want to show that Aristophanes' speech, presented by *the* "archetypal" writer of comedies, has profound intertextual connections to Sophocles' *Oedipus Tyrannus*, later canonized by Aristotle as his prime example of tragedy in the *Poetics*, and which must have been well known by Plato as well. Actually, on a certain level *Oedipus Tyrannus* constitutes the most serious competition to Plato's own struggle (or competition) against drama and theatre. Oedipus himself has the characteristics of a philosopher, but the premises for his vocation are almost diametrically opposite to those exemplified by Socrates. Oedipus and Socrates are therefore, I argue, the implied competitors in the battle between philosophy and the theatre. But the struggle between them is of quite a different nature than the contests presented in Plato's dialogue.

The fact that Aristophanes is suffering from hiccups when it is his turn to give his speech in praise of Eros has given rise to numerous interpretations and speculations.[16] In the dialogue itself, after giving some medical advice, the physician Eryximachus makes his eulogy, and afterward, when Aristophanes says he applied the Sneeze Treatment to get rid of the hiccups, Eryximachus comments, "You are making jokes before your speech, and you are forcing me to prepare for you to say something funny, and to put up my guard against you, when otherwise you might speak at peace" (472, 189a). To this Aristophanes retorts, "I'm not worried about saying something funny in my coming oration. That would be pure profit, and it comes with the territory of my Muse. What I am worried about is that I might say something ridiculous" (472, 189b). After presenting his eulogy, Aristophanes begs the others to be cautious, and "don't make a comedy of it" (476, 193d). Why is Aristophanes' speech so carefully framed by remarks about its generic classification? Does Plato imply that Aristophanes has already created some form of unification of tragedy and comedy, perhaps competing with the form of unification that Socrates, according to my reading, promotes in the final moments of the *Symposium*? And in which way is the narrative about the four-legged creatures related to other literary genres, in particular to tragedy, which is the most relevant one in the context of the *Symposium*?

What I argue is that Aristophanes' speech in the *Symposium* is closely related to Sophocles' *Oedipus Tyrannus*. They are both based on narratives about the transformation of the number of legs, raising the question "What is man?" Aristophanes presents a transformation of the legs from four to two, and the desire to become reunified into four-legged creatures. And Sophocles' drama is indirectly based on the "leg narrative" presented in the riddle of the Sphinx, in which a creature is portrayed as walking on four legs in the morning, two in the afternoon, and three in the evening. I will explore the riddle text in greater detail later. But instead of referring to the transformation in terms of the autochthonous "birth" of the human beings; that is, that man is originally not born from other humans but through a "cut" or division whereby the original mythological four-legged creatures become two-legged humans—as Aristophanes does in Plato's text—the riddle of the Sphinx presents the transformation of the number of legs as an expression of the human life cycle. As Claude Lévi-Strauss has pointed out in his analysis of the Oedipus narrative, one of its central ironies is that its hero actually behaves as if he were an autochthonous creature. This creature had grown like a tree, instead of being born from the womb of a woman, before being cut off from the ground and receiving the scars on his legs, which is reflected in his name.[17] Oedipus's scars "deceive" him into believing that he is an autochthonous creature.

Aristophanes' narrative also draws attention to the bodily scars—but not on the feet—from the cut that have transformed the four-legged creatures into two-legged humans, mentioning the physiological changes that had to be made after the original creatures were cut in two halves, "the way people cut sorb-apples before they dry them or the way they cut eggs with hairs" (474, 190e). After they had been cut in half, Zeus also told Apollo to turn the heads around, "so that each person would see that he'd been cut and keep better order" (474, 190e), something to which Oedipus with his scars on his legs obviously does not adhere. He hardly notices them. In addition Zeus asked Apollo in Aristophanes' narrative to heal their wounds on what we now call the stomach, leaving only a small scar consisting of a few wrinkles around the stomach and the navel, "to be a reminder of what happened long ago" (474, 191a). A truly autochthonous creature obviously does not have a navel. And only later, when Zeus realized that these divided creatures are gradually dying out because they refused to do anything without their second half, did he take "pity on them, and came up with another plan: he moved their genitals around to the front!" (474, 191b). Therefore: "Love is born into every human being; it calls back the halves of our original nature together; it tries to make one out of two and heal the wound of human nature (474, 191d).

The riddle of the Sphinx is based on a completely different configuration of the legs, presenting a profound cognitive dissonance between Oedipus's understanding of his name, his body, and his own self, on the one hand, and his philosophical insights, on the other. The riddle is a crucial component of the Oedipal narrative and of negotiating the transformation with respect to human legs. Significantly, though, the riddle has not been included in Sophocles' dramatic text (another important dissonance or division), but it appears in a number of other sources from the period. However, the repeated references to Oedipus's solving the riddle in Sophocles' drama indicate that it must have been quite well known among the audiences and readers of Sophocles' play. One of these sources, in the prefaces to Euripides' *Phoenician Women*, has the following poetic formulation:

Riddle:
There is on earth a creature with two legs, four legs and one voice:
three legs too. Alone it changes in form of creatures who exist
on earth, in air, on sea. But when it goes resting on more feet
then the strength of its limbs is weaker.

Answer:
Listen, like it or not, ill winged songstress of death
to my voice, which will end your folly.
You mean man, who crawling on the ground
at first is four footed, a babe from the womb
then in old age leans on a stick as third foot,
with a burden on back, bent double in old age.[18]

If in Aristophanes' narrative the four-footed creature is the strongest and most rebellious one, in the riddle of the Sphinx it is, together with the three-footed creature, the weakest. The two-legged creature is the mature human being in both.

However considering the fate of Oedipus as it is given literary, dramatic form by Sophocles, it is difficult to free oneself from the suspicion that the Sphinx somehow deliberately leads Oedipus to the trap of carrying out the second half of the Delphic oracle, marrying his mother and begetting children with her, intentionally "making" his solution of the riddle the right one. There had obviously been previous unsuccessful attempts to solve the riddle—because a riddle text must also have a "wrong" answer—but we do not know exactly what the "wrong" answers were. We only know what the "right" solution provided by Oedipus is.[19]

It is even possible to imagine an uncanny cooperation between the two supernatural creatures whose pronouncements are only appearing indirectly in Sophocles' drama. Thus imagine a collusion between the Delphic oracle and the Sphinx, or even between the Sphinx and Jocasta, deviously leading Oedipus into the incestuous trap of his mother's bed, clearly a tabooed form of Eros. The search for the missing half that characterizes the humans in Aristophanes' narrative clearly also contains an incestuous aspect, in that all humans are searching for the human being from which they have been separated at "birth," although in Aristophanes' story this does not refer to a mother specifically. The fact, however, that the Oedipal drama fully realizes this incestuous subtext further tightens the intertextual weave between the two leg narratives and between Aristophanes' speech and *Oedipus Tyrannus*. The separation at birth, which Oedipus's as well as Jocasta's incestuous drives so forcefully realize in Sophocles' drama, is based on a double separation, first when the child is born and the umbilical cord is cut, and then when the newborn baby is left alone on Mount Cithaeron.

Initially, Oedipus's solution to the riddle of the Sphinx leads to his triumph. It makes him the ruler of Thebes and the husband of the widow-queen, according to what could be considered a traditional riddling situation at weddings. The future husband, possessing abstract, "philosophical" knowledge, is rewarded with the carnal knowledge of the nuptial bed as well as frequently also with political power. In solving the riddle of the Sphinx, a riddle dealing directly with the human body and the identity of man, Oedipus in fact draws attention to the crucial difference—which for him becomes fatal—between his abstract, philosophical understanding of human identity and his own self-knowledge, or rather his lack of such self-knowledge. Although Oedipus successfully solves the intricate intellectual puzzle of man's universal identity, which obviously lies within the realm of philosophy, he does not know who he himself really is. This is most forcefully expressed by his inability to identify his own father at the place where the three roads meet, or his own mother in the nuptial bed after marrying her. Oedipus is thus incapable of fulfilling the famous dictum attributed both to Socrates and to the oracle at Delphi: Know thyself—*Gnôthi seauton*.

Oedipus's ability to solve the philosophical riddle while being unable to understand its practical implications as to which "man" he himself is, points to several important issues concerning the relationships between the philosophical and the thespian discourses. Whereas the Delphic oracle activates the narrative of Sophocles' play—after Oedipus's birth, when he is abandoned by his parents on Mount Cithaeron, as well as when he leaves Corinth for Thebes and the final realization of the oracle—the riddle of the Sphinx, on the other hand, is not a text to act on. It penetrates much deeper into the existential core of the play. It does not define what the hero is going to do—the *drama* in the Greek sense of this term, which means "to do"—it defines who he is, his being, and his self as a creature subject to constant transformation.[20] The riddle functions as the hidden philosophical subtext that has to be revealed and discovered. Adriana Cavarero has suggested that "faced with the Sphinx, Oedipus reveals himself to be a philosopher."[21] But then, after the first solution in which man is "found," the riddle has to be radically redefined and resolved at different junctions in Sophocles' play. This leads to the answer to the question "Who is Oedipus?"—just as the legs of man, according to Oedipus's initial solution to the riddle, undergo a constant transformation. The riddle of the Sphinx, referring to itself as a meta-text, is *one* text with *many* answers, just as man has *one* voice and *many* legs, an aspect of the riddle that all the known versions of the riddle include.[22]

Thus the riddle can be formulated in terms of an ongoing, dynamic dialectic between unity and multiplicity. This opposition between the one and the many on which the riddle text is based (and which is also echoed in the *Symposium* in Socrates' final supplication to the two playwrights)[23] is also a central issue in the plot of Sophocles' play, being directly related to Oedipus's possible responsibility for having killed his father, the old king Laius. This responsibility actually depends on the exclusive opposition between the one and the many—because the herdsman who witnessed the murder of Laius had, in order to protect Oedipus, always claimed that there were several murderers. Oedipus himself knew that he had been alone when killing an unknown man at the place where the three roads meet, and therefore he had not been considered or considered himself to be the murderer of the former king. When this difference becomes crucial in the play itself, Oedipus tries to defend himself against any possible accusation that he is the murderer by making the following proverbial statement, which also has obvious philosophical implications: "The one and the many cannot be one and the same."[24] Because of the new, hitherto hidden evidence brought forward by the herdsman—changing his previous testimony (through which he wanted to protect Oedipus) from *many* murderers to *one*—Oedipus soon discovers his own involvement in this crime.

From a strictly logical perspective "the one and the many cannot be one and the same" because "one" and "many" are mutually exclusive. But this contradiction seems to be overruled by the riddle of the Sphinx, asking what has one voice and many legs at the same time. There is also another opposition or reversal between one and many in Sophocles' play itself that is directly related to the paradox of containing both. Initially, there was only one witness (the herdsman) of the many robbers who had supposedly killed Laius. But in the play itself we learn that Tiresias had also been a kind of witness—at least he knows who had murdered the old king—whereas there was only one murderer: Oedipus himself. One of the central developments of the play is therefore a reversal in which the one witness turns out to be more than one and the many murderers become reduced to one.

The multileveled interactions between the one and the many, and the fact that the one and the many cannot be identical, is clearly not only an issue that has to be solved on the level of the dramatic plot in *Oedipus Tyrannus*, it is one of the central issues that ancient Greek philosophy confronted as well. The perception of the flux of the material world stands in a constant opposition with the attempts to find the unifying philosophical or metaphysical principle of being. The opposition between Parmenides' indivisible "one" and Heraclitus's universe of constant, multiple flux—the *panta rhei*—is an obvious example of this opposition as it was formulated by the pre-Socratic philosophers. However, the teaching Plato presents in his Socratic dialogues, in which the oneness of the Idea transcends the multiple appearances of the objects in the material world, is no doubt the most elegant and comprehensive philosophical formulation of this conflict in the Greek world of thought. It bridges the gap between unity and multiplicity, transforming the logical contradiction into a dialectical metaphysics and explaining the flux of the world in relation to the eternal Ideas.

Therefore the coexistence of unity and multiplicity in the riddle of the Sphinx, defining what a human being is, foreshadows the dialectics between unity (the eternal Ideas) and multiplicity (the individual objects partaking of them) in Plato's philosophy. The philosophical and the thespian discursive practices share a desire to find a solution to this basic inconsistency between the one and the many. In Sophocles' drama the riddle of the Sphinx accommodates this opposition, leading to the ultimate tragedy of Oedipus, who after his initial triumph—after solving the riddle—marries the widow-queen, his mother. The solution of the riddle of man leads to Oedipus's ultimate downfall because it makes the second part of the Delphic oracle come true. Plato, on the other hand, solves the logical contradictions between the one and the many through metaphysical premises. Also Socrates personifies the contradictions between them by being an ironic trickster, who not only unifies tragedy and comedy but also the human and the divine.

In book 7 of the *Republic*, in his discussion on arithmetic, Socrates claims that the apparent contradiction of the one and the many activates the process of thought itself:

If the one is adequately seen itself by itself or so is perceived by any of the other senses, then, as we were saying in the case of fingers, it would draw the soul towards being. But if something opposite to it is always seen at the same time, so that nothing is apparently any more than the opposite of one, then something would be needed to judge the matter. The soul would then be puzzled, would look for an answer, would stir up its understanding, and would ask what the one is. And so this would be among the subjects that lead the soul and turn it around towards the study of that which is. (1141, 524d–e)

And to this Glaucon responds, with an obvious echo from the riddle of the Sphinx: "But surely the sight of the one does possess this characteristic to a remarkable degree, for we see the same thing to be both one and an unlimited number at the same time" (1141, 525a).

According to Plato, when the search for true knowledge has been achieved, the opposition between the one and the many, just as the perception of the human being in the riddle, is supposedly given a philosophical resolution that allows for the differences between the human and the divine perspectives. There is however a radical difference between the philosophical and the thespian discourses in that the philosopher becomes purified by resolving this opposition. Meanwhile, according to Sophocles, Oedipus, who believes he possesses a divine perception, has to face his tragic fate for having solved the riddle of the coexistent one and many. Thus, not until it is too late, does he find out who he himself is. He too is one and many; one person who is both the son and the husband of Jocasta as well as the brother and the father to his four children. Only when he looks down at his own feet, discovering the scars, can he finally solve the riddle of his own identity.

Intertextual Bridges and Discursive Practices

The intricate intertextual bridges erected between philosophy and theatre on the basis of Oedipus's philosophical hubris and Socrates' desire to unify tragedy and comedy in philosophy—both emphatically activating notions of unity and multiplicity—are crucial for the basic arguments presented in this book. The philosophical inclinations of Oedipus are a prerequisite for Plato's activation of these dialectics. In his interpretation of Oedipus's paradoxical standing as a proto-philosopher, Jean-Joseph Goux takes a panoramic view of philosophy:

> The tragedy [*Oedipus Tyrannus*] explores and unsettles the scene of philosophy, bringing to light what philosophy does not know about itself, what it cannot glimpse within the terms of its own language. Sophocles produces a critique in the strong sense, tracing the limits to which philosophy can only remain blind, disclosing the posture, unthought by philosophy itself, that institutes it. This tragic critique—unnoticed even by those who, like Hegel, recognized that Oedipus's intelligence inaugurated philosophical consciousness—is more powerful, in the long run, than the one Heidegger undertook in his meditation on "Being." What the Oedipus plot discloses is the protophilosophic posture that generates the conquering orientation of philosophy up to Descartes and Nietzsche. The enormous interest of this posture with respect to modern conceptualizations is that it does not suppress the imaginal preconditions of the philosopher's position. It reveals their forgotten footings, their irreducible fiber. It allows us to trace the frontiers of the philosophizing attitude—frontiers of which that attitude itself is unaware—so we can more readily cross them and emerge on the other side of the enclosure where Heidegger's rumination confines and exhausts it. Let me make the point here and now, before returning to it in greater detail: what Western thought has had to acknowledge, since the Enlightenment, as another scene, foreign to the reflective subject, is precisely what the Oedipean posture—founding the subject as consciousness of self—excluded and denied. The gesture by which Oedipus situated himself so as to respond to the "riddling bitch," guardian of the initiatory threshold, and the belief that he could abolish her with the word "man" in a presumption of auto-initiation, are what institute, in a counter-effect, the difference between what will later be called consciousness and unconsciousness.[25]

According to this scenario, Sophocles' drama provides a quest for human identity and being that philosophy itself has not been able fully to provide. Doubtless, seen from this perspective, also for Plato's Socrates, the plays of Sophocles must have constituted an extremely difficult challenge. But at the same time, *Oedipus Tyrannus*—and this discussion can be expanded further by examining the relationship of *Antigone* as well as *Oedipus at Colonus* to philosophical discourses—also presents a revolting but flawed philosopher who becomes a tragic hero because of his blindness. He obviously lacks what the spectators in the theatre must possess: the ability to see and to judge. In his Theban plays Sophocles points to a form of philosophical hubris, even before philosophy had fully crystallized itself as a discursive practice. Likewise the *Symposium* presents an ultimately flawed philosopher-hero who appropriates the multivalent theatrical discourses of tragedy and comedy in his philosophy.

Charles Segal has provided some important insights based on a similar perception of Oedipus:

Oedipus confronts the mystery of being alive in a world that does not correspond to a pattern of order and justice satisfactory to the human mind. He places us in a tragic universe in which we have to ask whether the horrible suffering we witness is all due to design or to chance, whether our lives are random or entirely determined. If everything happens by accident, a view to which the modern reader is probably more inclined than the ancient, then life seems absurd. If it is all by design, then the gods seem cruel and unjust, and life is hell. Sophocles does not give us a final answer, any more than Shakespeare offers us a final answer for the final shape of Hamlet's life or for the death of Cordelia in *King Lear*.[26]

Segal also offers:

The deceptiveness of the senses and the concealment of ultimate reality beneath false appearances are dominant themes throughout the period in both philosophy and literature. *Oedipus* shares this concern with finding truth in a world of appearances and is influenced, even if indirectly, by the new theories about language that pose the problem of the relation of words to reality and emphasize the power of words to deceive, to win unjust causes, and to confuse moral issues.[27]

In *The Birth of Tragedy from the Spirit of Music*, Nietzsche also confronts in what sense Oedipus can be seen as a philosopher. He has solved the riddle of the Sphinx but at the same time is the murderer of his father and the husband of his mother. In explaining this "appalling trinity of the fate of Oedipus,"[28] Nietzsche refers to the ancient Persian belief:

According to which a wise magus can only be born from incest: which we, with respect to the riddle-solving and mother-marrying Oedipus must immediately interpret as follows—that whenever prophetic and magic powers break the spell of present and future, the inflexible law of individuation, and above all the real enchantment of nature, this must have been brought about by a monstrous transgression of nature—as in this instance incest; for how could nature be forced to give up its secrets otherwise than by a triumphant violation, that is, through the unnatural?[29]

In Nietzsche's view—and the seemingly inevitable formulation by Freud of his Oedipus complex—the wisdom achieved by Oedipus is therefore a Dionysian wisdom, an "abomination against nature"[30] that is radically different from the attempts of (Plato's) Socrates to find a harmonizing form of wisdom.

Both the philosophical and the thespian discourses are related to the riddle of the Sphinx. The riddle, apart from dealing with the dialectics between the one and the many, is actually a poetic formulation of one of the most fundamental issues in any philosophical system: the essential nature of man. The riddle of the Sphinx relates the nature of man to the transformation of his legs. With Aristotle's discussion of different kinds of definitions in his *Analytica Posteriora*, it is evident that even this most rational philosopher is able to cross the border of the strictly logical discourse and enter the ludic landscape of riddling. In his discussion about definition by division (just as the four-legged creatures in Aristophanes' story are divided), a procedure that Aristotle logically opposed, the following example is presented: "Thus to the question 'What is the essential nature of man?' the divider replies 'Animal, mortal, footed, biped, wingless.'"[31] This almost absurd definition of man as a "wingless mortal biped" also functions as an intertext with the riddle of the Sphinx as well as with Aristophanes' speech in the *Symposium*.

Oedipus Tyrannus can be seen as a painful parody on the dictum "Know thyself," in which the tragic flaw of Oedipus is not only that he does not know who he is, but that he does not really know his own legs—in spite of the fact that he has solved the leg riddle presented by the Sphinx. Oedipus's own body, and in particular his legs, are actually the riddle that he has to look at, interpret, and solve. The enigmatic inscription on his feet is of crucial importance. Several critics have drawn attention to the fact that Oedipus is the man with the swollen (*oidos*) foot who, punning on his name, knew (*oida*) how to solve the foot-riddle of the Sphinx. Although Oedipus, the first speaker in the play, uses his own name as early as the eighth line, he never asks why he has this name, why he has swollen feet (as we may perhaps conclude from this name), or why his feet are scarred as a result of what his parents had done to him just after his birth. Not even when Jocasta mentions that the baby born to her and Laius was exposed, with his feet pinned together, on Mount Cithaeron does Oedipus really look down at his own feet. And neither has his wife asked how he got his name—which she, even if she is also his mother, did not give him—nor how he has scarred and swollen feet.

The riddle of the Sphinx, which Oedipus has solved, focuses on the feet of man as a universal concept; Oedipus's name points to his own personal fate and his disfigured feet. However, when Oedipus asks the messenger if he, the infant Oedipus, was in pain when the messenger picked him up, the following conversation ensues:

> MESSENGER. Your ankles . . . they tell the story. Look at them.
> OEDIPUS. Why remind me of that old affliction?
> MESSENGER. Your ankles were pinned together. I set you free.
> OEDIPUS. That dreadful mark—I've had it from the cradle.
> MESSENGER. And you got your name from that misfortune too, the name's still with you.[32]

Oedipus, the famous solver of riddles, does not "look" at his own feet until the very end, in order to make the final, fatal connection between his name and his body, between the universal concept of man and his own particular subjectivity.

Aristophanes' story in the *Symposium* also interprets the inscriptions on the body, but these are the "birth-marks" of the human race, which are universal, not the personal wounds from which Oedipus suffers. Before his meeting with the messenger, Oedipus's failure to look at himself—either his feet or his name—in order to solve the riddle of his own identity is connected both to his metaphorical blindness (which after the painful discovery is willfully transformed into a real physical blindness) and his problematic status as a human being, as someone who has broken one of the most significant social taboos by marrying his mother.

Even Aristotle, who valorized *Oedipus Tyrannus* in his *Poetics* as the prime example of tragedy, has failed to look down at the scarred feet of Oedipus. In chapter 16 of the *Poetics*, examining the notion of recognition or discovery, *anagnôresis*, which is directly related to philosophical issues embedded in the theatrical discourse, Aristotle enumerated the least artistic forms of this device, "which poets mainly use through the poverty of their imagination," and which are external signs, such as birthmarks. Also what Aristotle calls "characteristics that we acquire after birth . . . . found on the body, for example, scars" are included in this category. The examples of scars Aristotle mentions are the two instances when Odysseus is "recognized through his scar in one way by the nurse and in another by the swineherds."[33] It is of course important to note in this context that Odysseus's scar is also situated on his foot. However—and it is tempting to designate this "blindness" as a transference from Oedipus—there is no mention in Aristotle's *Poetics* of the scar for which Oedipus was named and that has marked him for life. The most significant difference between Homer's and Sophocles' use of scars is that in the former the discovery is made by the people surrounding the hero, while Odysseus obviously knows who he is throughout. Oedipus, on the other hand, begins in a state of ignorance and his self-discovery constitutes tragedy in and of itself.

It is quite puzzling, though, that in Aristotle's treatise on tragedy, in which Sophocles' *Oedipus Tyrannus* serves as the prime example of excellence, the scars on Oedipus's feet are not even mentioned—in particular, because these scarred feet and the feet of the riddle are actually, together with the oracle, the prime "movers" of Sophocles' text. These scarred feet make him the lonely figure traveling on the roads. The main reason for this oversight is that for Aristotle, the intellectual (or rather philosophical) forms of *anagnoresis* are superior to those based on physical marks on the body. For the theatre, on the other hand, the presence and awareness of the body is crucial. Plato's *Symposium* contains complex dialectics between an abstract, philosophical discourse, in particular in Socrates' report from his meetings with Diotima, and the constantly recurring preoccupation with the human body. This is of course not a surprise in a text focusing on Eros. Frequently, strong, uncontrollable desires are revealed, like Alcibiades' profound disappointment with Socrates and the erotic competitions. In this context, the notion that performance is a form of scripted embodiment becomes powerfully realized. In particular, Aristotle has also failed to see Oedipus's scars, the written inscriptions on his body, just as Oedipus himself is blind to them until his meeting with the messenger who had saved his life on Mount Cithaeron.

Aristophanes' Protest

If it wasn't for one small detail in Plato's masterful text that has troubled me throughout my work on this dialogue, this would be the ideal point at which to end my already somewhat lengthy examination of the encounter between Socrates and the two playwrights in the *Symposium* and its intertexts. The detail I want to focus on is Apollodorus's description of what happened after Socrates had spoken:

> Socrates' speech finished to loud applause. Meanwhile, Aristophanes was trying to make himself heard over the cheers in order to make a response to something Socrates had said about his own speech. Then all of a sudden, there was even more noise. A large drunken party had arrived at the courtyard door and they were rattling it loudly, accompanied by the shrieks of some flute-girl they had brought along. (494, 212c)

With Alcibiades knocking at the door and making his entry, the dialogue takes a completely new turn, and Aristophanes never gets a chance to say what had bothered him in Socrates' presentation. Plato only indicates that it is related to Socrates' reference to what Aristophanes had said, but the dialogue does not reveal what his protest actually was. Just like Socrates' lecture about tragedy and comedy at the end of the *Symposium*, this is obviously a lacuna in Plato's text. But Aristophanes' inaudible protest has an even greater effect on the interpretation of Plato's dialogue than those final moments when the two playwrights as well as Aristodemus fall asleep. With Aristophanes' protest, Plato in fact undermines and even subverts Socrates' authority.

The point Aristophanes tries to make apparently refers to a short reference Socrates has made to the two-legged creatures searching for their missing halves that is crucial for Aristophanes. But it is actually not Socrates himself who makes this point, because Socrates has quoted Diotima, who in their conversations had supposedly said that "there is a certain story according to which lovers are people who seek their other halves" (488, 205e). And without waiting for Socrates' reaction, she adds "that according to my story, a lover does not seek the half or the whole, unless, my friend, it turns out to be good as well" (488, 205e). But regardless of whether such a half is good or not, Diotima seems to know more than is reasonable within the context created by the dialogue itself.

Therefore Aristophanes' protest raises a number of complex issues. The first question that has to be asked is how it could be possible for Diotima, within the fictional universe created by Plato, to make a reference to Aristophanes' story about the four-legged creatures. Aristophanes has already told the myth of the androgynes and the two other original sexes. He does so when Socrates presents his conversations with Diotima. And if these ideas had been commonly known and frequently discussed, this would arguably not cause any problems, because then Diotima would be referring to something most people at the time would know. However, these ideas do not seem to be common knowledge. The myth told by Aristophanes does not exist in any other contemporary Greek source and could even be Plato's own invention put in the mouth of Aristophanes. Therefore, if this is a myth that Plato wanted his readers to "hear" for the first time in the *Symposium*, it is strange that Diotima, who obviously was not present at the banquet and was quoted from her dialogues with Socrates, refers to it directly.[34]

This slippage, which dramatizes the crucial difference between new stories and stories that are repeated returns in the discussion on Benjamin as a storyteller, was no doubt also intentional on Plato's part. Every single detail in Plato's text must be subordinated to his comprehensive authorial vision, including Aristophanes' protest. So why has this detail been included? Aristophanes, who was an experienced author of comedies, clearly knew that if a character has not witnessed a certain event or has not been given a report about it, he or she cannot make any direct reference to it. Plato was obviously also aware of this. Did Plato wish to undermine Socrates' credibility, wanting his readers to draw the conclusion that Socrates had invented some of the things he is quoting Diotima as having said? Or can it be (and I write this with great hesitation) that Socrates has invented Diotima? And if this is the case, that Diotima is Socrates' fiction, is she fabricated in order to mystify the sources of his own philosophy? Plato has clearly added this small and seemingly insignificant detail in the text in order to create the basis for such a possibility. This does not mean that Plato totally undermines the philosophical ideas presented by

Socrates in his (at least partially imagined) dialogue with Diotima. But it definitely places Socrates in quite a different light as a character than he is generally depicted in Plato's dialogues.

These doubts concerning Socrates' personal integrity cannot be easily integrated within the more comprehensive theory of climbing the mystical ladder that Diotima has taught her pupil. But they are already implied by Socrates' earlier interrogation of Agathon, after Agathon has given his speech and before Socrates begins his own presentation. In the mode of irony typical of Socrates, reacting to the rhetorical exaggerations Agathon has just presented, Socrates says: "In my foolishness, I thought you should tell the truth about whatever you praise" (481, 198d). A little later he adds that after hearing Agathon's speech "it appears that this is not what it is to praise anything whatever; rather, it is to apply to the object the grandest and the most beautiful qualities, whether he actually has them or not" (481, 198e). And Socrates goes on, paraphrasing the line Euripides has put in the mouth of Hippolytus (in *Hippolytus*, 612) that "So 'the tongue' promised and 'the mind' did not" (37, 199a), in this case meaning that when Socrates agreed to eulogize Eros, he supposedly did not know that it meant making things up as he will also do.

Austin also quotes this line from *Hippolytus* in his preparatory discussion on the sincerity of utterances. When making a promise, Austin argues in *How to Do Things with Words*, "I must not be joking, for example, nor writing a poem."[35] Austin, who claims, "Accuracy and morality alike are on the side of the plain that *our word is our bond*," excludes "such fictitious inward acts as this"[36] (italics in the original). This confirms Austin's anti-theatrical approach, claiming somewhat later that "a performative utterance will, for example, be *in a peculiar way* hollow or void if said by an actor on the stage, or introduced in a poem, or spoken in soliloquy"[37] (italics in the original). In view of my reading of Socrates' character in the context of the *Symposium*, the debates concerning Austin and his use of this line in his own anti-aesthetic argument have to be reevaluated.[38]

Because it is likely that Socrates has also made up much of what he will just begin to tell, Plato has apparently subverted the Socratic irony as well as the authority of his teacher-hero. And finally, with the dramatic entry of the military commander Alcibiades—who, acting on the stage of history, experiencing the *agon* between life and death on the battlefield—

it becomes his task to draw attention to the enigmatic contradictions of Socrates' character. Alcibiades' depiction of Socrates in connection with the hollow statues of Silenus is also very revealing:

> If you were to listen to his arguments, at first they'd strike you as totally ridiculous; they're clothed in words as coarse as the hides worn by the most ridiculous satyrs. . . . He's always making the same tired old points in the same tired old words. If you are foolish, or simply unfamiliar with him, you'd find it impossible not to laugh at his arguments. But if you see them when they open up like the statues, if you go behind their surface, you'll realize that no other arguments make any sense. (503, 221e–222a)

Aristophanes, the writer of comedies, is not given a similar opportunity to expose Socrates' deceptions. Obviously, Aristophanes' protest, had it been heard and discussed, would have been much more effective in upsetting Socrates' argumentation than are the emotionally charged accusations Alcibiades fires at him. But Alcibiades' allegations are much more dramatic and theatrical than anything Aristophanes could have produced using the tools of logic to unmask Socrates.

The Final Exit

The final lines of Plato's *Symposium* herald the new day breaking:

But after getting them [Aristophanes and Agathon] off to sleep, Socrates got up and left, and Aristodemus followed him, as always. He said that Socrates went directly to the Lyceum, washed up, spent the rest of the day as he always did, and only then, as evening was falling, went home to rest. (505, 223d)

As the dialogue ends the focus is directed toward Socrates' healthy, self-contained body. His body, on the one hand, stands in opposition to the sleeping bodies of Aristophanes and Agathon, or Alcibiades' uncontrollable desires, and the scarred bodies depicted in Aristophanes' mythical narrative. On the other hand, the body of Socrates contrasts with Oedipus's self-maimed body and bleeding eyes. The philosopher is taking a bath, spending the day in accordance with his regular routines.

Nietzsche, in *The Birth of Tragedy from the Spirit of Music*, also draws attention to Socrates' daily routines, who after having spent the whole night in intensive discussions, torn between the men who compete for his intellectual as well as his bodily attention, takes care of himself. For

Nietzsche, however, the final moments of the *Symposium* point to something much more inclusive and final, the moments just before Socrates' own death, in which as Nietzsche expresses it,

> according to Plato's account, he [Socrates] approached death with the calm with which he left the symposium, in the early dawn as the last of the revelers; while behind him on the benches and on the floor his fellow carousers remained asleep, dreaming of Socrates, the true eroticist (*dem wahrhaften Erotiker*).[39]

As I argue in detail below, Nietzsche actually transforms Socrates into the ultimate tragic hero in the historiographical scenario that he suggests becomes the basis of the birth of philosophy from the ruins of tragedy. In spite of Nietzsche's valorization of the Dionysian life and his harsh critique of rational philosophy—in particular of Socrates as the cause of the ruin of tragedy—there is also a "subplot" in *The Birth of Tragedy from the Spirit of Music* that valorizes Plato's philosopher-hero for being "the true eroticist," the ultimate embodiment of Eros. After the tragic spirit born from the unification of the Dionysian and the Apollonian forces has collapsed from the onslaught of rational philosophy, represented by Socrates, Nietzsche actually shows that from this disintegration a new form of tragedy is born. It is the tragedy of Socrates leaving the two sleeping playwrights behind him, while he is already, and willingly, taking the path to his own death sentence. Thus Nietzsche implies that Socrates was victorious over the theatre. His philosophically integrated tragedy and comedy set against his death by poison are in fact reflections of each other, transforming him into the tragic hero.

Also for Walter Benjamin the *Symposium* was a text pointing to a deepened understanding of the relations between philosophy and art as developed in his "Epistemo-Critical Prologue" to *The Origin of German Tragic Drama*. Benjamin actually considers the *Symposium* as a potential blueprint for the mutual interdependence of these two discursive practices, because this text

> contains two pronouncements of decisive importance. . . . It presents truth—the realm of ideas—as the essential content of beauty. It declares truth to be beautiful. An understanding of the Platonic view of the relationship of truth and beauty is not just a primary aim in every investigation into the philosophy of art, but it is indispensable to the definition of truth itself.[40]

Benjamin also related directly to the final scene of the *Symposium*, declaring that Socrates is the true poet:

At the end of the *Symposium*, when Socrates, Agathon, and Aristophanes are seated alone, facing one another—why should it not be the sober light of his dialogues which Plato allows to fall over the discussion of the nature of the true poet, who embodies both tragedy and comedy, as dawn breaks over the three? The dialogue contains pure dramatic language, unfragmented by its dialectic of tragic and comic.[41]

The crucial question of course is whether it is possible at all to constitute such a pure dramatic language, and if it is, one has to wonder what form it will take.

2

"Who's There?"

HAMLET AS PHILOSOPHER AND THESPIAN

> What, has this thing appeared again tonight?
> —William Shakespeare, *Hamlet* (1.1.21)[1]
>
> There are more things in heaven and earth, Horatio,
> Than are dreamt of in your philosophy.
> —William Shakespeare, *Hamlet* (1.5.166–167)
>
> The tragic hero has only one language that is completely proper to him: silence.
> It has been so from the very beginning.
> —Franz Rosenzweig, *The Star of Redemption*[2]

Both the text of Shakespeare's *Hamlet* and its eponymous protagonist are strategically as well as liminally positioned between the discourses of philosophy and theatre. Hamlet aspires to be both philosopher and thespian, and this desire is actually a significant aspect of his tragedy. He relies on the theatre to solve existential philosophical issues, whereas his own subjective meditations and thoughts about the meaning of life are frequently highly theatricalized. He is not able to separate the two discursive practices, and the tension between them is highlighted by the use of soliloquy, the mode of address Shakespeare used to make Hamlet a true master. However Hamlet attempts to confront the tensions between who he is as a philosopher and as a thespian, striving to be both. Furthermore Shakespeare's play itself constantly oscillates between the discursive practices of the philosophical and the theatrical, in language, theme, and composition as well as in its numerous puns, allusions, and intertextual references. The play frequently juxtaposes the two discursive practices with and even against each other. This dimension of the play is introduced as early as its famous first line—"Who's there?"—which refers to the concrete situation of changing the guards and their fears that the ghost is appearing again that night. It also alludes to and probes the ontological status of the actors within the theatrical event itself. But my reading of Shakespeare's opening question can also be seen as referring to Hamlet's inner struggle between being both a philosopher and a thespian. "Who's there?" The answer is both philosopher and thespian. In this chapter, after offering my reading of this radical split between the philosophical and the thespian discourses in Shakespeare's play, I will briefly discuss its philosophical interpretations from Hegel to Marx to Derrida, "inviting" the ghost to play the role of Utopian figure.

As we have seen, in Plato's *Symposium* Socrates strives to create a form of philosophizing that integrates the theatrical, including both tragedy and comedy, through which the philosopher supposedly prevails over the arts as well as over the two playwrights. But as we have also seen, based on Aristophanes' protest, Plato introduces a complex critical irony with respect to his philosopher-hero, even subverting Socrates' victory. In *Hamlet* Shakespeare also creates an ironic perspective, but on a much larger scale, beginning with the famous first line of the play. This contrasts with Plato's carefully hidden narrative strategy. In *Hamlet* philosophy and theatre are not to be viewed as oppositional, as something through which individuals compete for attention and primacy. Instead the two discursive practices should be seen as a conflict occurring within the protagonist himself, illuminating each other from constantly shifting perspectives. Competitions usually end in victory or defeat, and in Plato's dialogue Socrates is victorious, regardless or even in spite of the sophistic means he uses. On the other hand, in *Hamlet* the opposition between the discursive practices is an internal competition. And as in any true tragedy there is no real winner except for Fortinbras, the marginalized representative of history whom Shakespeare gives neither time nor language to reflect on these matters. Therefore Shakespeare's *Hamlet*, like Sophocles' *Oedipus Tyrannus*, can be read as an indirect critique of philosophy, featuring a hero whose philosophizing constitutes a vital aspect of his hubris, leading to his final downfall.

Many of the intricate meta-textual conceits in Shakespeare's play both literally and figuratively take place "behind" Hamlet's back, repeating, reinforcing, and frequently even subverting the paradoxical encounters between the philosophical and thespian discourses. Thus Shakespeare's text frequently "performs philosophy" and "philosophizes performance" in ways in which Hamlet himself is totally unaware. Shakespeare's play points to the consequences of this multiple, divided focus on the basis of which both the character and the text "stage" numerous, simultaneous encounters and conflicting interactions between philosophy and theatre/performance. To the best of my knowledge, this has not been proposed by previous readers of the play.[3] For Hamlet, his attempt to unify the two discursive practices becomes an integral part of his tragedy, whereas in Shakespeare's play—which obviously also includes Hamlet's failure to combine these two discursive practices—the encounters between the character and the text become both highly charged and sometimes even quite complex and puzzling.

These multiple and constantly changing perspectives prompt a meta-dialogue between the dramatic characters—in particular Hamlet and Polonius—the protagonist and the implied authorial voices, which also includes the voice of the ghost "behind" and sometimes literally "beneath" the text, in the cellarage, as well as between the various actors on stage, at least in its first production. These sophisticated meta-dialogues between the actors, the characters, and the text are clearly in large part the reason Shakespeare's *Hamlet* has acquired its unique position within subsequent philosophical as well as theatrical discourses. But of course the play is also unique for its perceptions of subjective interiority developed by psychoanalytic theory and thinking.

These complex multiple perspectives were, I believe, also the reason, in his well-known essay "Hamlet and His Problems," T. S. Eliot argued that the play, because of the tensions between the character and the play, was a failure:

The levity of Hamlet, his repetition of phrase, his puns, are not part of a deliberate plan of dissimulation, but a form of emotional relief. In the character Hamlet it is the buffoonery of an emotion which can find no outlet in action; in the dramatist it is the buffoonery of an emotion which he cannot express in art. The intense feeling, ecstatic or terrible, without an object or exceeding its object, is something which every person of sensibility has known; it is doubtless a study to pathologists. . . . We must simply admit that here Shakespeare tackled a problem which proved too much for him. Why he attempted it at all is an insoluble puzzle; under compulsion of what experience he attempted to express the inexpressibly horrible, we cannot ever know.[4]

Eliot claimed that Shakespeare had not mastered the discrepancy between action and emotion involving both the character Hamlet and his author. I would argue that it is exactly this tension that has been one of the major reasons for the innumerable readings and interpretations of Shakespeare's *Hamlet*. Rather than buffoonery, as Eliot claims, the play, addressing the abyss of silence and death, presents a fascinating and even brilliant balancing act of kaleidoscopic changes in perspective.

I begin by examining this divided attention between philosophy and the theatre as it is expressed in the character of Hamlet himself. From the events during the first council meeting of the new king (the beginning of act 1, scene 2), after the funeral of Old Hamlet, and after both Claudius's wedding with Gertrude and his coronation, we learn that when Hamlet's father dies, Hamlet himself has been studying in Wittenberg and is called home to Elsinore for the funeral. The council meeting begins with Claudius taking care of some urgent diplomatic issues. After briefly consulting with Polonius, he grants Laertes permission to return to Paris, from where, as Laertes says, he had returned to Elsinore "to show my duty in your coronation" (1.2.53). Then Claudius turns to Hamlet, begging him to stay in Denmark:

> For your intent
> In going back to school in Wittenberg,
> It is most retrograde to our desire,
> And we beseech you bend you to remain
> Here in the cheer and comfort of our eye,
> Our chiefest courtier, cousin, and our son.
> (1.2.112–117)

Gertrude, Hamlet's mother and now also Claudius's wife, immediately seconds this request: "I pray thee stay with us, go not to Wittenberg" (1.2.119), to which Hamlet responds, "I shall in all my best obey you madam" (1.2.120). Shakespeare does not make any effort to justify their emphatic demand, besides wanting him to remain within observation: in "the comfort of our eye."

Hamlet's studies and his friends in Wittenberg are perceived as vaguely threatening to both Claudius and Gertrude. And he obviously has to stay in Elsinore for the plot to develop. Before they retire for their ceremonial drink, celebrating "this gentle and unforced accord of Hamlet" (1.2.123), as Claudius cynically expresses it, he repeats how pleased he is with Hamlet's "loving" and "fair reply," continuing in the next line with a highly charged and multivalent imperative. It begins with the verb "to be," *the* most philosophically charged verb of the play, at least for Hamlet: "*Be* as ourselves in Denmark" (1.2.120–121; italics added). A little earlier, when Gertrude tells Hamlet "'tis common, all that lives must die, / Passing through nature to eternity," which Hamlet confirms with "Ay madam it is common." She again retorts, "If it *be*, / why seems it so particular with thee?" (1.2.72–75; italics added). And Claudius immediately reiterates this point by saying, "For what we know must *be*" (1.2.98; italics added). The existential dimension of this verb, which will become crucial later for Hamlet's own philosophizing, is introduced during his first meeting with Gertrude and Claudius.

After their exit Hamlet remains alone on the stage for the first time, delivering his first soliloquy, beginning with "O that this too too solid flesh would melt" (1.2.129–159). Now he begins reflecting on the "canon 'gainst self-slaughter," which culminates much later with the "To be or not to be" soliloquy (3.1.56–88). Expressing his general disgust with the world—"How wary, stale and unprofitable / Seem to me all the uses of this world!"—Hamlet positions himself within a discursive universe in which philosophical and existential issues are of crucial importance, ending with an oath of silence: "But break, my heart, for I must hold my tongue." After the first visitation of the ghost, Hamlet asks Marcellus and Horatio three times to swear "never to speak of this that you have seen" (1.5.153; also with slight variations in 144 and 158). After saying to Horatio: "There are more things in heaven and earth, Horatio, / Than are dreamt of in your philosophy" (1.5.166–167),[5] Hamlet introduces the sense that "the time is out of joint" (1.5.189).

There are many oaths of silence in the play that point to the dangers of thinking and saying certain things. Most prominent is the oath Hamlet delivers after he has encountered the ghost for the first time. But the oath of silence ending his first soliloquy already presents a philosophical-existential stance clearly echoed later in his final words, after he has been mortally wounded by the poison sword tip: "the rest is silence" (5.2.337). And then, just after Hamlet's death, his words, "But break, my heart," from the first soliloquy, are reiterated by Horatio: "Now cracks a noble heart" (5.2.338). Shakespeare has evidently employed this structural feature in order to make sweeping connections among the central philosophical themes of his play.

Retrospectively, it is therefore appropriate that immediately after Hamlet's first soliloquy, Horatio enters, accompanied by Marcellus and Barnardo. The reader/spectator of the play has already become acquainted with both of them. They appear during the change of the guards in the first scene of the play. Now they have come to inform Hamlet about their encounter with the silent visage of the ghost. However, judging from Hamlet's questions to Horatio, this seems to be the first time they actually meet after the death of Hamlet's father, unless of course the ensuing dialogue between them is in jest. Even if this is a possibility, it seems quite unlikely. Their meeting even begins with a slight embarrassment, with Hamlet being so enwrapped in his own thoughts that he becomes confused and has to confirm that he remembers the name of his friend correctly: "Horatio—or do I forget myself" (1.2.162), as if he is unconsciously repeating the first line of the play: "Who's there?"

After having received Horatio's confirmation, that this is his name, Hamlet continues, "I'll change that name with you" (1.2.165). Perhaps it is the *ratio*—the *ratio*nality—in Horatio's name that attracts him, even if that quality, as Hamlet emphatically says to him after the encounter with the ghost, is actually lacking in Horatio ("There are more things in heaven and earth, Horatio/Than are dreamt of in your philosophy" [1.5.166–167]). Horatio's name as well as his basic rational philosophical understanding is a central issue for Hamlet. They are apparently both students of philosophy, and Hamlet confronts the issue of whether Horatio's rational capacities are sufficient for coping with the situation he is in. And just before his death, Hamlet returns to Horatio's name, saying: "O God, Horatio, what a wounded name" (5.2.323), which could mean that what has taken place is completely against the initial *ratio* in Horatio's name. At the same time it could also mean that after Hamlet's death Horatio will become the *orator* (H*oratio*) who will "speak to th' yet unknowing world/How these things came about" (5.2.358–359), even implying that the play itself could actually be the act of performing the irrational events leading up to Hamlet's death, repeating them again for the audience. For Hamlet "the rest is silence," whereas Horatio will continue to speak:

Of carnal, bloody and unnatural acts;
Of accidental judgments, casual slaughters;
Of deaths put on by cunning and forc'd cause;
And, in this upshot, purposes mistook
Fall'n on th' inventors' heads.
(5.2. 360–364)

In the first scene of the play, the verb "to speak" appears fourteen times, nine of which are imperatives used by Horatio in the encounter with the silent visage of the ghost. The dialectic between speech and silence as it has been developed by Shakespeare has profound philosophical reverberations.[6]

After the issue concerning Horatio's name has been resolved, Hamlet immediately asks: "And what make you from Wittenberg, Horatio?" (1.2.164). Moreover, after briefly greeting Marcellus and Barnardo, Hamlet repeats his question almost word by word: "But what in faith make you from Wittenberg, Horatio?" (1.2.168). Horatio's answer that it is his "truant disposition" (1.2.169)—where *truant* means both vagabond (is Horatio actually another traveler?) and someone who absents himself from school without leave—apparently does not satisfy Hamlet, so he repeats his question a third time: "But what is your affair in Elsinore?" (1.2.174). This time he uses the name of their present location instead of Wittenberg, the city they have both left because of the portentous events in Elsinore. Only after having been asked three times what his reason for being in Elsinore is, Horatio replies, "I came to see your father's funeral" (1.2.176), to which Hamlet cynically responds: "Do not mock me fellow student, / I think it was to see my mother's wedding" (1.2.178).

The sudden turns and almost obsessive repetitions of Hamlet's question to Horatio are both peculiar and perplexing. How is it possible that Hamlet and Horatio, who are obviously fellow students in Wittenberg— and will remain close friends until Hamlet's death—have not yet encountered each other in Elsinore? Their close relationship, based on their mutual trust, is crucial for the subsequent plot development. Because Horatio could identify the silent visage of the ghost as Hamlet's dead father, he must certainly have met him before they left for their studies in Wittenberg. Therefore it seems strange that just as Shakespeare's text does not clearly answer why Claudius and Gertrude are so stubbornly opposed to Hamlet's returning to Wittenberg, the play provides no explanation for why Hamlet and Horatio have not encountered each other in Elsinore. Neither did they see each other there during the funeral, to attend which Horatio says he returned to Elsinore, nor at the wedding of his mother and uncle and the coronation of the new king. There is nothing in the plot that prevents them from meeting before Horatio wants to inform Hamlet about the ghost, except it is logical for Horatio to break this news after Hamlet has been forbidden to return to Wittenberg, when his conflict with his uncle and mother has reached the imminent state of crisis that we have just witnessed.

The two short scenes (at the beginning and end of act 1, scene 2)—in which Claudius and Gertrude prevent Hamlet from returning to Wittenberg and Hamlet encounters Horatio for the first time after having left his studies there for the funeral of his father—draw attention to the high level of anxiety and uncertainty surrounding Wittenberg. Interestingly, one of the oldest German universities, founded in 1502—100 years before *Hamlet* was first performed—is still located there.[7] Even the ghost is indirectly connected to Wittenberg, because when it appears for the first time in the play, Marcellus says to Horatio: "Thou art a *scholar*, speak to it Horatio" (1.1.42, italics added), implying that only someone who has studied at the university can address the ghost in the appropriate manner. After his meeting with the ghost, Hamlet addresses Horatio and Marcellus as scholars (1.5.141), and after Hamlet has relegated Ophelia to the nunnery, she calls *him* a scholar in her short lament for the loss of his sanity (3.1.145).

There is a somewhat uncanny atmosphere connected with Wittenberg, a city that during Shakespeare's time had a large international student body and was most known for Martin Luther's nailing of his ninety-five theses on the doors of its castle church in 1517.[8] But Wittenberg is also the city of Dr. Faustus, a figure with whom Shakespeare no doubt was familiar from Christopher Marlowe's play and possibly from other sources as well.[9] Also Paul d'Eitzen, the first person to report that he had actually seen Ahasver—the Wandering Jew—outside Hamburg in 1564, had been a student of Luther and Philipp Melanchthon in Wittenberg. This first "report" about the Wandering Jew was published in 1602, more or less around the time *Hamlet* was first performed.[10] This legend with its strong roots in the anti-Semitic sentiments of Protestantism of the time—expressing another form of anxiety, the fear of the foreign—also pointed to the new mobility that was developing during the early modern period. These developments are also clearly reflected in Shakespeare's play, in which the characters are constantly traveling among Denmark, England, France, Germany, Norway, and Poland. *Hamlet* presents a map of European travel.

Wittenberg is where academic learning and argumentation became transformed into philosophical-theological debates about religious dissent as well as about the artistic creativity of literary legends and theatre. It is also where several other characters in the play have acquired their educations—in philosophy as well as in the theatre. Wittenberg, together with Elsinore, where the political struggle takes place, are the two main locations mentioned in Shakespeare's play. The challenge Hamlet confronts, and which I argue is a major motif in the play, is how to apply what he has learned in Wittenberg to the much more politically charged setting of Elsinore. For Laertes and Hamlet respectively, Paris and Wittenberg are represented as sites of erotic and academic freedom, whereas Elsinore is obviously restrictive in both.

Claudius has apparently sent for Rosencrantz and Guildenstern from Wittenberg, where they have also been studying with Hamlet and are, Claudius informs us, Hamlet's childhood friends, being "brought up with him, / And sith so neighboured to his youth and haviour" (2.2.11–12). They have been invited to Elsinore in order to spy on Hamlet. During their first meeting, which takes place after Hamlet has already encountered the ghost, Claudius makes one of his most well-known philosophical reflections: "What a piece of work is man!" (2.2.286), distantly echoing the "Ode to Man" in Sophocles' *Antigone*, a philosophical poem. According to Alfred Ferguson, this lament about human kind "serves roughly the same purpose in *Antigone* as in Shakespeare's play—a reminder to the spectators of the duality of human fate, the Janus-faced nature of human destiny."[11]

But Hamlet's amazement with man's supreme qualities, just as in his first soliloquy—"O that this too too solid flesh would melt"—quickly becomes transformed into a sense of repulsion and disgust. This speech, as well as Hamlet's constant philosophical quibbling with his two "friends," is a reflection of the routines and the jargon of their shared academic life in Wittenberg. And concerning the situation in Elsinore, Hamlet informs his fellow students, "'Sblood, there is something in this more than natural, if philosophy could find it out" (2.2.337–338). Philosophy in Hamlet's usage of the term is obviously a method for finding out the truth, even going beyond the occult practices of Dr. Faustus. However, the problems begin when Hamlet decides to substitute philosophical-theological investigations with theatre in his pursuit of truth. He uses the play to carry out his criminal investigation—or as he says at the end of the long scene where he first meets Rosencrantz and Guildenstern and the players: "The play's the thing / wherein I'll catch the conscience of the king" (2.2.556–557). The theatre seems to be a more enlightened and rational way to find out the truth than is relying on the testimony of a ghost, who Hamlet does not trust.

Many of the characters in *Hamlet* have been exposed to the theatre, both as spectators and active participants, before the action of the play begins. When Rosencrantz informs Hamlet that he and Guildenstern have passed the players "on the way, and hither are they coming to offer you service" (2.2.297), Hamlet asks to which players he refers. Rosencrantz responds: "Even those you were so wont to take delight in, the tragedians of the city" (2.2.304–305). This traveling theatre company has apparently visited Wittenberg on its tours, and now it too has been summoned to Elsinore, probably by Claudius, to serve as a distraction for Hamlet. We assume it was Claudius rather than Hamlet who called for the troupe because Hamlet does not respond to the information given by Rosencrantz. As the players arrive however it becomes clear that Hamlet knows them well, addressing one: "Oh my old friend! why, thy face is valanced since I saw thee last" (2.2.386–387), meaning that his beard has grown; whereas to a woman in the company Hamlet says, "Your ladyship is nearer to heaven than when I saw you last by the altitude of the chopine" (2.2.388–389). He is making reference to the thick soles of her shoes, similar to the high soles used in the performances of tragedy in late antiquity, but also to the fashion of shoes, popular in Shakespeare's own time, that protected their wearers from mud. It is also important to note that there were female actors in this troupe, though they were likely played by male actors in Shakespeare's own time. Thus a male actor plays a female actress (who is part of *Hamlet*'s fictional world), creating a complex defamiliarization process, "playing" with the social conventions as well as the ontology of the theatre. As we shall see later, this is not the only time Shakespeare created such a warp within the theatrical sign systems.[12]

The meeting with the actors simultaneously engages several theatrical levels, and Hamlet seems to be able to control all of them fully, even if Shakespeare is at times playing games behind his back. From the dialogue between the players and Hamlet, we learn that he has seen them perform a play based on "Aeneas' tale to Dido" (2.2.404–405), presenting Priam's slaughter. This is the first time after his encounter with the ghost of his father that Hamlet compares his own situation—having to avenge a father, as Pyrrhus did—with a theatre performance. This idea gradually develops into one of the major themes of the play, first and foremost in the performance of the playlet *The Mousetrap*. Hamlet says that the players will perform "something like the murder of my father" (2.2.548). Hamlet wants to examine his uncle's reaction to investigate whether Claudius is in fact guilty of murder. This approach raises several basic epistemological issues concerning the theatre and whether it can replicate what the ghost of Hamlet's father has reported to Hamlet about his murder: to "hold as 'twere the mirror up to nature" (3.2.18), that is, in this case the murder of his father. During his first meeting with the players, Hamlet recites a "dozen or sixteen lines" (2.2.494) from this play, a feat that impresses Polonius: "For God my lord, well spoken, with good accent and good discretion" (2.2.424–425).

Both Hamlet and Polonius have a keen interest in the theory as well as the practices of the theatre, and their pronouncements and exchanges on these topics have been carefully interwoven into Shakespeare's text. The most well-known speech in the genre of theoretical pronouncements about the theatre is Hamlet's instructions to the actors in the beginning of act 3, scene 2. Also, already before the players arrive, Polonius parodically introduces their abilities to Hamlet as being "the best . . . in the world, either for tragedy, comedy, history, pastoral, pastoral-comical, historical-pastoral, tragical-historical, tragical-comical-historical-pastoral; scene individable, or poem unlimited" (2.2.363–366). Hamlet responds by referring to the biblical figure of Jephtha's unnamed daughter. In so doing he alludes to a well-known ballad, a genre Polonius has not included on his list, as well as to the fact that Polonius has a daughter that he is constantly putting at risk, as Jephtha sacrificed his daughter. Polonius's exaggerated list obviously reflects the Renaissance debates about dramatic genres based on classical models. Thus also, at least indirectly, his list refers to the comments about tragedy and comedy made by Socrates at the end of the *Symposium*.

Somewhat later, just before the players perform *The Mousetrap* at the Elsinore court, Hamlet turns to Polonius, indicating that he possesses some important information about him: "My lord, you played once i'th'university you say" (3.2.87–88), to which Polonius answers: "That I did my lord, and was accounted a good actor" (3.2.89). Since Wittenberg is the only town in the play mentioned for its university, it is logical to assume that Polonius was also a student and an actor there, though it does not really matter if he in fact studied somewhere else. The important point is that Polonius is an experienced actor from the time he was studying at the university, and we have already seen that this goes for Hamlet too. And to Hamlet's question about what role Polonius played, he responds, "I did enact Julius Caesar. I was killed i'th'Capitol. Brutus killed me" (3.2.91–92). On a fictional level this prefigures Hamlet's stabbing of Polonius two scenes later, in Gertrude's closet. However in *Hamlet* Polonius is not playing a fictional character as he has supposedly done in the university production about Julius Caesar, just as the actress who Hamlet greets is not playing a fictional role, even though she is played by a male actor.

However, in tandem with Hamlet's questioning of Polonius about his career as an actor at the university, Shakespeare has staged a sophisticated meta-theatrical game behind the backs of his characters. The actors who played Hamlet and Polonius in the first performance of *Hamlet* communicated directly between themselves as well as with the audience about their roles in the performance. They therefore discussed their own acting careers, just at their fictional characters do. Critics have noted that John Hemmings, who had played Caesar (in Shakespeare's *Julius Caesar*, 1599–1600) also played Polonius (in *Hamlet*, 1600–1601), while Brutus and Hamlet in these two performances were both played by Richard Burbage.[13] Therefore, when Hamlet (Burbage) says to Polonius (Hemmings): "It was a brute part of him to kill so capital a calf there" (3.2.93), Burbage was at the same time addressing Hemmings and pointing to their careers as actors, saying that it was *brut*al (punning on his having been Brutus) to have killed him in the previous performance, even if he will perform this brute deed again a few scenes later, when Burbage's Hamlet stabs Hemmings's Polonius.[14] There are several references to the murder of Julius Caesar and its portentous consequences in *Hamlet*, which not only aims to draw historic parallels but also to remind the audience of the actor's previous performance.[15]

Shakespeare's contemporary audiences must have paid attention to these allusions, echoing the opening line, "Who's there?" on yet another level. This meta-communication between the two actors, leading up to the stabbing in the closet, has already commenced with the duel of words between Hamlet and Polonius, in an earlier scene. After Polonius says that he will take his leave, he gets the following response: "You cannot, sir, take from me anything that I will more willingly part withal—except my life, except my life, except my life" (2.2.209–210). As the contemporary spectators no doubt realized, it is Hamlet who will "take" Polonius's life. Or it is Burbage, playing the character of Hamlet, who will kill Hemmings's character in this performance, as Burbage kills Hemmings's Caesar in *Julius Caesar*.

Hamlet and Polonius are of course totally unaware of these allusions to the professional, meta-fictional, behind-the-stage realities of the performance. The pranks between the two actors with their comic, distancing effects are in direct opposition to the issue of the actors' emotional involvement. Hamlet brings up this emotionality in the long soliloquy following the meeting of the players that ends the second act, somewhat subverting its seriousness. In his soliloquy Hamlet asks how it is possible for an actor to become totally involved in his role while he himself is unable to mobilize the necessary emotions to carry out revenge as the ghost has demanded. He experiences an emotional paralysis as he faces his father's ghost and the demand to avenge his untimely death:

> Is it not monstrous that this player here,
> But in a fiction, in a dream of passion,
> Could force his soul so to his own conceit
> That, from her working, all his visage wanned,
> Tears in his eyes, distraction in's aspect,
> A broken voice, and his whole function suiting
> With forms to his conceit? And all for nothing!
> For Hecuba!
> What's Hecuba to him, or he to Hecuba,
> That he should weep for her? What would he do,
> Had he the motive and the cue for passion
> That I have?
> (2.2.503–514)

Thus, Shakespeare presented a carefully crafted dialectic between two perspectives of the actor as being both involved and/or distanced, leading to sophisticated tricks with the ontology and the emotional perceptions of actor and character.

It is worth noting that Polonius also has a philosophical education, which like his understanding of the theatre is parodied in the play. One prominent example is when Polonius, wanting to convince Claudius and Gertrude that Hamlet is mad, begins philosophizing about the essence of time, that which for Hamlet "is out of joint" (1.5.189).[16] But Polonius, instead of debating—"expostulate" is the word he uses—"Why day is day, night is night, and time is time, / Were nothing but to waste night, day, and time" (2.2.86–89), wants to get directly to the point, telling Gertrude, "Your noble son is mad. / Mad call I it, for to define true madness, / What is't but to be nothing but mad?" (2.2.92–94). Polonius obviously employs a circular proof to make his point, which leads him to the following conclusion: "If circumstances lead me, I will find / Where truth is hid, though it were hid indeed / Within the centre" (2.2.155–157). This is further parody of his philosophical schooling, which at the same time indicates that the play has an elusive centre.

Shakespeare's play presents a series of intricate competitions between Hamlet and Polonius concerning their knowledge and understanding of theatre and philosophy. But they also vie for Ophelia's devotion. This clearly represents a transformation of the rhetorical-theatrical as well as the erotic competitions as presented in the *Symposium*. Furthermore Hamlet and Polonius employ almost diametrically opposite modes of "theatricality" as models for their own behavior. Polonius is a flattering, calculated courtier, incapable of distancing himself from his official role in the court. Whereas Hamlet, as he says to his mother after having killed Polonius, "I essentially am not in madness, / But mad in craft" (3.4.188–189). Madness is a role he plays. I discuss in greater detail the more comprehensive implications of such a role, of playing or actually being insane or mad, in connection with the correspondence between Nietzsche and Strindberg. The conclusion that has to be emphasized at this point, however, is the powerful juxtaposition of Hamlet and Polonius in how they divide their attention between theatre and philosophy. Polonius, like Hamlet, mistakes the search for truth for a theatrical performance, most poignantly when he hides behind the arras in Gertrude's closet, which leads to his death. Polonius apparently believes that by hiding behind the arras he is "safely stored" as a spectator outside the theatrical fiction. Hamlet's problem, on the other hand, is that he is unable to fully enter the same state of strong theatrical emotion as the actor weeping for Hecuba.

Hamlet as Philosopher and Thespian 73

But if Polonius is constantly presented by way of parody and jest, then Hamlet is often presented as a confused and yet completely serious and very dedicated thespian, at least from Hamlet's own perspective. Role-playing and its effects is one of the most frequently discussed topics in Shakespeare's play. However, as the present discussion emphasizes, at the same time as Hamlet theatricalizes his thinking, presenting his own subjectivity in obvious performative terms, being "mad in craft," he employs the theatre for purely philosophical goals, in particular in *The Mousetrap* performance, to examine if the ghost has spoken the truth. The theatricalization of the self and the philosophical uses of the theatre are for Hamlet two sides of the same coin, contributing to his fatally configured liminality. He is both philosopher and thespian yet unable to distinguish clearly between the two.

One of the first examples presenting this confusion takes place just before Hamlet is forbidden to return to Wittenberg, when Gertrude demands of him to "cast thy knighted color off" (1.2.68) and "not forever with thy vailéd lids / Seek for thy noble father in the dust" (1.2.70–71), ending her request by asking why, because "all that lives must die . . . seems it so particular with thee?" (1.2.73–75). In his response Hamlet argues with an obvious philosophical twist: "Seems madam? nay it is, I know not seems" (1.2.76), evoking both ontological and epistemological arguments with regard to a person's inner self and subjectivity and its total independence from the outward signs, which are theatrical and can therefore not really give expression to a person's true self. None of the customary outward signs of mourning, like wearing black clothes, wetted eyes, "can denote me truly" (1.2.83), Hamlet continues, for "These indeed seem, / For they are actions that a man can play, / But I have that within that passes show" (1.2.83–85). This means of course that his inner self is his true self, whereas the outward, theatrical vestiges are not. What we can see of another person, Hamlet argues, is a misleading performance. The true self remains hidden from view.

After he has encountered the ghost of his father, however, Hamlet begins to pursue a course of action that, at the same time as he is developing these assumptions, partly refutes his own notion about the complete separation between the outer vestiges and the true inner life of a person. Toward the end of the long Hecuba soliloquy, Hamlet discloses his plan to employ the theatre as an epistemological tool—a kind of polygraph—to examine whether the king is guilty of the deed of which the ghost has accused him, or if the devil too has put on a performance by using his father's ghost. "I have heard," Hamlet says, nearing the close of his soliloquy,

> That guilty creatures, sitting at a play,
> Have by the very cunning of the scene
> Been struck so to the soul that presently
> They have proclaimed their malefactions;
> For murder, though it have no tongue, will speak
> With most miraculous organ, I'll have these Players
> Play something like the murder of my father
> Before mine uncle. I'll observe his looks;
> I'll tent him to the quick. If a do blench,
> I know my course.
> (2.2.541–551)

The theatre, which is based on outer signs and vestiges, can according to Hamlet touch the veiled parts of the human soul so that we unconsciously or against our own will reveal our secrets.

Hamlet returns to these fundamental issues several times in the play, most prominently in his speech to the actors (3.2.1–36), the longest prose passage in this Shakespeare play. This passage has been interpreted as Shakespeare's own tractate on the art of acting, in which he instructs the players to "suit the action to the word, the word to the action" (3.2.15), and "to hold as 'twere the mirror up to nature; to show virtue her own feature, scorn her own image, and the very age and body of the time his form and pressure" (3.2.18–20). These instructions, serving, it would seem, to display Hamlet's profound understanding of the art of the theatre, are followed by two performances, first the dumb show—the plot presented in pantomime—and then *The Mousetrap*, in which "The Murder of Gonzago" is played out with speaking actors. Included here is the "dozen or sixteen lines" (2.2.494) that Hamlet himself has written and given to the First Player. It is impossible to say exactly which lines Hamlet has added. But these activities point to Hamlet's deep commitment to the theatre. They are an expression of his somewhat naive belief that by creating theatre he can solve the moral and emotional conundrum he is facing.

For Hamlet, as well as for the tradition to which he typically belongs, the discursive practices of philosophy and the theatre converge in the theological question that he raises at the end of the Hecuba soliloquy. From this question he draws the inspiration to test the conscience of the king through a theatrical performance:

> The spirit that I have seen
> May be a devil—and the devil hath power
> T'assume a pleasing shape. Yea, and perhaps
> Out of my weakness and my melancholy,
> As he is very potent with such spirits,
> Abuses me to damn me. I'll have grounds
> More relative than this. The play's the thing
> Wherein I'll catch the conscience of the King.
> (2.2.551–558)

The devil plays tricks just as actors do. And before the performance, Hamlet tells Horatio to watch his uncle carefully, in particular during the scene that "comes near the circumstances / Which I have told thee about my father's death" (3.2.66–67), because "If his occulted guilt / Do not itself unkennel in one speech, / It is a damnéd ghost that we have seen" (3.2.71–73). Here again Hamlet returns to the double dilemma the play is supposed to solve, to find out if the king is the murderer and if the ghost is sent by Satan.

This is also the point in the play at which, on the one hand, philosophy, as a method for investigating the truth and raising moral issues, and theatre, as a form of representation, on the other, become conflated and even confused. Stephen Orgel has shown that the ideas Hamlet espouses were already in circulation when Shakespeare wrote the play, and that they were examined in the literature about a decade later, in 1612, by Thomas Heywood in his essay "Apology for Actors." Orgel points out that the essay based

> its concluding arguments on the assumption that drama is genuinely therapeutic, and he even manages to produce a few examples to prove the point. One of these examples concerns a woman who had murdered her husband and, seeing a play about a similar crime, was driven to confess in a paroxysm of repentant guilt.[17]

Shakespeare thus positioned Hamlet within the contemporary debates about the influence and the legitimacy of the theatre, drawing on arguments that had already been raised by Plato and Aristotle. Hamlet (the character), taking an Aristotelian stance, primarily focuses on the cathartic, epistemological effects of the theatre and how the art of acting stirs the emotions of the actor, which in turn influences the spectator. On the other hand, Shakespeare (the author of the play) draws attention to the ontological issues that were Plato's point of departure for his censorial critique of the theatre. Both Plato and Shakespeare obviously take the theatre seriously: the former (at least officially) in order to ban it; the latter to create a complex dialectic between its different layers of "being" by juxtaposing the theatre with Hamlet's naive belief in its power to expose and reveal the inner thoughts of the individual. This complex dialectic can also be distinguished, at least partially, in the discursive practices Plato presents in the *Symposium*.

Shakespeare has positioned his hero in a gyre, in which the philosophical and thespian discourses converge with emotional, moral, and theological import, making it impossible for Hamlet, despite all his exceptional poetic and philosophical sensitivities, to maneuver the situation in Elsinore, or as he himself says in the "To be or not to be" soliloquy: "to take arms against a sea of troubles" (3.1.59). This soliloquy, and many of Hamlet's pronouncements about philosophy and the theatre, reflect the academic milieu of Wittenberg with its ongoing discussions on theology and philosophy as well as its theatrical activities and frequent visits by traveling theatre companies. Hamlet tries to apply this knowledge in Elsinore. However, given the political turmoil and Hamlet's own personal crisis that result from his father's death, he conflates the two discursive practices. Hamlet interprets the philosophical issues concerning his own identity and other existential issues in theatrical terms and vice versa.

This profound ambiguity can be perceived already in the first lines of the play, during the changing of the guards on the ramparts of Elsinore castle. Barnardo, who is going to relieve Francisco from his guard duty, begins by asking, "Who's there?" He directs the question to the figure who he sees as he enters. Francisco, who is on duty, throws Barnardo's question back at him, asking, "Nay answer me. Stand and unfold yourself" (1.1.1–2). Regardless what the conventions are for who puts the question in situations like these, the opening question "Who's there?" is confusing. By directing the question "Who's there?" to the figure already on the stage, the actor playing Barnardo is also asking his fellow actor to say who he is playing. And by retorting, "Stand and unfold yourself," the actor playing Francisco wants the actor playing Barnardo to do the same.

A few lines later, after they have discussed the guard duty, the initial question of the play is repeated by Francisco in a somewhat more emphatic form: "Stand ho! Who is there?" (1.1.13), as Horatio and Marcellus appear and join Barnardo on his watch.[18] And after a few additional lines, we learn that the tension and caution expressed at the start of this scene are not only triggered by the change of the guard, but more important, by the experience of the prior few nights: they have seen "a dreaded sight" (1.1.25), an apparition. This is the reason why Marcellus (or according to the second quarto, Horatio) asks the guards who are going to be relieved: "What, has this thing appeared again tonight?" (1.1.21).[19] Many critics, among them perhaps most convincingly and creatively Herbert Blau, point to these lines as being highly charged with meta-theatrical energies, referring not only to the fictional situation—the change of the guards—but to the world of the theatre and performance. This question refers both to the appearance of the ghost and the appearance, again this night, of the theatrical performance itself. Beyond this, it reveals the complex theatrical mechanism whereby the theatre enables such supernatural phenomena to be seen night after night on the stage. The theatre itself has become a ghost.

Philosophy Reads *Hamlet*: The Worthy Pioneers

The philosophical afterlife of *Hamlet* has privileged interpretations of the ghost as an uncanny figure who is pointing toward a Utopian future. Such a position ought to have been reserved—at least ideally—for Hamlet, the son. But he claims *silence* for his final point of *rest*. It is the ghost of Hamlet's father—bearing the same name as his son—who repeatedly returns, appearing in this position. Thus the chronological sequence, with Old Hamlet naming his son after himself in order to assure his succession and a configuration of the future, has become paradoxically reversed.[20]

No other dramatic text, except perhaps Sophocles' Theban plays—and in particular *Antigone* and *Oedipus Tyrannus*—have received such a varied and philosophically oriented reception from a host of thinkers. Hamlet's struggle to be both philosopher and thespian—as presented thus far—has no doubt contributed to the extraordinary interest this literary character has received from psychoanalytic theorists like Sigmund

Freud and Jacques Lacan, and from authors like Johann Wolfgang von Goethe and James Joyce, as well as from philosophers like G.W.F. Hegel, Karl Marx, Nietzsche, Benjamin, and most recently Jacques Derrida.[21] But finally, in all of these cases, it is the superb sophistication of Shakespeare's play, making room for a unique hermeneutic freedom which has triggered the imagination of thinkers from almost all fields and schools, that has contributed to the remarkable afterlife of *Hamlet*.

In *Specters of Marx*, Derrida explores the complex intertextual dialogue between the *Communist Manifesto* and Shakespeare's *Hamlet*, asking: "How can one be late for the end of history?" And he immediately answers with the kind of enigmatic certainty that he was capable of, claiming that this is a "question for today . . . because it obliges one to reflect again, as we have been doing since Hegel, on what happens and deserves the name of *event*, after history; it obliges one to wonder if the end of history is but the end to a *certain* concept of history."[22] The question we need to ask is if it is Utopia that comes after what Derrida terms "a certain concept of history." What does it mean to reflect *again* as Derrida urges us to do? Is it really possible in view of Hamlet's supplication that "the rest is silence" (5.2.337) to "tell my [that is, "his"] story" (5.2.328), as Hamlet wants Horatio to do? And does it still make sense as Horatio then proposes to do, to tell "th'yet unknowing world / How these things came about" (5.2.358–359)? I hope it still does, and that we still care about the "cause" (to use Hamlet's own term) for his untimely death, which Hamlet wants Horatio to "report," although I have serious doubts about the effectiveness of such a report.

Trying to provide some very preliminary answers to these questions, I will focus on two issues. The first is how we relate to history when imagining and representing Utopias in the theatre or on the stage. The Utopias of the twentieth century have been based on complex combinations and linkages between the past and the future. On the one hand, the hoped-for Utopian condition has been perceived as a corrective for, or even a way of healing, the failures of the past. But at the same time, the Utopian condition has been viewed nostalgically, as a return to an idyllic past with its obvious associations of retrieving, or even some claim of reestablishing, a lost paradise.

The second issue, more directly related to the theatre itself, is how the appearances of ghosts on the stage simultaneously point toward these ambivalently perceived pasts of failure and nostalgia as they point toward the future. The appearance of a supernatural being on the stage frequently constitutes the concrete link between these pasts and the future. And on the stage, in stark opposition to what Hamlet claims before he dies, the rest is usually *not* silence. Instead the dead not only appear again as ghosts or spirits of all kinds, they are also constantly talking, presenting to the survivors real or imagined demands and threats.

The theatre and more recently also the cinema have taken on privileges for "materializing" the dead in forms that most of us would most probably deem impossible or even unacceptable in our daily lives. The Israeli playwright Hanoch Levin made one of his characters say that the dead can appear only in our dreams, and on special occasions, like anniversaries. But at the same time many of his performances were overcrowded by the physical appearances of the dead on the stage. We are willing to grant privileges to theatrical and cinematographic representations that conflict with our common sense and our rational understanding of the world in which we live.[23]

The ghost of Hamlet's father is the "worthy pioneer" that has come to signify both the different versions of the past as well as a Utopian future. The expression "worthy pioneer" is used by Hamlet after his solitary meeting with the ghost, which the audience has also witnessed. But when Horatio and Marcellus, who have not been present during this meeting, return to the stage, Hamlet begs them to "Never make known what you have seen tonight" (1.5.144). This command is obviously changed as Hamlet is nearing his death, when he asks Horatio to speak, emphasizing the almost unbridgeable tensions between speech and silence. When Hamlet asks his friends to swear on his sword to be silent, the ghost echoes this demand from its position under the stage, in the so-called cellarage, the scenic metaphor for Purgatory. To this Hamlet quickly responds: "Well said old mole, canst work i'th'earth so fast? / A worthy pioneer" (1.5.162–163).

The primary meaning of "pioneer" in Shakespeare's time was of a military nature, referring to someone who was a member of an infantry group going ahead of the army or the regiment to dig trenches, repair roads, and clear the terrain for the main body of troops. But "pioneer" had already received a more abstract meaning as well, referring to a person who goes before the others to prepare or to open up the way, beginning a new enterprise or course of action. This is where the Utopian dimension comes in, lending to the word "pioneer" the meaning "avant-garde," which entered the French aesthetic discourse in the mid-nineteenth century and in the beginning of the twentieth century. "Pioneer" is synonymous in English with "innovator," particularly in the arts, and was already used in Shakespeare's time, though not by Shakespeare himself, for someone who goes before the troops. The ghost of Hamlet's father is a pioneer in all of these senses. And the military attributes of this ghost are mentioned explicitly by Horatio. He emphasizes that when he saw it the first time, it was wearing full military uniform, from head to foot.

But letting the ghosts enter the stage is not sufficient for this forward look into a Utopian future to become fully materialized. However, pointing directly to such a possibility is Derrida's reading of *The Communist Manifesto* from 1848, in particular of its now proverbial opening sentence: "A spectre is haunting Europe—the spectre of Communism" (*Ein Gespenst geht um in Europa—das Gespenst des Kommunismus*).[24] In "The Eighteenth Brumaire," Marx is even more explicit, saying,

> The revolution is thoroughgoing. It is still travelling through purgatory. It does its work methodically. By December 2, 1851, it had completed half of its preparatory work; now it is completing the other half.... And when it has accomplished this second half of its preliminary work, Europe will leap from its seat and exult: Well burrowed [grubbed or dug; in German *Brav gewühlt*], old mole![25]

And in a later speech, from 1856, Marx even claims that "the old mole that can work in the earth so fast, that worthy pioneer [is] the Revolution."[26]

At the same time as the ideas of Marx point toward his own Utopian visions, they echo Hegel's explication of the ghost of Hamlet's father in his "Lectures on the History of Philosophy." Here the ghost figures as the transformation of poetry into pure spirit, which is almost, according to Hegel, like a volcanic eruption or even an earthquake:

> It [the old mole/the ghost] always comes forward and to the fore, because spirit alone is progression. Often it seems to have forgotten who it is, to have gotten lost. But, internally divided, it works its way forward—as Hamlet says of his father's spirit, "Well done, old mole"—until, having gathered strength, it pushes through the crust of earth that has separated it from its sun, its concept, and the crust collapses. When the crust collapses, like a rundown, abandoned building, spirit takes on new youthful form and dons seven-league boots. This labour of spirit to know itself, find itself, this activity is spirit, the life of spirit itself. Its

result is the concept that it grasps of itself; the history of spirit yields the clear insight that spirit willed all of this in its history.[27]

This passage depicts the movement from the inner regions of the earth toward the light, pointing to the end of history as a progression from darkness to light, a revelation. Looking backward at this genealogy of worthy pioneers, from Derrida to Marx and from there back to Hegel and Shakespeare himself, we become "involved" in a "revolving" motion, in the sense of a repeated revolutionary movement. We therefore are gesturing toward Utopia by looking forward through the figure that represents the past, which as Marx claimed in his frequently quoted passage from *The Eighteenth Brumaire*, becomes farcical: "Hegel remarks somewhere that all great world-historic facts and personages appear, so to speak, twice. He forgot to add: the first time as tragedy, the second time as farce."[28] This, echoing the dialectics between tragedy and comedy in the *Symposium*, means that the reappearance of the ghost—and it obviously appears again, because that is what Shakespeare's play is about—is a farce, at least in the way it depicts history.

Another curious feature of these readings of the "old mole" is that both Hegel and Marx are misquoting Shakespeare. Instead of quoting Hamlet's original "Well said, old mole," Marx presents the phrase as *"Brav gewühlt, alter Maulwurf,"* with *brav gewühlt* basically meaning "well dug." And before him Hegel had shifted to the more abstract *"Brav gearbeitet, wackerer Maulwurf,"* with *brav gearbeitet* translating as "well done" or "well labored."[29] The German translations of Shakespeare that they used are probably one the reasons for these changes. Peter Stallybrass refers to the Schlegel/Tieck translation that Marx knew and that erases the verb, becoming *"Brav, alter Maulwurf."*[30] This shift of emphasis from *saying* to forms of *doing*, as in "digging" or "laboring," needs to be explored in a broader context than is possible here. Let me draw attention again to the twentieth-century philosophers of language, most prominently J. L. Austin and John Searle, but also Judith Butler, who makes some important distinctions between saying and doing. But among them, Austin in particular is very hostile to the complex combination of saying and doing on which the theatre is based.[31]

The hypothetical modes of expression of the theatre, just like Utopian discourses, disregard the commonsense criteria for sincerity, authenticity, and truth stipulated by Austin in order to confirm for example that those saying "I do" during a wedding ceremony really mean what they say. Without these sincerity criteria, Austin argues, the performativity in the saying of this phrase becomes void. However in her recent book, *Antigone's Claim*, Butler, also following Hegel, makes a great effort to bridge the paradoxical gap between saying and doing by examining the legal contexts Sophocles' play provides. Butler focuses on the question of what it means to make a "claim," and from this we can learn how law and theatre are related. One of the features legal discourses and theatrical modes of representation have in common is their close relationship to the Utopian imagination.[32]

Also, but from a very different perspective, it is necessary to account for a military "pioneer" besides the ghost in Shakespeare's play. I am referring to Fortinbras, the Norwegian prince, who is perhaps less "worthy" than the ghost, but no doubt more of a pioneer. The wars initiated by young Fortinbras, whose father bore the same name and lost the wars against Old Hamlet, are briefly mentioned in the first act of the play. The wars remain a potential threat to the stability of the kingdom throughout. Fortinbras belongs to the world of politics, and his wars and conquests serve as the backdrop to the tragedy of Hamlet. They are obviously not the tragedy itself but history in its crudest and most violent form. However, only in the last scene of the play, when Fortinbras himself arrives, does this explicit historical / political presence cross the threshold of the stage, invading its core. And when Horatio, after Hamlet's death, says that he wants to "speak" about the things that have taken place, Fortinbras nonchalantly responds, "Let us haste to hear it" (5.2.365), but is neither capable of listening to nor reflecting on what *we* have seen. Fortinbras does not even pay attention to the details of the tragedy that has just come to a close with Hamlet's death. Instead he briskly commands: "Take up the bodies. . . . Go bid the soldiers shoot" (5.2.380, 382). Horatio on the other hand has just requested that the bodies be put "high on a stage" (3.5.357) in order to transform into theatre the grim spectacle we have witnessed, invoking the flights of angels that will now sing Hamlet to his rest. Whereas Horatio only sees Hamlet's tragedy, not the broader historical context, these are the angels that for Walter Benjamin will eventually become the angel of history, the *Angelus Novus*.

The ghost of Hamlet's father also constitutes a peril to the stability of the kingdom, but on a completely different level, threatening Hamlet with demands for revenge, rather than as Fortinbras does, by invading the borders of Denmark. We therefore have to account for the fact there are actually two worthy pioneers in Shakespeare's *Hamlet*. First there is the ghost, which for Hamlet represents the more private tragedy, and which has become the focus of attention for the commentators I have referred to previously. But the ambitious young general Fortinbras, who represents the political events that change history, is also a pioneer. This fusion between tragedy and history—making room for both of these "pioneers," even creating a tension between them—has become a major mark of modernity, and even more I would argue, of postmodernity. Fortinbras undermines the Utopian vision toward which the ghost, according to Hegel and Marx, is supposedly pointing.

Georg Büchner's *Danton's Death*, with its critique of the French Revolution, is an important milestone in the emergence of such a dystopian fusion between history and tragedy. In Heiner Müller's reinterpretations of the classics, this fusion is a constantly recurring feature. His *Hamletmachine*, a radical adaptation of Shakespeare's play, begins with the words: "I was Hamlet. I stood at the shore and talked with the surf BLABLA, the ruins of Europe in back of me."[33] This is no doubt an expression of the destructive gyre where history and tragedy converge and where Utopia is given a technical knockout. Echoing Walter Benjamin's depiction of Klee's *Angelus Novus*, the helpless angel of history, situated in the middle of the debris where the storm of history is repeatedly taking its tragic course, which I return to later, Heiner Müller depicts a situation in which it has become impossible to hear the gradually enfeebled voices of the Horatios who are telling us how these things came about after Hamlet has declared that "the rest is silence." And then there is the noise of the ocean.

In *The Birth of Tragedy from the Spirit of Music*, Nietzsche proposes a diametrically opposite reading, arguing that the figure of Hamlet finally becomes transformed by a paralysis of action, a standstill containing "a *lethargic* element in which all past personal experience is submerged. / . . . that / separates the world of everyday reality from that of Dionysian reality." And Nietzsche continues, "as soon as that everyday reality returns to consciousness, it is experienced for what it is with disgust: an ascetic mood which negates the will is the fruit of those conditions." This is true for Nietzsche of the Dionysian man as well as of the character Hamlet, who "both have at one time cast a true glance into the essence of things, they have acquired *knowledge*, and action is repugnant to them; for their action can change nothing in the eternal essence of things, they feel that it is laughable or shameful that they are expected to repair a world which is out of joint." There is no "worthy pioneer" in view here, and this, he adds, leads to a situation in which "no consolation is accepted, the longing goes beyond the world after death, goes beyond even the gods, now existence, together with its glittering reflection in the gods or in an immortal world is negated." From this negation of the gods, Nietzsche goes on claiming that this is a state of extreme danger in which art becomes an enchantress who "comes to rescue and heal" by reshaping "that disgust at the thought of the horrific or absurd aspects of life into notions with which it is possible to live." Nietzsche, repeating Socrates' insistence that there is a philosophical blueprint based on a unification of the two dramatic genres, points to the *"sublime,* the artistic taming of the horrific, and the *comic,* the artistic discharge of disgust at the absurd" (italics in the original).[34] The horrific and the absurd are the two sides of the same Nietzschean coin, of which Hamlet with his sometimes even optimistic drive forward is not fully aware. Or as he says after having confronted the ghost for the first time:

> The time is out of joint. O cursed spite
> That ever I was born to set it right!
> Nay, come, let's go together. (1.5.189–191)

At this point at least, in spite of the fact that "time is out of joint"—or rather because this is the case—it still makes sense to "go together," joining forces.

And as I will argue in the next chapter, it is not at all certain that art and the freedom of the spirit that Nietzsche strives to achieve can maintain and support this kind of redemptive potential for the philosopher of Dionysian ecstasy. Rather, by magnifying Hamlet into a Dionysian figure, Nietzsche sets the stage for a much more powerful confrontation with madness and insanity than Hamlet himself does. Already when he wrote *The Birth of Tragedy from the Spirit of Music,* Nietzsche apparently sensed that it is not possible to hide behind "an antic disposition" (1.5.172) as Hamlet does, even if he evokes those "things in heaven and earth" that Horatio has not even dreamed of.

These "things" that are appearing again tonight, as Benjamin concludes in *The Origin of German Tragic Drama,* are no doubt based on the Christian theological substratum of Shakespeare's play (bringing the learning and theology of Wittenberg to Elsinore), but they must also be viewed, he adds, from a broader historical perspective. In his book Benjamin opens one of his discussions of Shakespeare's play by quoting Hamlet's last soliloquy: "How all occasions do inform against me." Hamlet asks again, with an almost direct reference to Sophocles' *Oedipus Tyrannus*:

> What is a man,
> If his chief good and market of his time
> Be but to sleep and feed? A beast, no more.
> Sure he that made us with such large discourse,
> Looking before and after, gave us not
> That capability and godlike reason
> To fust in us unus'd. (4.4.33–39)

Here Benjamin perceives not only "an element of German paganism and the grim belief in the subjection of man to fate," which he could just as well label the classical Greek world view, but also something new: "an empty world," which both Calvinism and Lutheranism viewed with great suspicion. For Benjamin, beyond Nietzsche's introspective reading of *Hamlet*, this play problematizes larger historical developments.

But for Benjamin, Shakespeare's play also protests against the acts of faith introduced by the reformations, indicating that life "is overcome by deep horror at the idea that the whole of existence might proceed in such a way." Instead,

> [t]he idea of death fills it [that is, "life"] with profound terror. Mourning is the state of mind in which feeling revives the empty world in the form of a mask, and derives an enigmatic satisfaction in contemplating it. Every feeling is bound to an *a priori* object, and the representation of this object is its phenomenology. Accordingly the theory of mourning, which emerged unmistakably as a *pendant* to the theory of tragedy, can only be developed in the description of that world which is revealed under the gaze of the melancholy man.[35] (italics in the original)

Here, in Shakespeare's *Hamlet*, the unique dramatic language that Benjamin had already found in the *Symposium* has disintegrated, leaving us with the "melancholy" man who

> alone is a spectator by the grace of God; but . . . who cannot find satisfaction in what he sees enacted, only in his own fate. His life, the exemplary object of his

mourning, points, before its extinction, to the Christian providence in whose bosom his mournful images are transformed into a blessed existence. Only in a princely life such as this is melancholy redeemed, by being confronted with itself. The rest is silence.[36]

For this melancholy man—and apparently, this is also true of Socrates—the redemptive dimension that Nietzsche has abandoned can still be retrieved. Or as Socrates himself says in the *Phaedo*: "Those who apply themselves in the right way to philosophy are directly and of their own accord preparing themselves for dying and death."[37] The silence of that moment for Hamlet is both theatrical and philosophical.

Ludwig Wittgenstein's *Tractatus Logico-Philosophicus* (*Logische-Philosophische Abhandlung*), published in 1921, and written during the First World War, with the author's preface dated 1918, has a similar narrative structure as Shakespeare's *Hamlet*. Wittgenstein's treatise begins with this enigmatic sentence: "*Die Welt ist alles, was der Fall ist*" (The world is all that is the case). The German word *Fall*—meaning, "the case"—as I show later, carries a much more pointed connotation than the English translation of Wittgenstein's text would have us believe. It is closely connected to the accidents and catastrophes we call history, at the same time as it contains a Utopian, even mystical dimension, ending with the short and enigmatic statement to which Wittgenstein gave the number seven: "*Wovon man nicht sprechen kann, darüber muß man schweigen*"[38] (What we cannot speak about we must pass over in silence). That about which we cannot speak still exists, because we must pass over it, as a pilot over "a sea of troubles" against which we can still "take arms," as Hamlet says in his "To be or not to be" soliloquy, "and by opposing end them" (3.1.58–59), a gesture that has Hamlet immediately turning to thoughts of suicide. Wittgenstein's treatise has a "Hamletian" structure, beginning with an account of the world, asking "Who's there?" and ending with a paraphrase of Hamlet's famous last words: "The *rest* is silence." These aspects of philosophy, performance, and history are directly and profoundly related to that "rest" that comes after the silence—both as a *place* of rest and as what *remains* afterward—the debris of history, which according to Wittgenstein, we pass *over* in silence, again.

3

Stagings of the Self

THE NIETZSCHE-STRINDBERG
CORRESPONDENCE

> I have used these weeks to "revalue values." Do you understand this expression? When you come right down to it, the alchemist is the most praiseworthy of men: I mean the one who changes something negligible or contemptible into something of value, even gold. He alone enriches, the others merely exchange. My task is quite singular this time: I have asked myself what mankind has always hated, feared, and despised the most—and precisely out of this I have made my "gold."
>
>   If only I am not accused of counterfeiting! Or rather, I'm bound to be.
> —Friedrich Nietzsche, letter to Georg Brandes, Turin, May 23, 1888[1]

The correspondence between Friedrich Nietzsche and August Strindberg consists of fewer than a dozen letters written during a period of not more than approximately six weeks. This intense exchange of letters ended abruptly with a short letter of eight words from Nietzsche, dated January 8, 1889, and signed *"Der Gekreuzigte"* (the crucified). It signaled the onset of his final insanity. The first direct communication between the two men was Nietzsche's dedication of his book *Götzen-Dämmerung* (*Twilight of the Idols*), which he sent to Strindberg, via the Danish critic Georg Brandes, in November 1888. The dedication reads: "Shouldn't someone translate this? It's dynamite (*Sollte man das nicht übersetzen? Es ist Dynamit*)." It is signed *"Der Antikrist."*[2] What for Nietzsche had begun as something explosive that should be translated ended in total chaos with the short letter signed *"Der Gekreuzigte."* This total reversal of roles—from *"Der Antikrist"* to *"Der Gekreuzigte"*—frames the complex performance-dialogue. Each correspondent, in his own very different way, dramatizes the elusive borderline between sanity and madness through his epistolary "staging" of himself.

Strindberg, who respectfully tried to follow and respond to the quick and sudden turns of Nietzsche's letters, did not fully understand the implications of what he had become involved in. At this time Strindberg had just published his own French translation of *The Father* (written in Swedish in 1887), which he had sent to Émile Zola. Strindberg had received a letter from Zola criticizing the play for its abstractness. This letter had been included in the French translation, which Strindberg later sent with a dedication to Nietzsche. And Strindberg's *Miss Julie*, written in the summer of 1888, was published during the same week in which his correspondence with Nietzsche began. In both of these plays the main characters meet death—*Father*'s captain by stroke and *Miss Julie*'s title character by suicide—after having crossed the border to insanity.

However, Nietzsche's epistolary outbursts were apparently of a different magnitude from anything Strindberg had previously encountered or created himself, and as we shall see they shocked and even scared him. This exchange of letters crossed the European continent, going back and forth, almost with the speed of e-mail. Nietzsche wrote in German from Turin, Italy, and Strindberg posted in French from the small village of Holte, near Copenhagen. The correspondence presents two very different understandings and realizations of the elusive boundaries where sanity ends and madness begins. Clearly, Strindberg "plays the role" of Hamlet, being "mad in craft" (3.4.189), whereas Nietzsche "acts out" Ophelia, unable to control his final outburst of insanity.

The first section of this chapter examines the brief correspondence between Nietzsche and Strindberg, but also the role of the Danish critic Georg Brandes who was involved as a major participant in the more extended drama. It was actually Brandes who introduced Nietzsche and Strindberg to each other, after having described one to the other in several letters. But also after the direct contact between them had been established, Strindberg continued to consult Brandes concerning the meaning and intentions of what he perceived as Nietzsche's sometimes irrational communications. Although Strindberg and Nietzsche never met face-to-face, Brandes and Strindberg, who at this time were living close to each other in Denmark, no doubt did.

The second section of this chapter examines a letter from Strindberg to Siri von Essen, written on June 20, 1876, more than twelve years before the Nietzsche-Strindberg correspondence began. On this day von Essen, an aspiring actress, was officially divorced from her first husband, Carl Gustaf Wrangel, an officer in the Swedish army, enabling her to marry Strindberg. They had become romantically involved during Strindberg's numerous visits as a family friend to the Wrangel home. As the marriage between Strindberg and von Essen was breaking down a decade later, Strindberg was writing three of his major plays, *The Father*, *Miss Julie*, and *The Creditors*—in which Tekla, the femme fatale, confronts both her former and her present husbands. Von Essen served as the model for Laura, the satanic wife in *The Father*; for the young noblewoman Miss Julie; and for Tekla. In these plays Strindberg served as his own model for the male protagonists. These characters include the captain—Laura's husband in *The Father*—and the servant Jean, at once seduced by and seducer of Julie, as well as Adolf, Tekla's second husband.

At the time of his correspondence with Nietzsche, besides presenting the breakdown of his marriage in *The Father*, *Miss Julie*, and *The Creditors*, Strindberg first depicts the details of the doomed marriage with von Essen in his autobiographical novel, *The Defence of a Madman*, originally written in French and published in 1887. And as a final act of public exposure of his wife, Strindberg had von Essen play the role of Miss Julie in the first production of the play, which was staged in Copenhagen on March 14, 1889. The letter from Strindberg to von Essen from the summer of 1876 serves as a baseline for the correspondence a decade later, as well as a point of departure for examining the complex combination of deception, seduction, and creativity practiced by Strindberg. Besides being written at an important juncture in Strindberg's life, this letter outlines a dream that serves as the blueprint for another of his major plays, *A Dream Play*, written twenty-five years later, in 1901.

And finally, the third section of this chapter goes even further back in time, presenting a reading of Nietzsche's first major work, *The Birth of Tragedy from the Spirit of Music*, published in 1872. Appropriate to our purposes, this book has the character of a letter, as it is dedicated and addressed to Richard Wagner. The complex relationship between Nietzsche and Wagner also has to be taken into consideration when examining the interactions between the philosophers' and thespians' respective discursive practices. Nietzsche's initial admiration of Wagner, his detachment from him, and their ensuing animosity bear witness to a conflict in German culture, in particular when viewed retrospectively. I hope in view of the conclusions I reach (in the following chapters) with regard to the crisis and collapse of pre–World War II Modernism, it will be possible to revisit this troubled relationship, and not only on the level of the personal.

My own reading of Nietzsche's book suggests that it is a self-dramatization of Nietzsche's own personal development. After Attic tragedy has disintegrated and the union between the Dionysian and Apollonian forces is dissolved, Nietzsche, I argue, finds the model for fashioning himself as a philosopher in the figure of Socrates, the tragic figure who is prepared to risk everything, even his own life. Nietzsche's relationship to the figure of Socrates, generally understood as an outright rejection of the philosopher, is complex and ambivalent. In spite of the sometimes virulent criticism of Socrates in *The Birth of Tragedy from the Spirit of Music*, it is possible to read this book as an allegory depicting the birth of the philosopher (Nietzsche himself) from the death of tragedy. This rebirth, like so many other aspects of Nietzsche's writing, is amplified by contradictions and paradoxes. However it also constitutes his first declaration that the form of philosophy and cultural critique he was beginning to develop contains a highly theatricalized modality of dialectical thinking.

The aim of returning to these earlier moments in the lives and writings of Nietzsche and Strindberg—with their brief correspondence fresh in mind—is to illuminate their individual modes of self-dramatization. For Strindberg the epistolary form of communication was a laboratory, a liminal form of mental experimentation, in which he gradually transformed the people he corresponded and lived with into characters of his own creative writings. The borders between the fictional world and Strindberg's own life are elusive. An anecdote poignantly illustrates this: after encountering one of his enemies in the street, Strindberg supposedly parted by saying, "See you in my next play!" This formula could even be applied to Strindberg's transforming of Nietzsche into a fictional character, having him appear as mad Caesar in his play *To Damascus*, written in 1899. Nietzsche's penultimate letter to Strindberg was signed "Nietzsche-Caesar."

Whereas for Strindberg, integrating his life into what he wrote was more of a literary technique, for Nietzsche it became the core of his philosophy: a constant quest for his own unique identity and thinking as the basis for truth, transforming his life into thoughts and words. Nietzsche's writings are authentic expressions of his innermost deliberations. At the same time they constitute an integral part of his philosophical thinking. The exchange of letters between Nietzsche and Strindberg can be read as a drama demonstrating the lack of communication and misfired expectations between a philosopher and a playwright. Finally, for Nietzsche, their correspondence led both to a huge sacrifice and to a far-reaching catharsis in his last years, during which he was insane. For Strindberg their exchange of letters constituted a laboratory.

The French philosopher Pierre Klossowski, one of the more perceptive readers of Nietzsche, has even suggested that "Strindberg—unwittingly, it is true—confirmed Nietzsche in his Turinesque vision of the world, and thereby helped prepare for Nietzsche's own transfiguration and his elevation into an absolutely fabulous region. Strindberg's pathos sustained Nietzsche's paranoia."[3] This may indeed have been the case, even if Strindberg's willingness to play a role in this complex drama was, as I will show, more complicated than Klossowski suggests. And just as Strindberg perhaps assisted Nietzsche to make his leap, the *Sprung*, Nietzsche became a haunting shadow for Strindberg in his much more methodological and controlled struggle with the "powers." This includes the period in which he was suffering from a psychological crisis, the so-called Inferno crisis, after which, unlike Nietzsche, he reemerged with renewed creativity. The fundamental difference between the playwright and the philosopher in this case was how Strindberg gradually overcame his mental crisis, revolutionizing European drama with his post-Inferno plays, whereas Nietzsche never recovered. Nietzsche succeeded in revolutionizing European philosophy, but he did so by way of a postcrisis thrust in which he could no longer actively participate. Therefore, the correspondence between the two men, rather than a true encounter, must be read more as a modern "drama" of how two individuals develop their own unique creativity on the brink of and beyond the borderline to insanity.

The Correspondence

In April and May of 1888 the Danish critic Georg Brandes gave five public lectures in Copenhagen introducing Friedrich Nietzsche and his philosophy to gradually growing audiences. These lectures were, according to Ernst Behler, the first major international recognition of Nietzsche and his thinking.[4] Brandes presented Nietzsche's philosophy as a form of "aristocratic radicalism," emphasizing the philosopher's atheist tendencies, something which, judging by Nietzsche's enthusiastic response in the letters he wrote to Brandes, delighted him. In one of his lectures Brandes introduced Nietzsche as "a diviner, a seer, an artist less fascinating by what he does than what he is."[5] This was certainly of interest to the writer August Strindberg, who during that spring was living in Holte, near the Danish capital, and read the reports of the Brandes lectures in *Politiken*, the influential Copenhagen daily newspaper. It is even possible that Strindberg attended some of these lectures himself.[6] In any case, Nietzsche's ideas, which the Swedish author felt were very close to his own, immediately made a very strong impression on him.

The initial contact but not yet back-and-forth correspondence between Nietzsche and Strindberg would commence several months later, in November 1888. But judging from the many extant letters to and from other correspondents, the philosopher and the playwright had already been indirectly introduced to each other during that summer. These "preparations" for the actual correspondence is an integral part of the "drama" that I am reconstructing. Already on April 3, 1888, even before Brandes gave his Copenhagen lectures, he wrote to Nietzsche, saying, "If you read Swedish, I'd like to draw your attention to Sweden's singular genius, August Strindberg. When you write about women, you very much resemble him."[7] And the first time Strindberg actually mentioned Nietzsche by name was in a letter to his Swedish writer-colleague Verner von Heidenstam, from May 17, 1888, about a week after the last newspaper report about the Brandes lectures had been published. In this letter Strindberg mentioned Nietzsche with the following enthusiastic instruction: "Buy a modern German philosopher called Nietzsche, about whom G.B. [Georg Brandes] has been lecturing. Everything is there! Don't deny yourself this pleasure! N. is a poet as well."[8] Strindberg had no doubt already become deeply enthralled with Nietzsche's ideas, and during the summer, as he devoted his time to the writing of *Miss Julie*, his enthusiasm grew.

On September 4, 1888, Strindberg sent quite a remarkable letter to Edvard Brandes, the younger brother of Georg Brandes. Edvard was a critic in his own right but is best known for taking an active part in the

Danish left coalition, which was struggling for full parliamentary government during the latter part of the nineteenth century. In this letter, Strindberg elaborated his very personal impressions of Nietzsche, and made the following amazing statement:

> However, the uterus of my mental [spiritual] world has received a tremendous ejaculation of the sperm from Friedrich Nietzsche, so that I feel like a bitch with a full belly. He's the man for me! Give my regards to Georg Brandes and thank him for introducing us! (Woman-hater, of course, like all talented men!)[9]

Strindberg's reaction to Nietzsche's ideas—probably after reading *Der Fall Wagner*—was quite visceral, giving rise to unbridled homoerotic feelings and confirming Strindberg's own ideas about women. His reaction can even be compared to the combination of spiritual and physical feelings that arises between the men discussed in the *Symposium*. The letter to Brandes shows that in his imagination Strindberg had already been more than introduced to Nietzsche, even if there had not yet been any direct contact between them.

The first time Nietzsche himself actually mentions Strindberg is in a letter to Heinrich Köselitz from October 14, 1888. In the letter, Nietzsche says that Brandes "gave a copy of my text [*Der Fall Wagner*] to the greatest Swedish writer, who reportedly has been wholly won over to my side, August Strindberg, he calls him a 'true genius,' just somewhat mad."[10] This is an almost literal repetition of a letter from October 6, a week earlier, when Brandes had written to Nietzsche saying, "I gave a copy of the book [*Der Fall Wagner*] to the greatest Swedish writer, August Strindberg, whom I have wholly won over to your side. He is a true genius, just a bit mad like most geniuses (and non-geniuses)."[11] And in a letter to Brandes from October 20, probably referring to *Götzen-Dämmerung*, of which Strindberg, as mentioned before, received a dedicated copy, Nietzsche asks Brandes "to send a copy to the Swedish man you introduced with such words of praise. Only I don't know his place of residence.—This text is my philosophy *in nuce*—radical to the point of criminality."[12]

And almost a month later, on November 18, in another letter to Köselitz, Nietzsche mentions he has received "a truly brilliant work of a Swedish man, the August Strindberg introduced to me by his greatest admirer Dr. Brandes. . . . It's called 'Les Mariés,' Paris 1885.—Very strange, we are in absolute agreement concerning 'woman'—it had already struck Dr. Brandes."[13] And two days later, on November 20, in a letter to Brandes, Nietzsche adds, "With great delight I read Mr. August Strindberg's "Les Mariés" two days ago at home. My sincere admiration, unhindered save by the feeling of slightly admiring myself in it."[14] The Strindberg book Nietzsche refers to in these letters is *Giftas* (*Married*), a collection of short stories about marriage, the first part of which had been published in 1884. Because of the way Strindberg had depicted the Holy Communion and the transubstantiation in this book, he had been sued and brought to trial, but was eventually freed from these charges. Strindberg's critical relationship to religion no doubt found strong support in Nietzsche, enabling him to admire himself, as he expresses in his letter.

On October 2, 1888, Strindberg had already written to Brandes and thanked him for sending Nietzsche's *Der Fall Wagner*.[15] Then on November 29, a short while after the Nietzsche letters about *Giftas*, Strindberg wrote to Brandes and thanked him for sending the dedicated copy of *Götzen-Dämmerung*, because Nietzsche's books, Strindberg added, "are well beyond my means," mentioning that he had "sent Nietzsche *The Father* 8 months ago,[16] care of his publisher! Am now sending another copy."[17] And a few days later, on December 1, slightly impatiently, Strindberg sent a short letter to Brandes, referring to Nietzsche as "an astoundingly brilliant master, but he's asked me if I can get him translated!" (no doubt referring to the dedication) and asked for his advice: "What should one say to him?"[18] Even if the question *"Sollte mann das nicht übersetzen?"* was put generally, and in a negative modality, it was hardly a direct invitation to Strindberg to translate the book. The theme of translation, however—which is also a form of transformation—gradually becomes one of the central themes in the ensuing correspondence between Nietzsche and Strindberg.

Strindberg ends his short letter to Brandes from December 1, asking if he has read his "re-evaluation (*Umwertung*) of the servant Figaro a year before 1889,"[19] referring to Jean in *Miss Julie*. By adopting this Nietzschean term, included in the first paragraph of *Götzen-Dämmerung*, which Nietzsche had also used in his letter to Brandes in May 1888 (quoted as the epigraph to this chapter), Strindberg was on the one hand signaling to Brandes that he had become a disciple, and on the other that he had already developed "Nietzschean" ideas on his own. He claims that he had worked out these ideas while writing *Miss Julie*, long before he had actually read Nietzsche's writings, although he must initially have been acquainted with them through Brandes's lectures. Strindberg's constant flickering between being a disciple of and a precursor to Nietzsche can be clearly distinguished both in the correspondence between them and in Strindberg's letters to Brandes—also in the letters after Nietzsche had become totally incapacitated.

Nietzsche wrote his first letter to Strindberg on November 27, 1888, after he had read Strindberg's French translation of *The Father* that Strindberg had sent him. This letter begins with the following overdetermined sentence: "I suspect our mail has [or, *our missions have*] crossed paths?" (*Ich denke, unsre Sendungen haben sich gekreuzt?*).[20] It is however not only their books and their opinions about each other in their letters to their friends that had been crossing in the mail. The word *gekreuzt*, in addition to meaning "crisscross," means "to be crucified." Nietzsche signed his final letter to Strindberg—as well as letters to several other people from those days—"*Der Gekreuzigte*" (the crucified). The signature says something about the way in which Nietzsche apparently imagines his communication with Strindberg: not only as a crisscrossing of letters and books, but as a form of crucifixion as well. Another relevant meaning of *gekreuzt* is "crossbreed," or something that is hybridized, to which Strindberg had referred in his letter to Edvard Brandes, about his spiritual/physical intercourse with Nietzsche's ideas, and which makes him feel like a bitch.

The correspondence between Nietzsche and Strindberg contains a highly eroticized subtext in which it is difficult to distinguish who is the seducer and who is the seduced in their hybridizing relationship (as in the union of an aristocratic woman and a servant in *Miss Julie*). Even the word *Sendungen* ("mail" and "missions"), referring to the books that both of them sent to each other more or less simultaneously, are indistinguishable. And this indistinguishability can also be understood in connection with Strindberg's homoerotic letter to Edvard Brandes, even though Nietzsche obviously did not know about it. There may however have been something in Strindberg's dedication in *The Father*, which has not been preserved, that led Nietzsche to begin his letter in this ambiguous way. In his first letter to Strindberg, Nietzsche admitted that reading *The Father* had been an intense experience for him: "I have twice read your tragedy with great emotion; it surprised me beyond all measure to become acquainted with a work in which my own conception of love—in its means, war; at its heart, the hatred unto death of the sexes—has been given such magnificent expression."²¹ Nietzsche encounters himself when reading Strindberg, just as Strindberg did when reading Nietzsche.

When Strindberg wrote his first letter to Nietzsche, he had probably not yet received the first letter Nietzsche had written. It was not dated by Strindberg himself, and the editors of his letters have connected it to December 4, 1888, but it was probably written a day or two before that date. Strindberg begins this letter by paraphrasing a sentence from Nietzsche's *Götzen-Dämmerung* ("I have given mankind the most profound book it possesses, my *Zarathustra*; shortly I shall give it my most independent"²²), the book he had received through Brandes claiming, "Without a doubt, you have given mankind the most profound book that it possesses." Strindberg continues his letter by referring to the dedication: "You wish to be translated to Greenlandish! Why not to French or English? You may judge of our intelligence when you hear that they wanted to commit me to an asylum because of my tragedy, and that so tough and rich a spirit as M. Brandes has been reduced to silence by this loutish majority." Strindberg connects translation and madness to the reception of his own play, pointing to the limitations of his own countrymen. Also he involves Brandes, who brought them together. And he ends his first letter with the following admiring words:

I end all my letters to my friends: read Nietzsche! That is my *Carthago est delenda*!
    Yet the moment you are known and understood, your stature will be diminished. And the sacred and revered rabble will address you with familiarity as their equal. Better to preserve your diminished solitude, and allow us ten thousand other élite spirits to make a secret pilgrimage to your sanctuary in order to imbibe at our pleasure. Let us protect your esoteric teaching by keeping it pure and inviolate, and not divulge it except through the medium of your devoted catechumens, among whom I sign myself
August Strindberg²³

It seems that Strindberg has already transformed Nietzsche into a saint and himself into one of his disciples.

Strindberg apparently received Nietzsche's first letter only after he had already mailed his own first letter to Nietzsche. Thus instead of responding, on December 4, 1888, Strindberg sent Nietzsche's letter to Brandes, updating him and seeking his advice, which Strindberg would continue to do for all of his contacts with Nietzsche. Strindberg began his letter to Brandes by referring to Nietzsche's comments on *The Father*, adding, "Let us remember that in such times of strong, awakening self-consciousness as these, it is only to be expected that, in comparison with others, a great force like him should find that his spirit is the greatest and the strongest, and that having discovered this, he should be overcome by the temptation to say so." After a long and detailed critique of Christianity, emphasising its barbarity and primitiveness (for example, "I regard Christianity as a retrograde step"), Strindberg goes on:

> To me, therefore, Nietzsche is the modern spirit who dares to preach the right of the strong and the wise against the stupid and the small (the democrats), and I can imagine the suffering of this great spirit under the sway of the petty host which dominates this feminized and cretinous age. And I hail him as the liberator, ending my letters to my literary friends like the catechumen with: Read Nietzsche!

Strindberg ends his letter to Brandes by saying that "the hatred unto death of the sexes" (*der Todhass der Geschlechter*) Nietzsche reacts to in *The Father* can also be seen in *Miss Julie*, repeating some of the ideas that Strindberg had already written in his homophobic preface to that play. Strindberg very carefully implies that on some level Nietzsche's ideas are not new to him, while at the same time—as the final paragraph of the letter to Brandes clarifies—he is aware of and made self-conscious by the philosopher's innovative qualities: "Strange that through Nietzsche I should now find the method in my madness of 'opposing everything.' I reassess and put new values on old things! (Unmask.) That's what no one has understood. Hardly even myself!"[24] Strindberg somewhat self-righteously saw himself as experimenting with the reevaluation of values, which he apparently confused with the "madness of 'opposing everything.'"

Brandes responds by returning the Nietzsche letter together with a polite letter dated December 5, 1888, saying that he is "pleased to have brought two so important men as you and him together and to have made my contribution to your understanding of each other." And, Brandes continues, somewhat sourly diminishing Nietzsche's ideas:

> You know how highly I rate Nietzsche, also how deeply I have felt the injustice of his languishing almost unknown. Meanwhile, I personally disagree with a great deal in his teachings, however much there is in them to admire.
>
> There are many things in him which seem less new to me than they appear to you and to himself. His antagonism towards Christianity cannot of

course—as I am sure you will admit—make a particularly profound impression on a man who for more than 20 years—much of that time alone—has borne the odium of being the Nordic Antichrist.

Brandes evidently also feels that he has had the same ideas as Nietzsche and ends his letter by giving some fatherly advice to Strindberg, indirectly also characterizing Nietzsche:

It seems wise to me to give other people something complimentary about themselves—and besides being wise, it is—in good taste. Those with the most powerful self esteem are probably too proud to indulge in self praise, so indifferent to the judgement of others that they say nothing about themselves. But such things are a matter of feeling and taste.[25]

Strindberg receives Nietzsche's second letter, dated December 8. Nietzsche begins somewhat impatiently by asking, "Did a letter from me get lost?" (*Ist ein Brief von mir verloren gegangen?*). The fear of having lost something now enters their communications. The reason for this worry is that Strindberg had not yet responded to Nietzsche's comments on *The Father*. Thus in his second letter Nietzsche repeats that Zola should produce this play. Gradually, however, Nietzsche's letter becomes very personal, even intimate:

But now five words just between us, emphatically just between us! When your letter reached me yesterday—the first letter in my life to have reached me—I had just finished the last manuscript revision of "Ecce Homo." As there is no longer any such thing as coincidence in my life, so consequently are you, too, no coincidence. Why do you write letters that arrive at such a moment? . . . Ecce homo should in fact appear simultaneously in German, French and English.

Nietzsche unknowingly touches on the anxieties—powers that cannot be accounted for by rational means—that brought Strindberg to the brink of madness, while at the same time letting the erotic undertones flourish, with expressions like "consequently are you, too, no coincidence."

Nietzsche, obviously encouraged by Strindberg's play, asks if Strindberg, whose own French translation of *The Father* Nietzsche had found so impressive, would be willing to take on the translator's task: "In case you wanted to take up the French translation yourself, I wouldn't know how to consider myself fortunate enough for that miracle of profound coincidence. For, just between us, a first-rate writer is required for translating my 'Ecce homo.'" And after discussing the practical and economic details of such an undertaking, Nietzsche continues with a somewhat eccentric remark: "In order to secure myself against German acts of brutality ('confiscation'), I will, prior to publication, send the first copies to Prince Bismarck and the young Kaiser together with a letter declaring war: then military officers won't be allowed to respond with police measures.—I am a psychologist. . . ." Nietzsche ended his letter by urging Strindberg to accept the offer: "Consider it, esteemed Sir! It is a matter of first importance. For I am strong enough to break the history of mankind in two."[26]

Strindberg very quickly responds with a letter dated December 11, which besides thanking Nietzsche for the "approval from your master's hand about my badly misunderstood tragedy," addresses the issue of translation that Nietzsche has taken up in his letter. Strindberg warns Nietzsche about the high cost of translation and at the same time indirectly introduces himself and his life situation: "Translating your work is an expensive business, and I am a poor devil (wife, three children, two servants, debts, etc.)." And Strindberg adds, "If the considerable expense doesn't deter you, you may count on me and my talent!" ending with, as Strindberg formulated it, the expression of his "most distinguished feelings."[27]

Nietzsche's next letter to Strindberg is undated, but it has been estimated to have been written a few days before Christmas 1888. Nietzsche opens this letter by saying "I am likewise getting my friends interested in the father of the father," just as Strindberg had urged his friends to read Nietzsche. Also Nietzsche alludes to the distinct male genealogy of Strindberg's play—the father in *The Father*—reinforcing the homoerotic subtext of the correspondence as well as echoing the homoerotic birth of tragedy from the union of two male gods depicted in his own book on this subject. Nietzsche continues by recommending that Strindberg send the play directly to Antoine at Théâtre Libre, and not to Zola, because Antoine is an actor who will no doubt want to play the role of the captain. The goal, Nietzsche implies, is to seduce Antoine to play this male role.

Returning to the issue of translation, Nietzsche informs Strindberg that Hippolyte Taine has promised to take care of the French translation of *Götzen-Dämmerung*, thus freeing Strindberg from this task. In his next letter, from December 27, Strindberg thanks Nietzsche for sending him "the grandiose *Genealogy of Morals*," adding, "I am once again disturbing your tranquility with a poetical piece." Strindberg now sends his short story "Samvetskval" ("Pangs of Conscience") to Nietzsche—which Strindberg says contains "my abortive speculations on the problem of Remorse, written before I was acquainted with your works," again implying that Nietzsche's ideas are not really new to him. The short letter ends with best wishes for a happy 1889.

Nietzsche's response, dated New Year's Eve 1888, first acknowledges that he has received the short story Strindberg sent him, which according to Nietzsche, "goes off like a gunshot" (*wie ein Flintenschuss*), whereas the remainder of the letter seems penned from beyond the borders of sanity:

I have ordered the princes to convene in Rome, I wish to have the young Kaiser executed by firing squad.
Until we meet again. For we shall meet again . . . Une seule condition: divorçons [*On one condition: we divorce*].
Nietzsche. Ceasar[28]

Strindberg, who must have learned by now that Nietzsche could become impatient, responds immediately, writing a letter mainly in Latin but also in some Greek:

Holtibus pridie cal. Jan. MDCCCLXXXIX
Carissime Doctor!
Jelw, Jelw manhnai!
Litteras tuas non sine perturbatione accepi et tibi gratias ago.
Rectus vives, Licini, neque altum
Semper urgendo, neque dum procellas
Cautus horrescis nimium premendo
Litus iniquum.
Interdum juvat insanire!
Vale et Fave!
Strindberg (Deus, optimus maximus).

[Carissime Doctor!
I want, I want to be mad!
I received your letter not without emotion, and I thank you for it.
Better wilt thou live, Licinius, by neither
always pressing out to sea, nor too closely
hugging the dangerous shore in cautious fear of storms[29]
However, it is a joy to be mad!

Farewell and goodbye!
Strindberg (God, the best and the highest)][30]

In this letter, with its strange mixture of languages, even when Strindberg writes, "I want to be mad," he is actually quoting in Greek the ancient choral lyric *Anacreontea* to make this claim. He had already quoted these exact words many years earlier in a letter to Siri von Essen dated March 12, 1876, a few months before the letter to her that I will examine in the next section of this chapter. This quotation is apparently a part of Strindberg's performative repertoire; it is hardly an authentic expression of insanity.

Strindberg is now beginning to recognize that Nietzsche is not playing a game. On January 3, 1889, he sends an additional letter to Brandes accompanied by the three previous letters from Nietzsche, saying he knows he is pestering Brandes. But now Strindberg adds, "I believe our friend Nietzsche is mad, and what's worse, that he can compromise us," unless, he continues, "the crafty Slav . . . isn't playing a trick on us all." After expressing his astonishment at the sudden turns in his correspondence with Nietzsche, Strindberg asks Brandes in German: "What should be done?" [*Was thun?*].[31] It is possible that Strindberg had already sent Nietzsche his letter with the quotes from the von Essen letter when he writes to Brandes, but in his letter to Brandes, Strindberg obviously does not mention that he is in fact "playing" along with Nietzsche's "games," even if it is clear that Strindberg situates his own "madness" (in Greek) in a literary, fictionalized context, perhaps trying to test if this is also Nietzsche's strategy.

The next day, on January 4, 1889, Brandes writes to Strindberg that he wants to keep Nietzsche's letters a few more days. In his response, Brandes situates Nietzsche's letters in a broader context, concluding:

As far as I can judge, the first two do not seem to go further than one might expect from the man's ever-increasing self-importance, which *I* criticised and *you* defended. I do not understand the last one. I do not see that this can be meant symbolically. And if not, then the man is stark raving mad. And that would be a true and great misfortune. Such a splendid intellect, so rare, so rich—struck by megalomania!

However, I still have a little hope. When, like me, one has spent more than twenty years as a doctor in the great hospital of the sick, wounded, unbalanced, fatuous vain creatures who collectively represent what is called literature—one is no longer amazed by any expression of self-adulation in a writer, especially in one so long misunderstood.[32]

In conclusion Brandes also mentions that the same week he had received from a Russian princess a letter asking after Nietzsche's health. Nietzsche had signed his letter to the princess: *"Der Antichrist."* "Yet," Brandes ends his letter to Strindberg, "I still believe the best."[33]

Nietzsche's final letter to Strindberg, estimated to have been written on January 8, 1889, contains a definitive answer to any possible doubts about Nietzsche's mental situation. It is one of the eight letters Nietzsche signed "The Crucified One" (*Der Gekreuzigte*), and it says: "Herr Strindberg / Alas? . . . Are we no longer to divorce?" (*Herr Strindberg / Eheu? . . . Nicht mehr divorçons?*).[34] Nietzsche's final letter to Brandes was even more direct: "After you discovered me, it was no great trick to find me: the difficulty now is to lose me" (*Nachdem du mich endeckt hast, war es kein Kunststück mich zu finden: die Schwierigkeit ist jetzt die, mich zu verlieren*). It was also signed *"Der Gekreuzigte."*[35] Nietzsche had taken a full step into the unknown (what Klossowski had termed) "Turinesque vision of the world."

After this point in early 1889, there are no letters preserved between Strindberg and Brandes for more than a year. Their correspondence apparently came to a halt. Because Strindberg continued to live just outside of Copenhagen for several more months, they may have met to discuss Nietzsche's tragic situation, if indeed they were familiar with the details. However they may have felt too embarrassed or ashamed to discuss the matter between themselves in writing. They knew of course that even their private correspondence might become public, at least for posterity. The first time Strindberg mentions Nietzsche again in a (preserved) letter is on January 28, 1889, writing to the Swedish author Ola Hansson. Hansson was gradually becoming an ardent follower of Nietzsche's philosophy. He had moved to Berlin in 1889 and had published books about Nietzsche's influence on and importance to the Scandinavian and European literary and cultural movements. In this letter, showing that Nietzsche's insanity had made a deep impression on him, Strindberg writes to Hansson:

I think Nietzsche is blinding me, my brain is like a wound! From overwork! But he is certainly driving me crazy too! Because the incredible self-esteem in his books has induced a similar feeling in me! Which won't prevent my grey matter from cracking, as it probably will! If the French Republic—such as it is—should fall, we shall have no manhood or old age, but end up living in a moral prison till we die! Was thun? Nichts! We shall all doubtless meet in Gheel![36]

Just as in the earlier letter to Edvard Brandes, Strindberg confesses that Nietzsche affected him both physically and mentally, also driving him toward madness.

Strindberg's (preserved) correspondence with Brandes resumes on April 12, 1890, when Strindberg was living in the Stockholm archipelago. After receiving a letter from Brandes (which has not been preserved) asking about Strindberg's understanding of his own intellectual development—Brandes was apparently preparing to write about him—Strindberg replies:

Thus, as early as 1885, following my trial, I began to sever myself from the remnants of theism, deism and democracy in my bloodstream, where they appeared in the form of categorical imperatives. I also experimented with socialism, in which my old Christianity resurfaced during a period of sickness, and purged it in "Kampf der Gehirnen" [battle of brains].

When I found the whole movement formulated in Nietzsche, whom I partly anticipated, I adopted his standpoint, and intend henceforth to experiment with that point of view, to see where it leads.[37]

Brandes answers on April 20, 1890, saying, "You should not really study Nietzsche so deeply. There is one element in him which could be used, another which drives thought and feeling to lack of control"[38] (my translation). Strindberg's response from April 22, 1890, shows that what matters most to him at this point is that he anticipated Nietzsche's ideas:

You mustn't therefore believe that I am uncritical of Nietzsche, but since he entered my life immediately after I had struggled to arrive at his position, without my knowing him, his program coincided with mine. You will recall saying to me once in Kungens Nytorv [a central place in Copenhagen]: "Well Strindberg, as someone who hates 'the small' you will surely like N-e." Thus acknowledging that I had anticipated the man.[39]

The following year Strindberg divorced Siri von Essen, and after a short-lived marriage to Austrian journalist Frida Uhl, Strindberg entered the period of his life called the Inferno crisis, which lasted between 1892 and 1897. During this time he experienced several psychological breakdowns.

The "drama" between Nietzsche and Strindberg that I have attempted to reconstruct, by presenting selected passages from the letters between them and commenting on major turns of this drama, does not contain a discussion about the discursive practices of philosophy and the theatre in the strict sense. It is a drama about the strategies for establishing the contact between them—a phatic relationship— rather than about the practices themselves. What I think it shows in the larger context of this study is that to establish an interaction between these discursive practices certain basic issues of sanity and madness have to be addressed. The border crossings between philosophy and theatre are of course not the only cultural sites in which such discussions take place. But they seem to be particularly pertinent when questions of truth and simulation are posed around the table in Agathon's home or at the court of Elsinore—or in the philosophy of Nietzsche and the writings of Strindberg.

Strindberg's Deceptive Dreams

Strindberg no doubt learned something important about madness from his correspondence with Nietzsche. It touched a creative nerve, presenting the Hamletian dilemma of real versus feigned madness and deception. The analysis of Strindberg's June 1876 letter to Siri von Essen (who was to become his wife a year and a half later) enables me to take a closer, and I think unique, look at Strindberg's creative process.[40] In this letter he describes a dream. Its opening words are "I had such a remarkable dream last night!" (my translation). And it is dated the same day von Essen's divorce from her first husband, a baron and an officer in the Swedish army, had become final.[41] But there is no hint about this in the letter itself. The initially secret love affair between Strindberg and von Essen, by this time, had been going on for more than a year, and according to the myth about their relationship, she aspired to realize her potential as an actress through their intimate relationship, knowing that with a young and promising writer by her side this was possible.

The context for writing to her was that Strindberg was spending the second half of June 1876, which included his attending the Midsummer festivities, in Stockholm, while von Essen was at a mansion called Äs, approximately thirty miles south of the city. The letter was written a few days before Midsummer, and it is interesting to note that *Miss Julie*, written twelve years later, also takes place on Midsummer's Eve. This was the play, modeled on von Essen and their relationship, Strindberg was completing as he first became acquainted with Nietzsche's ideas.

Strindberg's letter to his future wife was a combination of seduction and manipulation, as well as a tool for Strindberg to exert his power over her. The puzzling and almost uncanny aspect of the dream Strindberg recounts in his letter is that it was an invention, though parts of it may have had their basis in actual dream imagery. In addition—and this is what makes the letter so interesting—the dream Strindberg describes to the woman who will become his first wife bears a very strong resemblance, both in structure and in some of its manifest content, to *A Dream Play*, written twenty-five years later, in 1901. The intention was to have his third wife, the young actress Harriet Bosse, play the role of Indra's Daughter. It is even possible to see this letter as an *ur*-version of *A Dream Play*.[42]

Strindberg's dream letter, just as the first scene of *A Dream Play*, after the descent of Indra's Daughter from heaven, begins with a detailed description of a frontal view of a building, in this case a two-story stone building—including two wings, one on each side of the house—with a steep roof and a staircase leading to the main door. This, Strindberg writes to her, must be the house where she, von Essen, is spending the holidays. He has never been there, but still he is meticulously providing her the details of the facade with its six windows on the first floor, mentioning specifically that two of these, on both sides of the main door, are situated at exactly the same height. There are yet two more windows, one on each side, in addition to the two aligned windows. These, Strindberg emphasizes, are positioned somewhat lower. These details, as we shall see later, are very important in order to show that Strindberg had made up parts of the dream.

Both the letter and *A Dream Play* continue with the dreamer entering a large house. Strindberg's conquest of his future bride is obvious. In the letter Strindberg says that he believes this building had previously been a monastery, a detail that perhaps entered Strindberg's *To Damascus*, written just before *A Dream Play*, featuring the mad character Caesar, a direct remnant of his correspondence with Nietzsche. The entrance into the growing castle in *A Dream Play* signals a return to childhood and innocence. In the dream, once inside the building, Strindberg reports that there were paintings on the walls; one of them depicts the Tower of Babel, signed 1594, and another has a white horse as its subject. He is even able to identify the names of the painters in the dream. After that, Strindberg continues, he suddenly finds himself in an orchard with different kinds of apples as well as different kinds of rare fruits. Through the Tower of Babel that appears in the painting and his arrival in an orchard that closely resembles the Garden of Eden, Strindberg is brought back to some kind of mythical beginning. One of the varieties of apples he sees in the garden is a *paradisäpple*, Swedish for "apple of paradise."

Strindberg continues his dream narrative; he rushes into a park that ends at the foot of a mountain approximately two hundred meters high. Then he comes to what in Swedish is called *ättestupa*, a suicidal precipice. Climbing down this precipice, Strindberg comes to a small cave where he meets an old woman or a hag (in Swedish *käring*, with the same root as the word for "being in love"), with whom he has a long conversation. These episodes are clearly early versions of the episodes with the female doorkeeper and Fingal's Cave in *A Dream Play*, where Indra's Daughter meets the poet who will free her from the sufferings of this world. This is of course Strindberg's own role in his play. Approaching the precipice, Strindberg asks the old woman, "What is the name of this mountain?" (my translation) and she answers, "*Vigsberget*," an unusual term in Swedish, meaning something like "Marriage Hill." He also asks about the price of the mansion, as well as the prices of the other houses and farms that he points out, asking for their names too. Indra's Daughter repeats this *gestus* of inquiry several times in *A Dream Play*, asking where she has arrived after entering this world.

Strindberg continues his letter to von Essen saying that in one of the houses there is a guest, a beautiful woman with blond hair shining like the sun and with very small fingers and feet. This is perhaps von Essen as an early version of Indra's Daughter. In the dream, however, Strindberg fiercely argues that no other woman in the world is as beautiful as his own beloved and he takes up a stone in order to hit the hag on the head, but "at this point the mountain collapses and she disappears" (my translation). At this enigmatic point, lacking any clear reason why this happens, Strindberg concludes his dream narrative: "I woke up!" (my translation). Just like in *A Dream Play*, which ends with the burning of worldly goods, the narrative in the dream letter comes to a close through a destructive action that takes place within the dream itself.

Strindberg then asks von Essen to describe the mansion at Äs in detail and to confirm that what he has dreamed actually corresponds to reality, proving his psychic powers. The letter goes on to tell von Essen how empty and gloomy the city is without her, adding that the blinds have been drawn in the home of Tor Hedberg, indicating that he had returned to the city. Hedberg was the director of the Royal Theatre in Stockholm and was to be influential in giving her roles to play on the stage. And with an obvious erotic allusion, Strindberg continues: "Let's see if I won't meet you in the cave in Marriage Hill under the precipice on the day after midsummer. Let's see if there is a cave and a hill" (my translation). He ends with a few everyday matters and a farewell suitable for a yearning lover.

The claim that Strindberg invented at least parts of this dream, that he, to put it bluntly, was actually bluffing, can be substantiated in the following way. A Swedish book by F. Richarts and Olof Eneroth, with the publication date of 1864–1869, called *Mansions and Castles in Södermanland* (Södermanland is the province where Äs is situated), contains an etching of the mansion. According to Hans Lindström, Strindberg had borrowed this book from the National Library where Strindberg worked at the time.[43] In the etching of the mansion in Äs, the windows are situated exactly as in Strindberg's dream, with the outer windows on the first floor located somewhat lower than the two other windows. In reality, however, as stated in a 1939 interview with the then owner of the mansion—and I have not actually visited this house, nor have I studied its architectural history in detail—the windows on the first floor have apparently always been in a straight line, and not as they are described in Strindberg's detailed narrative in the letter nor as they appear in the published drawing. The properties and their prices Strindberg mentions in his dream are also cited in the library book, which Strindberg no doubt must have consulted when writing his letter.[44] This does not of course contradict that he may have had a dream about the place where von Essen was at the time, but it is obvious that the exact details about this place had a source in addition to the dream itself.

It took another twenty-five years, however, before Strindberg wrote *A Dream Play*, one of his major contributions to twentieth-century theatre. It was based on a metaphysical dimension made manifest through the feminine presence of Indra's Daughter. This metaphysical dimension can be traced back to *Miss Julie*, where just before she goes off to her suicide there is a heavily charged sunrise through which everything becomes illuminated with a heavenly light. But the divine empowerment of the female figure in *A Dream Play* stands in stark opposition to the views of the feminine Strindberg held during the time he wrote *The Father* and *Miss Julie*. These views correspond closely with Nietzsche's ideas. In *A Dream Play* Strindberg openly and directly acknowledges the presence of such a metaphysical female force on the theatrical stage—this in a world where the belief in such a metaphysical dimension had already been declared dead by Nietzsche himself. *A Dream Play* is in this respect a very Platonic play, based on Plato's notion of the migration and rebirth of souls. Indra's Daughter attains the same position of ultimate wisdom as Diotima in the *Symposium*, giving the Poet in the play, Strindberg's alter ego, the role of Socrates. The important difference is, however, that Strindberg invites his representative of divine feminine wisdom to enter the stage of action.

Strindberg confronts a contemporary dilemma. The death of God and the supposed end of metaphysics that results made it possible for the theatre to focus its attention more closely on the theatrical machineries themselves and to investigate in a more playful, meta-theatrical manner how the supernatural apparatus, in this case the feminine *"dea" ex machina* represented by Indra's Daughter, appears.[45] Or as Jürgen Habermas emphasizes in his commentary on Ernst Bloch and the notion of Utopia, a spatial metaphor is mobilized for understanding the Utopian spirit in a world where God is no longer present. According to Bloch, Habermas argues,

God is dead, but his locus has survived him. The place into which mankind has imagined God and the gods, after the decay of these hypotheses, remains a hollow space. The measurements in-depth of this vacuum, indeed atheism finally understood, sketch out a blueprint of a future kingdom of freedom.[46]

In Strindberg's play Utopia is conceived of as a female supernatural presence, which while briefly visiting this world recognizes the magnitude of its human suffering and returns to the heavenly spheres. She is no doubt more of the young Hamlet, not Old Hamlet's ghost, appearing again every night, demanding revenge, but a much more benevolent metaphysical reality that the theatre can realize. But how free the blueprint of the modern theatre as a performance reality can make the spectators, and if, indeed, we are even able fully to appreciate and interpret it, remains an open question. The modern theatre, and our more contemporary performance traditions in particular, is attempting to fill the void, mainly by making us painfully aware of the dimensions of this vacuity. But can our contemporary theatre still function as the "locus" where the "kingdom of freedom" can be imagined, even if there is a deep and growing awareness that the kingdom itself might never be reached? Regardless of our answer to this question, the possibility that Indra's Daughter may appear again points to an option that is radically different from Hegel's and Marx's interpretation of Old Hamlet's Utopian dimensions; or to highlight another example that addresses this issue: the fact that Godot will not appear again tonight.

Strindberg and Kierkegaard

Strindberg is profoundly aware of the repetitive dimensions of this metaphysical/theatrical narrative. Therefore, before ending the discussion on Strindberg, I want to draw attention to one additional detail in *A Dream Play* that is of great relevance in the context of the encounters between the philosophical and the thespian discourses I examine. Strindberg's play contains a very conscious allusion to Søren Kierkegaard's book *Repetition: A Venture in Experimenting Psychology*, published in 1843 under the pseudonym Constantin Constantinus. In one of the central scenes of his play, Strindberg three times uses the Danish word *gentagelsen* (meaning "repetition," literally "to take again"), which is the title of this remarkable and at the time quite widely read book. In the same passage Strindberg uses at least ten Swedish synonyms for "repetition," but because the Danish word is completely different from the broad paradigm of Swedish cognates designating the notion of "repetition," which Strindberg also uses, it very clearly stands out on the page.

In this particular scene the difficulties of the marriage between Indra's Daughter, now with her earthly name Agnes, and the lawyer are depicted in terms of discord and mutual distrust. Indra's daughter realizes that earthly life only leads to suffering and humiliation, and begins to prepare for her return to the heavenly abodes where her journey began. At this crucial point the lawyer harshly reminds his wife of her duties to him and to the household, saying: "Repetition! [*gentagelsen*]—Retakes!!—Go back! Redo the homework!—Come!"[47] After telling her that these dull domestic duties will only become pleasant after they have been fulfilled, the lawyer continues, saying:

I wake up in the morning with a headache; and then the repetition [*gentagelsen*] begins, the perverse repetition [*gentagelsen*] though. In such a way that everything that was beautiful, pleasant and invigorating last night, today in the morning appears in my memory as ugly, foul and stupid. The pleasure becomes rotten and the joy disintegrates. (77)

And a little later he adds: "You must return in your footsteps, take the same way back . . . and suffer retakes, re-writings, repetitions . . ." (79). But Indra's Daughter has already decided to make her own "repetition" by refusing to accept her husband's domestic demands and going back to the heavenly spheres she originally came from.

Strindberg's use of the term *gentagelsen* focuses on the marriage crisis between the lawyer and his wife, and the burdensome routines of a weary relationship, even if it also has profound metaphysical implications for her return to heaven. Kierkegaard's book is more directly related to the issues I examine in the discursive practices of philosophers and thespians, and therefore also—because Strindberg no doubt read this book and absorbed its more general, philosophical implications—it is of twofold interest in this context. I do not however examine all the complexities of Kierkegaard's book.

One of the central themes in Kierkegaard's *Repetition* is spectatorship in the theatre. The book as a whole is conceived as a psychological self-experiment carried out by its fictitious author Constantin Constantinus—a name that hints at something that is unchanging—who is investigating, in a series of detailed everyday actions and experiences, whether it is possible to solve the paradoxes that stem from experiencing something that happens repeatedly. Or in Kierkegaard's words:

The dialectic of repetition is easy, for that which is repeated has been—otherwise it could not be repeated—but the very fact that it has been makes the repetition into something new. When the Greeks said that all knowing is recollection, they said that all existence, which is, has been; when one says that life is a repetition, one says: actuality, which has been, now comes into existence. If one does not have the category of recollection or of repetition, all life dissolves into an empty, meaningless noise.[48]

In an attempt to examine this complex psycho-philosophical issue, the author sets out on a trip to Berlin, where he has been before. He takes the same lodgings near the *Gendarmenmarkt* he has taken before and goes to see exactly the same performance of a farce at the Königstädter Theater that he had seen on his previous visit to the city. But as he carefully examines the same room he lodged in, eats in the same restaurant, and goes to see exactly the same performances, he seriously begins to doubt the possibility of repetition.

There are some short, fleeting moments when Constantin Constantinus admits that repetition is possible, like in the restaurant he has returned to, where the guests, completely unaware of their behavior and habits, give him the impression of "the same sameness" (170). But when he goes to the theatre, the art form where this "thing" is supposed to appear again that night, he immediately draws the conclusion that "the only repetition was the impossibility of repetition" (170). The theatre contains an element of the accidental, which apparently leaves the spectator in doubt about whether what is seen on the stage is actually repeated. "The accidental," Kierkegaard proposes, "is second only to the ideal." But, he continues, "the accidental is preferable in every way, because it sets the imagination in motion" (162). From this Kierkegaard concludes, "If there is to be a representation of a person in the theatre, what is required is either a concrete creation thoroughgoingly portrayed in ideality or the accidental" (162). Kierkegaard tackles what is no doubt one of the most complex issues of theatrical representation: the endeavor to achieve the purity and clarity of an ideal form—expressed by the Socratic turn toward an all-inclusive drama—that enables the ladder of wisdom to be scaled, on the one hand, and, on the other, theatrical representation to be embedded in the accidental, and even catastrophic, turns of history.

Nietzsche's project, to which I turn now, was to situate this ideal theatrical form in a pre-Socratic context, in which the maelstrom of history is at least partly embedded, even if Walter Benjamin later criticized him for not sufficiently recognizing this. Nietzsche took the completely opposite route from that of Kierkegaard in searching for the uniqueness of a certain event or action. According to Alexander Nehamas, "Socrates had succeeded in living as 'instinctively' as Nietzsche claimed he had lived himself," and therefore Socrates, who had already broken away from everything that went before him, "constituted an immense problem for him." If Nietzsche, as Nehamas interprets him, also strove to achieve such a break, he would be repeating what Socrates had already done, and goes on to claim that because of this Nietzsche could never be sure that his own project was not also the project of the character who animated the tradition against which he defined himself. He could therefore never be sure that his project was not the same as the project of the tradition he denounced.[49]

Kierkegaard found unique individuality while experimenting with repetition, whereas Nietzsche, through his anxiety, found that searching for the total and unique break from tradition means finding repetition, a repetition that involves breaking away from tradition through the act of revolt itself, just as Socrates had done.

These two possibilities clearly complement each other, but neither can fully resolve the issues at stake. However, the point that must be made in this context is that the theatre—which ideally is both unique and repetitive—was perceived both by Kierkegaard and Nietzsche as the privileged testing ground for their philosophical questions. In this respect both Kierkegaard and Nietzsche were repeating Hamlet's gesture of applying methods and ideas from the theatre for solving philosophical and existential issues. They created a vital, ongoing dialectic between the discursive practices of both, but without becoming directly involved in the theatrical activities themselves, as Hamlet does, or denying their contribution to the vitality of the Utopian polis, as Plato prescribed.

The Birth of the Philosopher from the Ruins of Tragedy

> Like a blank sheet, Socrates invites us to write; like a vast stillness, he provokes us into shouting. But he remains untouched, staring back with an ironic gaze.
> —Alexander Nehamas, *The Art of Living* (9)

Nietzsche's *Geburt der Tragödie aus dem Geiste der Musik* (*The Birth of Tragedy from the Spirit of Music*), originally published in 1872, is an enigmatic and multifaceted text that has received many different and even contradictory interpretations.[50] At the same time as it presents Nietzsche's own version of the birth of tragedy through a union constituted by "the duality of the *Apollonian* and the *Dionysian*: just as procreation depends on the duality of the sexes, which are engaged in a continual struggle interrupted only by temporary periods of reconciliation,"[51] it is,

I argue, also a text about the birth of philosophy, and in particular about the autochthonous birth of Nietzsche himself as a philosopher.

This second birth takes place after the Dionysian and the Apollonian energies—whose union had previously resulted in the birth of tragedy—have crumbled, leaving the brilliance of early Greek culture in a chaotic demise. But at the same time as this collapse—on the overt level characterized by Nietzsche as catastrophic for Western civilization—had taken place, a new stage in the development toward self-reflection and critique had in fact been born. In spite of some very critical pronouncements of protest and even aversion against this development, Nietzsche, I argue, closely identified himself with it in his ongoing attempt to create a discursive space wherein the remnants of tragedy become transformed into philosophy. Whereas Socrates had initially constructed his philosophical discourse through a unification of the dramatic genres of tragedy and comedy, Nietzsche's philosophical thinking was born out of the collapse of tragedy.

This ambivalent position enabled Nietzsche to take on the role of mediator between the discourses of tragedy and philosophy as an expression of the human spirit and its recurring stages of development. It is only, Nietzsche seems to be saying, when philosophy "remembers" its origins stemming from the performative energies of tragedy that it can achieve the aim of "revaluing values," in the sense he aspired to achieve through his more comprehensive philosophical project. This was certainly not what Plato's Socrates had advocated when he appropriated both tragedy and comedy for the sake of philosophy. Nietzsche's project was instead to create a mechanism of "generational" bridges between the philosophical and the thespian discursive practices. But still, Socrates constantly reappears as a powerful ghost for the demise of tragedy in Nietzsche's text. At the same time as he rejects Socrates' rationality, Nietzsche admires his presence, in particular during the moments before Socrates' death. Actually, to put this situation in pictorial terms, when Nietzsche looks at himself in the philosophical mirror set up in *The Birth of Tragedy from the Spirit of Music*, he sees the image of Socrates, who—in the words of Nehamas, quoted in the opening to this section—even if he "provokes us into shouting . . . he remains untouched, staring back with an ironic gaze."[52] Nietzsche is in this sense a reincarnation of Alcibiades.

Nietzsche's text begins with a description of sexual procreation stemming from the tidal waves of struggle and reconciliation between two divine figures, both male. Classical tragedy was born of the homoerotic tie between these divine figures; but also, as we learn later in Nietzsche's text, the renewal of art in Nietzsche's own time (as exemplified in the work of Wagner) depends on the reunification of these two male forces. The Apollonian, plastic art of the sculptor with its dream images (*Traumbilder*) and the formless, intoxicating Dionysian art of music are, according to Nietzsche,

> two very different drives [that] run in parallel with one another, for the most part diverging openly with one another and continually stimulating each other to ever new and more powerful births, in order to perpetuate in themselves the struggle of that opposition only apparently bridged by the shared name of "art"; until finally, through a metaphysical miracle of the Hellenic "will," they appear coupled with one another and through this coupling at last give birth to a work of art which is as Dionysian as it is Apollonian—Attic tragedy. (19)

Nietzsche models his narrative of the birth of tragedy, basically referring to the work of Aeschylus and Sophocles, on the mythical pattern of Eros presented by Aristophanes in the *Symposium*, with the difference that Nietzsche's imagination creates a union of two divine figures.

In the "Attempt at Self-Criticism," the 1886 preface to the second edition of *The Birth of Tragedy from the Spirit of Music*, looking back at the writing of the first edition from a fifteen-year distance—and closer in time to his correspondence with Strindberg—he returns to the process that had given birth to the ideas in his book. This preface begins by stating, "Whatever may lie at the bottom of this questionable book; it must have been a question of the greatest interest and appeal, as well as a deeply personal question" (3). Since it was written during the Franco-Prussian War of 1870–1871, he reflects that "while the thunder of the battle of Wörth died away over Europe, the exasperated friend of perplexing puzzles who was to father this book sat in some corner or other of the Alps, very perplexed and puzzled, at once very careworn and carefree, and wrote down his thoughts on the *Greeks*" (3; italics in the original). The German word Nietzsche uses when pointing at himself as the person who had engendered this book is *Vaterschaft*, or "fatherhood." After presenting this paternal relation Nietzsche adds, further emphasizing the analogy between the general political situation and his own private one, that at the same time "as peace was being negotiated in Versailles, he [the author] made his peace with himself and, during a slow convalescence from an illness brought home from the field of battle, completed the definitive version of the 'Birth of Tragedy from the Spirit of *Music*'" (3). The illness he refers to probably contains the seeds that will erupt in January 1889, leading to his final insanity.

To substantiate my interpretation of *The Birth of Tragedy from the Spirit of Music*, it is in particular necessary to examine how Nietzsche depicts the transformation from the phase of tragedy into that of philosophy. In the first ten chapters of his book, Nietzsche describes the Dionysian and the Apollonian forces as well as the union between them as elements from which tragedy was born. Here, often in a figurative language richly embedded in detailed cultural associations from many fields and disciplines, Nietzsche describes the role of the various formal components of tragedy, like the chorus, the images, the dialogue, the masks, and in particular the music. He further describes how they receive their unique expressive potentials of tragedy through the union of the Apollonian and the Dionysian energies. The Apollonian component originates in the "reality of the dream" to which the "artistically sensitive man" responds "in the same way as the philosopher responds to the reality of existence" (20). On the other hand, the Dionysian element is based on intoxicating and ecstatic sources: "Man is no longer an artist, he has become a work of art; the artistic force of the whole of nature, to the most intense blissful satisfaction of the original Unity, reveals itself here in the shudder of intoxication" (23). However the Dionysian component is constantly given primacy over the Apollonian one, because

> [a]ccording to an incontrovertible tradition, the suffering of Dionysus was the sole subject of the earliest form of Greek tragedy, and for a long time there was no other available stage hero than Dionysus himself. And we may maintain with equal assurance that up to the time of Euripides Dionysus remained the tragic hero, and that all the famous figures of the Greek stage, Prometheus, Oedipus, and so on, are only masks of that original hero Dionysus. That behind all these masks a deity is hidden is the essential reason for the typical "ideality" of those famous figures, so often a source of wonder. (59)

The cultural revolution signified by the unification of the Dionysian and the Apollonian energies had been reached by what Nietzsche terms the "feeling for myth" (61); that is, resisting a development in which the "mythical presuppositions of a religion are systematized as a finished sum of historical events under the strict rational eye of a dogmatic conviction" (61).

This resistance led to the remarkable renaissance through which the

reborn genius of Dionysian music took hold of this dying myth: and in its hands it bloomed once again, with colours never seen before, with a scent which aroused a longing presentiment of a metaphysical world. After this last radiant appearance, the myth collapses, its leaves wither, and soon its faded and ravaged flowers are scattered by the wind in all directions, pursued by the scornful Lucians of the ancient world. Through tragedy, myth achieves its deepest content, its most expressive form; it rises once again, like a wounded hero, and the whole excess of its force, together with the calm wisdom of the dying man, burns in its eyes with the last powerful gleam. (61)

It is at this point, when tragedy itself—like a dying hero, collecting its last and final forces, realizing a moment of final glory—also crumbles and falls silent. In the following paragraph, Nietzsche describes the fatal turning point, when Euripides "sought to force this dying myth once again into [his] service" (61) by bringing, as Nietzsche expresses it, "the *spectator* onto the stage" (63; italics in the original). Later that other spectator is also introduced. It is Socrates himself. The theatrical self-reflexivity combined with the pedestrian everyday realities that these two spectators introduce, "fought and conquered Aeschylean tragedy" (69) by presenting "cool paradoxical *thoughts*—instead of Apollonian visions—and fiery *emotions*—in the place of Dionysian raptures—and they really are highly realistic imitations of thoughts and emotions devoid of any trace of the ether of art" (70; italics in the original). This, Nietzsche concludes, is "the essence of *aesthetic Socratism*" (70; italics in the original).

But at the same time that Socrates is introduced as an enemy of the arts in the Platonic dialogues—and Nietzsche has not spared rhetorical fireworks to take him to task for that—Nietzsche gradually begins to focus his attention on another aspect of Socrates: the person who, while he was waiting to drink the hemlock after being sentenced to death, rewrote some of Aesop's fables in verse and composed "premiums," that is, the introductions that precede recitals by rhapsodists. "It was something resembling a daemonic warning voice which forced him to undertake these exercises," Nietzsche concludes. They were, Nietzsche goes on, the only sign of an apprehension on his part about the limits of the logical nature; he must have asked himself the following question—perhaps whatever is not intelligible to me is not immediately unintelligent? Perhaps there is a domain of wisdom which excludes the logician? Perhaps art is even a necessary correlative of and supplement to science? (80)

From this point in his treatise, Nietzsche gradually begins to panegyrize the dying Socrates, whose influence he says

has extended down through posterity to this very moment and indeed stretches out into the future in its entirety, like a shadow which grows in the evening sun, as the same influence again and again necessitates the re-creation anew of *art*—of art in the already metaphysical, broadest, and deepest sense—and how its own infinity guarantees the infinity of art also. (80; italics in the original)

This is the Socrates who, in Nietzsche's view,

approached death with the calm with which he left the symposium, in the early dawn as the last of the revelers; while behind him on the benches and on the floor his fellow carousers remained asleep, dreaming of Socrates, the true eroticist. The *dying Socrates* became the new ideal, never seen before, of the noble Greek youth: above all the typical Hellenic youth, Plato, threw himself down before this image with all the fervent devotion of his enthusiast's soul. (76; italics in the original)

This is also the Socrates who, even if he was denied "the sweet madness of artistic enthusiasm" (76) and even if he represented a decline, became a model, through his philosophical project, for the regeneration of the arts. This is the role Nietzsche himself performs in the transitional stage he believed his own culture was situated in, positioning himself in the same ambivalent position Socrates had placed himself vis-à-vis the arts:

If we look with eyes strengthened and refreshed by the sight of the Greeks at the highest spheres of that world which surges around us, then we perceive how the craving of an insatiable optimistic knowledge, which appears in an exemplary form in Socrates, is transformed into tragic resignation and need for art; while admittedly this same craving in its lower stages must express itself as hostile to art and must have a particular inner aversion to Dionysian-tragic art, as illustrated for example in the struggle of Socratism against Aeschylean tragedy. (84–85)

Only the person who has closed the door is capable of opening it again.

4

Walter Benjamin and Bertolt Brecht Discuss Franz Kafka: Exilic Journeys

> When I returned
> My hair was not yet grey
> And I was glad
> The travails of the mountains lie behind us.
> Before us lie the travails of the plains.
> —Bertolt Brecht, "Observation," in *Poems 1913–1956* (written in Berlin, February, 1949)

The fourth and last encounter I examine—between Walter Benjamin and Bertolt Brecht—presents a unique challenge for several reasons. Their multifaceted relationship points to an almost overwhelming number of personal, intellectual, and historical threads bundled together, leading simultaneously in several, even contradictory, directions. It can hardly be characterized as an "encounter" in the sense I have used this term so far. Therefore the narrative I present does not claim to be exhaustive. It takes one particular conversation between them as its point of departure. This particular conversation—during which they discuss Franz Kafka's short story "The Next Village" (*"Das Nächste Dorf"*)—took place in Svendborg, Denmark, on August 29, 1934. It was briefly documented by Benjamin in his diary, which was published posthumously as "Notes from Svendborg, Summer 1934."[1]

Benjamin and Brecht met in Berlin in 1929 and collaborated closely on the plans for a journal. With the rise of Hitler to power they both escaped into exile; Brecht and Helene Weigel had already fled Berlin the day after the Reichstag fire, on February 28, 1933, first to Prague, then to Zurich, and in November to Paris. Meanwhile Benjamin left Berlin for Paris on March 17, 1933. After Brecht's arrival in that city, they stayed in the same hotel. During this time Benjamin and Brecht had planned to write a series of detective stories together, but it seems they never did. In December 1933 Brecht and his entourage found refuge in Skovsbostrand, a Danish village on the outskirts of the small town Svendborg. The town is on the southern shore of the Danish island of Fyn, situated only a few dozen kilometers from the German coast and the city of Kiel. Even if he made many trips from there, this was Brecht's residence for almost six years, until April 1939. Soon after his arrival in Svendborg, Brecht wrote to Benjamin in Paris, offering to bring large parts of Benjamin's library to Denmark. And when much of it had been shipped to Svendborg, Brecht tried to persuade Benjamin to come and work there. After hesitating more than once, Benjamin finally came to visit over the summer of 1934. Ultimately, he decided to visit again, during the summers of 1936 and 1938.

My exploration of the relationship between Benjamin, the philosopher, and Brecht, the thespian, focuses on Benjamin's first visit to Svendborg during the summer of 1934. Benjamin arrived on June 20, and until October of that year he lived in a small pension called Stella Maris, not far from the farmhouse where Brecht was living. They spent most of their time reading and writing, while the evenings were devoted to listening to German and Austrian radio broadcasts, to discussions, and to playing chess, the latter usually in complete silence.

In a short postscript to a letter from Brecht to Benjamin, from May 4, 1934, renewing his invitation to Benjamin to come to Svendborg, Margarete Steffin, one of Brecht's collaborators and lovers, to make the invitation even more attractive, adds that "B is getting a new car next week (ridiculously cheap, 350 Kr.) and since I am *probably* getting a driver's license, I promise to take you to the café as often as you want—even if Weigel cooks wonderful coffee which you are invited to begin with"[2] (italics in the original; my translation). Brecht, who had a great passion for cars, received an old Model T Ford about a week later. And as we shall see, this passion for cars, besides making it possible for Steffin to drive Benjamin to the café, makes its way into Brecht's thinking as well as into his theatrical practices. The fact that Brecht had previously been involved

FIGURE 1. Bertolt Brecht (left) plays chess with Walter Benjamin at the playwright's home in Skovsbostrand, Denmark, in 1934. (Photographer unknown. Source: Bertolt Brecht Archives, BBA FA 07 / 027.)

in a dangerous car accident, in May 1929, adds a significant dimension to Steffin's letter.

The preparations and expectations for Benjamin's visit took many forms. In a letter to Brecht dated May 21, 1934, not long before his departure for Svendborg from Paris, Benjamin asks:

Are you familiar with Go, a very ancient Chinese board game? It is at least as interesting as chess—we should introduce it to Svendborg. You never move any pieces in Go, but only place them on the board which is empty at the start of the game. It seems to me to be similar to your play in this regard. You *place* each of your figures and formulations on the right spot from whence they fulfill their proper strategic function on their own and without having to act.[3] (italics in the original)

The play Benjamin is referring to is the final stage version of *Roundheads and Peakheads* that Brecht had completed about six weeks prior and that Benjamin now wanted to recommend for a London production. However, it would be three years before it would premiere in Copenhagen. But Benjamin's comment about Brecht's dramatic technique is very telling. Benjamin indicates that Brecht places his figures "on the right spot," from which they can statically fulfill their "proper strategic function," as in the Chinese board game. In Go, the game pieces are strategically arranged but do not move as they do in chess. Benjamin's comparison between the game of Go and Brecht's dramaturgical principles foreshadows their discussion about the Kafka story, and following that, the scenic conception of Brecht's mature epic plays, in particular *Mother Courage and Her Children*.[4]

Benjamin's Kafka Essay and Narratives of Exile

One of the texts Benjamin brought with him on his first visit to Svendborg and that he was eager to discuss with Brecht, was his Franz Kafka essay, written on the occasion of the tenth anniversary of Kafka's death. This essay was later published in *Jüdische Rundschau*, in December 1934, a few months after Benjamin had left Svendborg for Paris and Italy, and it is one of the first major interpretations of Kafka's work. It relates to the notion of exile on a number of different levels, reflecting the concrete life situations of Benjamin and Brecht themselves, for whom exile had at this time become very concrete. Their interpretations of "The Next Village" not only put into focus the fact of their exilic circumstances—exile as each of them viewed it—but pointed to something that was crucial for their creative work and thinking. In Brecht's case, his interpretation of the Kafka story can be seen as an early blueprint for his creative work during his years of exile, and also for his work after his return, his "homecoming," to Berlin after the war.

During his years of exile in Denmark, Brecht significantly widened and expounded upon the notion of the Epic Theatre, and he began to work on what were to become some of his major artistic projects: *Mother Courage and Her Children*, *The Life of Galileo*, and *The Good Person of Szechuan*, all of which were only fully completed, however, after he had left Denmark. Toward the end of his stay in Denmark, Brecht also started work on *The Messingkauf Dialogues*, intended to become his most comprehensive statement on the relations between theatre practice and theory, including a philosophical understanding of the theatre. But about a year before his death, he gave up on the project. Brecht had his *Messingkauf Dialogues*, his uncompleted magnum opus, as Benjamin had his *Passagen-*

Werk. Kafka's short story contains the seeds for all of these projects; it can even be viewed as the most concentrated formulation of their common deep structure, a highly concentrated reflection on exile.

Because Brecht and Benjamin decided to focus their discussion on "The Next Village," this text was obviously very significant for Benjamin himself. Specifically, the interpretation Benjamin offers in his discussion with Brecht in Svendborg, to which I later refer in detail, reflects the philosophy of history he was gradually developing at this time, which would culminate in his fragmentary pronouncements in both "On the Concept of History" as well as in certain sections of the *Passagen-Werk*. "The Next Village" is presented in the last section of Benjamin's essay on Kafka. This section begins with a story about a beggar that is not by Kafka himself, but as can be seen from its opening sentence—"So the story goes"—is evidently quoted from another source. Because this story is important to Benjamin's presentation of the Kafka story, contextualizing it within a messianic context as well as within the context of several exilic travelers, I quote it in full here. But I will defer the more detailed analysis to the discussion of Benjamin's performative storytelling techniques in the last chapter of this book. One of the distinguishing features of these storytelling techniques is the dense weaving together of stories from several sources, in this case framing Kafka's enigmatic narratives in a broader context of associations and constellations.

It is virtually impossible to enumerate all the relevant contexts leading up to Benjamin and Brecht's discussion of the Kafka story in Svendborg. In any case, here is the story that opens the last section of Benjamin's essay:

In a Hassidic village, so the story goes, Jews were sitting together in a shabby inn one Sabbath evening. They were all local people, with the exception of one person no one knew, a very poor, ragged man who was squatting in a dark corner at the back of the room. All sorts of things were discussed, and then it was suggested that everyone should tell what wish he would make if one were granted him. One man wanted money; another wished for a son-in-law; a third dreamed of a new carpenter's bench; and so each spoke in turn. After they had finished, only the beggar in his dark corner was left. Reluctantly and hesitantly he answered the question. "I wish I were a powerful king reigning over a big country. Then, some night while I was asleep in my palace, an enemy would invade my country, and by dawn his horsemen would penetrate to my castle and meet with no resistance. Roused from my sleep, I wouldn't have time even to dress and I would have to flee in my shirt. Rushing over hill and dale and through forests day and night, I would finally arrive safely right here at the bench in this corner. This is my wish." The others exchanged uncomprehending glances. "And what good would this wish have done you?" someone asked. "I'd have a shirt," was the answer.[5]

According to Benjamin, "This story takes us deep into the household that is Kafka's world,"[6] and immediately afterward he goes on to reflect on the mission of the Messiah to set right the distortions (*Entstellungen*) of his own time. This desire to banish life's defects, Benjamin adds, Kafka himself must also have considered, just as Benjamin no doubt did, and according to his notes from his discussions with Brecht in Svendborg, was even taken to task by his close friend for doing so. As I will show in detail below, Kafka's "The Next Village" brought to light some profound differences between Benjamin and Brecht concerning their basic viewpoints on life and art. This short text can even be seen as a test case for many of the ideas concerning the discursive practices of performance/theatre and philosophy presented in this book.

Immediately following the Hassidic tale about the beggar, Benjamin quotes Kafka's "The Next Village," but significantly, without the short introductory presentation of the grandson. The story in full reads as follows:

My grandfather used to say: "Life is astoundingly short. As I look back over it, life seems so foreshortened to me that I can hardly understand, for instance, how a young man can decide to ride over to the next village without being afraid that, quite apart from accidents [*unglücklichen Zufällen*], even the span of a normal life that passes happily may be totally insufficient for such a ride."[7]

Kafka's short text is extremely complex and dense, and before presenting the interpretations of Benjamin and Brecht, I want to take up two other issues. First I want to touch upon the notion of the *unglücklichen Zufällen*, usually translated as the "accidents" that can take place on the road. Had the young man who set out on the journey listened carefully to his grandfather, he probably would not even have begun the ride to the next village, and not out of fear of potential accidents. Even if it is the brevity of life itself, not accidents, that seems to be the main reason for the rider not reaching the next village, accidents are something that have to be taken into consideration, should the rider for some reason believe he can reach this goal. The possibility of an accident is a factor that has to be reckoned with in the complex subjunctive state of affairs Kafka has depicted. And even if *Zufall*, the German word used by Kafka, is closer to the English word "coincidence" than it is "accident"—the word *Unfall* means "accident." Together with *unglücklichen*, meaning "unhappy" or "unfortunate," the collocation *"unglücklichen Zufällen"* certainly comes very close to meaning what we in English call an accident. I mention this detail because the notion of "accident" is central to the modernist debates about the interaction among art, technology, and ideology to which both Benjamin and Brecht made important contributions, and which I examine in the next chapter.

Second, to contextualize the notion of exile Benjamin developed in his essay, it is helpful to look briefly at some of the additional stories of exile and travel he refers to. These narratives and associations, together with the story about the beggar's wish and Kafka's story about the rider, relate in different ways to Brecht's creative concerns. In his Kafka essay Benjamin refers to the village situated at the foot of Castle Hill in Kafka's *Das Schloss* and compares it to the village in a Talmudic legend about the coming of the Messiah:

It is the village in a Talmudic legend told by a rabbi in answer to the question why Jews prepare a festive evening meal on Fridays. The legend is about a princess languishing in exile, in a village whose languages she does not understand, far from her compatriots. One day this princess receives a letter saying that her fiancé has not forgotten her and is on the way to her.—The fiancé, so says the rabbi, is the Messiah; the princess is the soul; the village in which she lives in exile is the body. She prepares a meal for him because this is the only way in which she can express her joy in a village whose language she does not know.—This village of the Talmud is right in Kafka's world. For just as K. lives in the village on Castle Hill, modern man lives in his own body: the body slips away from him, is hostile toward him. It may happen that a man wakes up one day and finds himself transformed into vermin.[8]

This is also a story about going from one place to another, of the attempts to overcome an exilic situation that triggers the yearning for the Messiah. Apparently, for Benjamin there is the possibility for redemption, whereas Kafka's world, despite Benjamin's reading, seems to be completely dystopian. In his Epic Theatre Brecht integrates something of this Kafkaesque, dystopian vision, primarily by problematizing the identity of the subject, whereas Benjamin more clearly favors the messianic interpretation.

"The Next Village" is also mentioned somewhat earlier in Benjamin's Kafka essay, in the context of quoting a fragment attributed to Lao-tzu, which as well relates to the distances between countries and the idea of traveling. According to Lao-tzu, "Neighboring countries may be within sight, so that the sounds of roosters and dogs may be heard in the distance. Yet people are said to die at a ripe old age without having traveled far."[9] There are echoes from this fragment about the difficulties of "traveling far" in one of Brecht's poems from *Svendborger Gedichte* called "Legend of the Origin of the Book Tao Te Ching on Lao-tzu's Road into Exile."

This poem, with its obvious autobiographical subtext, has been dated to May 1938, several years after Benjamin's first visit to Denmark, but the subject itself may very well have been something Brecht and Benjamin raised in their discussions about the Kafka essay.[10] The poem tells the story of an old man who, because in his home country "goodness had been weakening a little," decides to leave, making a journey, only bringing with him the absolute necessities for the journey and a young companion. After four days he reaches a border crossing where he needs to declare the valuables he has brought with him. The young boy accompanying him explains that the old man is a teacher, only carrying his knowledge, that "soft water" can "grind strong rocks away." As they begin to move on, the customs man wants them to stay, to explain who "wins or loses," and he asks the boy to write the answer down for the time when the old man is gone. The old man stays for seven days and dictates his wisdom to the boy, eighty-one sayings, and then he and the boy travel on, thanking the customs man for his hospitality. The poem ends with a reflection that a customs man can take wisdom as easily as he takes money as payment for passing the border: "So the customs man deserves his bit. / It was he who called for it."[11]

Fredric Jameson has interpreted this poem as a discussion about "the distance which distance maintains from itself,"[12] related also to Brecht's play about Galileo, in which it is the pupil, Andrea, who is going into exile, leaving his revered teacher, Galileo, behind to die but taking his wisdom with him over the border.[13] Besides measuring distance, the crucial moment during Lao-tzu's temporary sojourn on his journey into exile takes place when some form of knowledge is revealed and passed on through the encounter between the teacher and his pupil, without obliterating their mutual independence. The story about the beggar in the inn, telling his wish, is about a similar brief moment of rest and insight during the ongoing exilic journey, when it becomes totally clear that "quite apart from accidents, even the span of a normal life that passes happily may be totally insufficient for such a ride." Talking about Kafka, Benjamin and Brecht both serve as teacher and pupil on their uncertain travels between two villages.

Benjamin and Brecht Interpret Kafka's Rider

On August 5, 1934, Benjamin writes in the diary entry, posthumously published as "Notes from Svendborg," that "three weeks ago I gave Brecht my essay on Kafka to read. He doubtless read it, but did not allude to it on his own accord; and on the two occasions when I brought the subject up, he responded evasively" (785).[14] Brecht apparently had some reservations about the work of Kafka or Benjamin's essay, or about both. After Benjamin had already taken back his manuscript, it is noted that "yesterday, he [Brecht] suddenly referred to the essay. With a somewhat abrupt and forced transition, he remarked that I, too, could not entirely escape the charge of writing in diary form, in the style of Nietzsche" (786). Brecht claims that Benjamin was looking "at the work as if it—and likewise the author—were a product of nature and isolated it from every possible context, even the author's life" (786). For Brecht, on the other hand, Benjamin observes in his notes the questions raised by Kafka: "What is he doing? How does he behave?" (786). Brecht admits that some of Kafka's images are good, but "the rest is just mystery-mongering. It is nonsense. You must ignore it. You cannot make progress with depth. Depth is simply a dimension; it's just depth in which nothing can be seen" (786). This pronouncement confirms that Brecht understands a literary work as described in Benjamin's letter about the Chinese board game, in which the pieces are placed on the empty board and "fulfill their proper strategic function on their own and without having to act."

To test their respective views on Kafka, Benjamin notes in his diary, they decided to discuss Kafka's "The Next Village." A few weeks later, on August 31, there is a long entry reporting that "[t]he day before yesterday, a long, heated debate about my Kafka" (787). Among other things Brecht had argued that his essay promoted "Jewish fascism" (787) instead of shedding light on Kafka himself. This accusation was perhaps triggered by Benjamin's tendency to interpret Kafka from a messianic perspective. The story about the beggar's wish and the Talmudic legend about the Messiah confirm this. But regarding the short story itself, the interpretations of Brecht and Benjamin, as reported by Benjamin, are more balanced, like one of their chess games, consisting of moves and counter-moves. This is how Benjamin summarizes their respective readings of Kafka's text:

> Brecht said it was a companion piece to the story of Achilles and the tortoise. A rider can never reach the next village if he divides the journey up into its smallest components—even aside from any incidents en route. Because life is too short for such a journey. But the error lies in the concept of "a rider." For you have to divide up the traveler, as well as the journey. And since in this you abolish the unity of life, you likewise do away with its brevity. However short it may be. This doesn't matter, because the man who started out on his journey is different from the man who arrives.—For my part, I proposed the following interpretation: the true measure of life is memory. Looking back, it runs through life like lightning. The speed with which you can turn back a few pages is the same as the speed with which memory flies from the next village back to the place from which the rider decided to leave. Whoever like the Ancients, has seen his life transformed into writing, let him read this writing backward. Only in this way—in full flight from the present—will he be able to understand it. (788)

Benjamin's interpretation of Kafka's story is consistent with his understanding of history presented in various contexts, culminating in his essay "On the Concept of History," in particular in the well-known passage on Paul Klee's painting *Angelus Novus*, another text that I analyze in detail in the last chapter, devoted to Benjamin's performative storytelling techniques. The journey to the next village is for Benjamin a journey backward through memory to the time/place—a Bakhtinian "*chronotopos*"—where the journey began. The angel, in Benjamin's text about the Klee watercolor, personifies this backward, melancholic gaze, at the same time as the angel itself is propelled into an unknown future by the storm that is caught in its wings.

Brecht's Interpretation and His Epic Theatre

According to Brecht's interpretation (as reported by Benjamin), the Kafka story shows us that besides the fact that life is too short for the rider to complete, the journey, the "error" as Brecht terms it, "lies in the concept of 'a rider.'" Not only the journey itself but the traveler, the individual subject, has to be divided up in its smallest units, and therefore Brecht adds, "The man who started out on his journey is different from the man who arrives." This approach radically changes the conditions for interpreting the Kafka story, because Brecht draws attention not only to the notion of the *Verfremdung*, the alienation of the subject from itself—that is, the character alienated from itself as well as the actor from himself or herself—but also to the interaction between the acting subject and the spatial conditions in which this subject performs or moves, a precondition for the theatre. The possibility that it is a different person who arrives than the one who set out on the journey—like the poem quoted in the epigraph to this chapter, written after Brecht's return to Berlin after the Second World War—introduces a moral assessment of the journey: If it were possible for someone to reach the next village, which changes has this person been forced or chosen to submit himself or herself to? These issues can perhaps be most clearly distinguished in *Mother Courage and Her Children*.

Brecht started writing this play during his stay in Denmark and decided to open his renewed theatre career by directing it in Berlin, in January 1949, a few months after his return to this city after the war. This production, which was the beginning of the collective of actors that was to become the famous Berliner Ensemble, was performed in the building where the Deutsches Theater is located today—Schumannstraße 13a—and where the theatre led by Max Reinhardt had been located before he went into exile. When in the opening scene of the *Mother Courage* production, the "wagon is rolled forward against the movement of the revolving stage,"[15] as Brecht prescribes in his so-called "Mother Courage Model," two opposite circular movements are superimposed on each other. The revolving stage turns clockwise, whereas from the point of view of the audience, the wagon moves counterclockwise. As a result of this superimposition of one circular movement onto another, one movement in opposition to the other, the spectators are watching one movement contradicting another—each revolving in opposite directions—perceived as stasis. The wagon actually remains in one place.

These two opposite circular movements are the basis for complex dialectics that can be perceived and formulated simultaneously in terms of motion and stasis, or as Benjamin writes in his notes for the *Passagen-*

Werk: "Image is dialectics at a standstill."[16] The standstill as an image in movement becomes literal. Furthermore, the theatrical machinery, and in particular the revolving stage, not only provides the support, or background, against which the movements and the actions of the characters gradually evolve, but it can also be viewed as an active participant, a kind of resistance, or even a real hindrance, against which the characters have to struggle. In the postscript to his short essay "Stage Design for the Epic Theatre," from 1951, which was also included in the fragments for *The Messingkauf Dialogues*, Brecht notes, "It is more important nowadays for the set to tell the spectator he's in the theatre than to tell him he's in, say, Aulis. The theatre must acquire *qua* theatre the same fascinating reality as a sporting arena during a boxing match. The best thing is to show the machinery, the ropes and the flies."[17] The theatrical machinery, in this case the revolving stage, becomes an active participant in the theatrical action, delineating the central *Gestus* of Mother Courage as a stage figure, who simultaneously moves and stands still. Despite her constant movement she does not, and neither does the rider in Kafka's story, make any progress from one point to another, never reaching the next village. And even if she and her entourage supposedly move from one battlefield to another, she remains fixed in one and the same spot on the stage, always situated in the middle of the war with its totally unpredictable progress and what Kafka in his story about the rider termed *unglücklichen Zufällen*.

By incorporating the theatrical machinery as an active participant in the dramatic action of *Mother Courage and Her Children*, Brecht took advantage of the fairly new stage technologies and transformed them into an integral aspect of the meaning he wishes to communicate.[18] Brecht developed the theatricalizing use of this stage machinery even further than had been done before him. According to David Richard Jones, a complex ensemble of circles was the most prevailing image that gradually developed in this production:

> On the floor was a large circle. Around the back of the circle ran the cyclorama, and at the front was the arc of the footlights. The sets were placed on this circle, scenes were acted on it, and the traveling—a central production image—took place around its great circumference. The circle was the world of Mother Courage.[19]

It is no doubt also significant that in his own production, Brecht chose to disregard the opening dialogue between the Recruiter and the

Sergeant, with which the printed version begins.[20] Instead, when the performance began, by drawing the curtain halfway, the turntable was already moving and the wagon gradually came into view. The wagon—which was simultaneously "moving" and "not moving," as it is drawn by the two sons serving as "horses"(!), with Mother Courage herself and her mute daughter Kattrin seated on the wagon—was the first image the spectators saw in this performance.

The 1960 film version of *Mother Courage and Her Children*—which was directed by Peter Palitzsch and Manfred Wekwerth, and intended to document the work of Brecht and pay tribute to it—was based on the two Brecht productions of the play (there was also a production of the play from 1951). In the film the revolving stage was not used, but it is possible to study several other details from the performance closely throughout the film. In the opening scene, Mother Courage is seated on the wagon and singing the triumphant march "Christian, Revive!"[21] At the same time as she is simulating the marching itself, swiftly swinging her left leg back and forth in the air, the wagon is drawn by her two sons. In spite of its revolving wheels, it does not move anywhere; Mother Courage's marching leg only stirs the air.

The wagon, each time drawn by a different constellation of people, is central to the performance. The first act ends with the wagon being pulled by Kattrin, who was seated by her mother in the opening scene. And in the last image of the performance, after covering her dead daughter with a blanket, Mother Courage is alone on the stage with her carriage. And when, after some hesitation she begins to move the carriage, the triumphant march with which the performance began can be heard again, but this time from offstage. What has in fact "happened" during the performance is that while she has been marching round and round with her wagon on the "same" spot, demonstrating the paradoxical dialectics of movement and stasis the Kafka story brings out so forcefully and paradoxically, she has lost her three children in the terrible "accident" called the Thirty Years' War.

The war does not lead anywhere, except to loss and despair. Mother Courage, who from the very beginning has unknowingly been caught in the *perpetuum mobile* impasse of a destructive treadmill, neither sees nor is able really to express the tragic significance of these events. In the production at the Berliner Ensemble, the call for revival under a Christian banner or any other banner, after the Second World War, was undoubtedly viewed in an extremely ironic light. After having seen this performance, George Steiner observed, "We cannot detach ourselves from the play and merely pass cool judgment on her faults. We too are hitched to the wagon, and it is beneath our feet that the stage turns."[22] The two concentric circles moving in opposite directions representing the journey between two villages, and the dialectics between them, are the potent *Gestus,* enabling Brecht in *Mother Courage and Her Children* to express the insoluble tensions articulated in Kafka's "The Next Village."

Mother Courage is somehow doomed to a never-ending movement around the circle, which neither has a beginning nor an end, nor makes it possible to arrive at a closure, even if the circle in itself is a harmonious and complete geometrical figure. The mental configuration of the circle was the figure through which Brecht was able to express these conflicts, enabling the movement around a center to become the point of rest on the journey that besides the movement itself has no final goal.

It is thus finally up to the spectators to experience the inner change that the war has led to, an experience that certainly must have been familiar to the Berlin audiences at the time. Elizabeth Wright very aptly has formulated this central issue of the audience reaction to Brecht's theatre: she claims that his "utopian wish was to produce an audience who would rejoice at the contradictions of a necessarily estranged world—the uncanniness of a world in flux, the constant shifting of figure and ground in a dialectical movement."[23] Brecht had returned to make theatre in the city that he had left sixteen years previously, having made his own circle around the world, much like the one Mother Courage does in his own play. In Brecht's case, to make a living, he flees the war instead of chasing after it. To the question about reaching "the next village"—from the poem "For Helene Weigel," which he wrote on the evening of the 1949 premiere of *Mother Courage and Her Children*—he provides a partial, but more personal answer. In this short poem Brecht asks his companion-rider wife, and the actress for whom he had written this role, to "step in your easy way/ On to the old stage in our demolished city/ Full of patience, at the same time relentless/ Showing what is right." In the final verse of the poem, he asks her to show the "unteachable . . . With some slight hope/ Your good face."[24]

The Caucasian Chalk Circle, which Brecht directed in 1954, is constructed from exactly the same components as is *Mother Courage and Her*

Children, even if their meanings have been modified and even reversed. Both these plays are about testing motherhood in times of war within the figure of a circle. Mother Courage obviously fails in this test, not from any fault of her own but rather as a result of the surrounding circumstances. On the other hand, Grusha, in *The Caucasian Chalk Circle*, gradually internalizes the notion of motherhood, even if she is not the biological mother of the contested child, and she gets some help from Azdak. *Mother Courage and Her Children* depicts a movement in space wherein Mother Courage is pursuing the war, to make a living from it, even at the prospect of losing her children. In the case of the *The Caucasian Chalk Circle*, Grusha is described as constantly fleeing the war to save the child and to keep out of reach of the war, which is "chasing" her. In both productions of these plays, in which the "geometry of motherhood" is explored, Brecht used the revolving stage in the same way. When Grusha flees with Michael over the mountains to her brother, the stage revolves in the opposite direction to her movement, fixing them as a static image at the front of the stage, just like the wagon of Mother Courage was fixed in the production of that play, showing how difficult and complex the travel is. But instead of making a "static" journey that leads to "nowhere" on an empty stage, as in *Mother Courage and Her Children*, in *The Caucasian Chalk Circle*, following common wisdom, if Grusha cannot reach the village, the village will come to Grusha. Thus she finally reaches her temporary goal with the assistance of the revolving stage. Both women are pieces placed on the board in a game of Go.

Brecht's use of the circle as a central scenic image is compelling. The circle creates a complex interaction between an individual human being (trying to reach the next village or even some form of Utopia), on the one hand, and the stage machinery, a technological invention, on the other. This interaction between man and machine prevents the completion of the journey, regardless of whether it is the road itself or the changing identity of the traveler that prevents this. However, at the same time as Brecht is transforming the abstract form of the circle into a concrete theatrical image, he is beginning to elaborate upon the circle's theoretical and metatheatrical aspects. This can be most clearly seen in *Life of Galileo* (and I will only examine the written text of this play here) and by extension also in *The Messingkauf Dialogues*, both of which in and of themselves present a sophisticated interplay between philosophy and performance.

Brecht was constantly striving toward a scientific notion of the theatre, and in *Life of Galileo*—about this scientist-hero, actually, Brecht's own alter ego—he combines the dramatic-theatrical and the theoretical-philosophic formulation of his "aesthetics" of the circle. And furthermore, the aesthetic principles of this play are a dialectical reflection of the structure of the universe, as it has been revealed by scientific laws and the principles of scientific experimentation, but also a reflection of social life as it has been determined by ideological forces. The fundamental principles of such an aesthetics based on the Copernican understanding of the universe can be described as a dynamic network of circular movements around an infinite number of different centers. In fact each individual subject in the world constitutes such a center around which all other bodies move. This subject position cannot become static because then, according to the view presented by Galileo/Brecht, there is an immediate regression to the Ptolemaic world picture, which because it positions the earth (and the pope) as its static center, is authoritarian and inflexible. *Life of Galileo* thus presents a dynamic view of the "center" as a subject position that has to be constantly redefined and reevaluated within a larger perceptual and ideological framework. This also follows from Brecht's interpretation of the Kafka story about the unreachable next village and the idea that the rider who arrives is not the same one who set out on the journey. As Galileo attempts to open up the perceptual and ideological possibilities, however, he is also forced (and willing) to make some humiliating compromises.

This concern with circles and the possibility of transforming any particular point in the universe into a center can be seen as early as the opening lines of *Life of Galileo*. Here Andrea, Galileo's pupil, says that the milkman must be paid "or he'll start making a circle round our house" (5),[25] which Galileo, while he is busy washing himself, immediately corrects by saying, "Describing a circle" (5), a more abstract and more scientific formulation. No matter the formulation used, the house has become a center. The description of the bailiff, who will come for the money in a straight line, the shortest distance between two points, and who will therefore also reach his goal (because no center is needed to do that), draws attention to the fact that Galileo and Andrea are living in a world based on the laws of geometry. It is a matter of finding the specific geometrical model that most fully elucidates this world, not only the house in which they live and study, but also the social world surrounding them, with its already existing and quite fixed hierarchies of power.

Life of Galileo presents two basic theoretical models competing with each other. In the very beginning of the first scene, Galileo makes a demonstration of the Ptolemaic system, exemplified by a wooden model that shows "how the planets move around the earth, according to our forefathers" (5), with the earth in the center and eight rings situated "one inside another" (6). After throwing the towel, with which he has been drying himself, as if to demonstrate the laws of gravity to Andrea, Galileo explains what the limitations of the old system are, while Andrea rubs his back, thus making Galileo, his teacher, the center of his "universe." According to Galileo the old Ptolemaic system, on which the hierarchical social norms have also been based, is "walls and spheres and immobility! For two thousand years people have believed that the sun and all the stars rotate around mankind. Pope, cardinals, princes, professors, captains, merchants, fishwives and school kids thought they were sitting motionless inside this crystal sphere" (6). But, continues Galileo, "We are breaking out of / the crystal sphere /, Andrea, at full speed. . . . Because everything is in motion, my friend" (6).

In the long and enthusiastic speech that follows, Galileo explains to his pupil that a new time has begun, pointing out when and how these changes began. But Galileo is also concerned with how these changes will affect the future:

> It is my prophesy that our own lifetime will see astronomy discussed in the marketplaces. Even the fishwives' sons will hasten off to school. For these novelty-seeking people in our cities will be delighted with a new astronomy that sets the earth moving too. The old idea was always that the stars were fixed to a crystal vault to stop them falling down. Today we have found the courage to let them soar through space without support; and they are traveling at full speed just like our ships, at full speed and without support.
>
> And the earth is rolling cheerfully around the sun, and the fishwives, merchants, princes, cardinals and even the Pope are rolling with it.
>
> The universe has lost its centre overnight, and woken up to find it has countless centres. So that each one can now be seen as the centre, or none at all. Suddenly there is a lot of room. (8)

The new understanding of astronomy, heralded by Copernicus and developed by Galileo, is not limited to the natural sciences, and as we know, the reason Galileo has to recant his ideas is not "geometric" but rather that these ideas threaten the existing social order.

The interaction between science and ideology is closely connected to the ideas of teaching and learning, which can be seen in the relationship between Galileo—the teacher—and his pupil Andrea. To teach Andrea about the new perception of the world, Galileo stages a small, highly theatricalized demonstration. He places Andrea on a chair, which, within the framework of the short play within a play that evolves, Galileo says represents the earth. Then Galileo asks Andrea how it is possible for the washstand, which represents the sun, to rise on one side of the earth and to sink on the other side. Andrea, quite logically, argues that by moving the washstand from one side to the other, "I can see with my own eyes that the sun goes down in a different place from where it rises" (9). It is however quite simple for Galileo to show Andrea, that by turning the chair instead of moving the washstand, there is an alternative way for the "sun" to move from Andrea's left side to his right. This small scene is constructed exactly like two alternative scientific experiments, showing that the answers can be given according to two alternative and plausible hypotheses, depending on how the circle is drawn. Either the washstand can be moved or the chair turned. And the scientific experiment, showing how the universe is constructed, has become a theatrical performance in which Galileo is the director and Andrea is both actor and spectator.

But Andrea, and Brecht too, clearly understands that "examples always work if you are clever" (11) and that Galileo's demonstrations do not prove anything unless there is a hypothesis that can be tested by examining the real world. Performance strategies cannot be considered empirical, no matter how sophisticated they are. Galileo—and implicitly also Brecht himself of course—are interested in showing Andrea, as well as the spectators, that these demonstrations, just like theatrical performances, are only models that have to be critically and empirically examined on the basis of the physical and social realities of the world itself. Performance is not science, and such is the initial tension from which the dialectics of the theatre stem; or as Galileo says to Andrea at the end of the first scene, "Look at Felicia down there outside the basket-maker's shop breastfeeding her child: it remains a hypothesis that she's giving it milk and not getting milk from it, till one actually goes and sees and proves it. Faced with the stars we are like dull-eyed worms that can hardly see at all" (18). The important point, however, is that Andrea gradually learns to see the world through these demonstrations, and not merely by "gawping"

(9), as Galileo complains when his student does not understand how the two alternative solutions to the chair and washstand demonstration work. The theatrical experiment—combining theatre and science and making the theatre scientific—enables Andrea to see the world dialectically. And *Life of Galileo*, ending with Andrea saving the *Discursi*, which Galileo has kept hidden inside the globe, for the world, presents an optimistic aspect of these complex dialectics. Andrea, like the bailiff, learns to make a straight line, something that apparently enables him to cross the border, and hopefully also to reach the next village.

In his unfinished *Messingkauf Dialogues*,[26] Brecht distinguishes between two basic models of the theatre: the merry-go-round and the planetarium. The merry-go-round, the so-called *k-typus* (from the German *Karussell*), is based on the Ptolemaic conception of the universe. It is a theatre that has a fixed center, with everything moving around it, causing dizziness to everyone situated in the theatre. This for Brecht is represented by the Aristotelian theatre, aiming at catharsis, in which the spectators identify with the events and characters on the stage. According to Brecht this was the model Stanislavski used.

The planetarium model, or *p-typus* (from the German *Planetarium*), is based on Copernicus's visual conception of the universe, in which the center is constantly redefined and reidentified. It is supposed to enable the spectators, first of all, through a demonstration, to observe and to understand, and only afterward to judge and draw conclusions. This is for Brecht the model he wished to realize through his own scientific conceptions of the Epic Theatre. In this form of theatre, the point from which the theatrical space is observed can change, depending on which aspect of the fictional universe is exposed and represented. Also the planetarium model enables the audience to observe the circular movements of the heavenly bodies "objectively," while at the same time allowing them to discern the truths about the universe from their exclusively "subjective" points of view as individual spectators who are at the central, but far from exclusive, point in the universe.

Ideally, *p-typus* liberates the perception of the fictional universe from the constrictions that buildings and cities, social strata, and ideologies impose on the spectators when they move around in the real world. Finally, the aim of Brecht's epic planetarium is to free the spectators from such limitations so they might sharpen their abilities to perceive the real world and to critique it. *Life of Galileo* is a dialectical play confronting these issues on two levels. The first level is the acute awareness that theatre itself is a model in the same sense that the Ptolemaic and the Copernican conceptions of the universe are models that have to be constantly reexamined in relationship to the universe. Such a reexamination also constitutes a form of demonstration, as for example what Galileo and Andrea do with the washstand and the chair. And such a demonstration is in itself a theatrical performance that functions meta-theatrically as a play within a play.

Furthermore, on the second level, *Life of Galileo* is actually a dialectical play in the sense that it contains elements of both *k-typus* and *p-typus*, the two forms of theatrical perception, which are not only perceived on the scientific level of astronomy, but are placed in opposition to each other on the social, ideological, and, most important, aesthetic levels. *Life of Galileo* can also be seen as a linear play, showing a middle-aged scientist who has just finished his breakfast in the first scene and who, in his old age, is having his supper in the last scene of the play. But at the same time it is also a historical parable about the cyclical reappearance or repetition of certain constellations at different times in history.

The circle and the line are the abstract, geometric level on which Brecht envisaged the dramaturgical "curves" of the theatre, serving as an abstract blueprint for the journey toward anything that could be situated between the next village and a Utopian ideal. These geometrical figures following from the Kafka story about the rider setting off to the next village were also deeply personal for the two friends positioning themselves in relation to this story. Benjamin was to interrupt his own journey by ending his life, never reaching "the next village." And I believe that Brecht was torn between two beliefs. On the one hand, he felt it was possible to make such a journey toward a Utopian ideal, no matter whether it was a radically changed person who finally reached the goal—and it actually had to be such a changed person, because that was the aim of the Revolution. On the other hand, he was keenly aware that his own village (Berlin) had changed so much that it would be impossible to recognize it when it was ultimately reached. That was an option neither Benjamin nor Brecht took into consideration as they were discussing "The Next Village." But then again, there were many things they knew nothing about and were not even able to imagine when they were discussing Kafka during the summer of 1934.

PART TWO

CONSTELLATIONS

5

Accidents and Catastrophic Constellations

PERFORMATIVE AGENDAS

> It is not that what is past casts its light on what is present, or what is present its light on what is past; rather, image is that wherein what has been comes together in a flash with the now to form a constellation.
> —Walter Benjamin, *The Arcades Project*

From Encounters to Constellations

In "The Next Village" Kafka depicted a *condition humaine* in which, regardless of the *unglücklichen zufällen* that may occur while traveling from one village to the next, life itself is perceived as being too short ever to reach this goal. Even if there is no direct causal relationship between such potential accidents and the brevity of life, in Kafka's fragmentary fictional world they are inevitably perceived as being very closely related. However, the grandfather's repeated reflection transmitted by the grandchild's telling of the story presents the accidents and the shortness of life as closely interacting with each other. The uncanny proximity of the possibility of accidents and the impossibility of reaching the next village for other, unknown reasons, made a deep impact on the creative work and thinking of both Brecht and Benjamin. And whether Kafka's text was the chicken or the egg—if it inspired them to new modes of creativity or rather confirmed what they had already experienced and expressed through their previous work, or most likely both of these options—is not the main issue.

Kafka's short and enigmatic narrative (as well as many of his other writings) profoundly coincided with the aesthetic and philosophical-ideological agendas of both Brecht and Benjamin at a time when they, together with a gradually growing number of intellectuals and Jews (or both) were seeking refuge in the insecurities of exile that culminated with the Second World War. Beginning with Hitler's rise to power, and in particular the Reichstag fire, the number of individuals experiencing the hazards of travel was constantly on the increase. Travel became more dangerous as the profiling of individuals crossing the border increased and borders themselves were tightened. And the physical dangers inherent in the act of traveling itself were constantly on the rise. Within a few years many of Brecht's and Benjamin's close friends and relatives became the victims of exile, whereas those who for various reasons decided to stay in Germany often faced even greater danger than those who fled. They did not even consider the option of beginning the journey.

The perceived hazards of traveling in this heightened, symbolic, and paradigmatic sense—long after Oedipus had traveled the roads to the place where the three roads met—indirectly led to the death of Benjamin. On his last trip, on foot as Oedipus had been, Benjamin unsuccessfully attempted to cross the Franco-Spanish border near Port Bou, the small village where he would be buried.[1] And Brecht—after traveling around the globe, making a journey that was even more extensive than that of his own Mother Courage—returned to Berlin after the war and established the now famous Ensemble named for the city. He began a new career there by directing his play about Mother Courage. Brecht's return to his own "village" no doubt brought a certain closure to his creative mission, although much of it remained unfinished. After returning to Berlin, Brecht himself somewhat enigmatically expressed his situation in the poem "Observation," from 1949 (which is presented in the epigraph to the previous chapter): "The travails of the mountains lie behind us. / Before us lie the travails of the plains."

However no matter how minutely the encounters between philosophers and thespians can be reconstructed, there are still many issues concerning the relations between the creative endeavors of theatrical/performative practices and philosophical thinking—in particular those resonating with and emanating from the meeting between Brecht and Benjamin—that must be examined more in depth. In the last chapter, I focus my attention on the more detailed historiographical specificities of the particular direct encounter between them, and how their discussion of Kafka reverberates within the larger contexts of their work and thinking—in particular the work of Brecht. Therefore in the last two chapters I shift focus to discuss some more wide-ranging constellations emerging from the discursive practices of philosophy and performance and how the historical events of the time affected the two men's perceptions and ideas: how the Zeitgeist is reflected in their work.

My reading of the letter from Strindberg to his future wife and my interpretation of Nietzsche's *The Birth of Tragedy* have already moved in this more general direction. But the issues I raised in that context were of a more private nature and did not directly confront the sense of the continental landslide demolishing everything in its path, which Brecht and Benjamin tried to find creative ways to confront. One of the methods for finding such a double reflection is by looking for what Benjamin himself, most prominently in his notes for *The Arcades Project* (*Das Passagen-Werk*), termed "constellations."

For Benjamin the notion of constellation was a mode of thinking intended to respond to the crisis he perceived at the time, framing it within a broader cultural, historical, and philosophical context.[2] The primary association of this term is connected to the stars in the sky, configured and brought together in seemingly arbitrary constellations, like, for example, the Big Bear and Andromeda, creating order within the overwhelming expanse of the starry skies. Constellations are the composite images that emerge in the sky by bringing heavenly bodies together. For Benjamin, though, the term was not primarily connected with celestial phenomena. He gave it a broader cultural, even historiographical and philosophical, scope, gradually laying the basis for his own philosophy of history. As we have also seen, Bertolt Brecht's *Life of Galileo* is not only a play about the sky and the celestial bodies, but about the significance and philosophical implications of the movements of these heavenly bodies, as well as how human bodies move and influence one another within the social and cultural-ideological spheres. And in *The Messingkauf Dialogues*, Brecht theorized the dynamics of the planetarium, through which constantly new aesthetic, ideological, and philosophical constellations emerge. In his play about Galileo, which was also planned to be included in *The Messingkauf* project, Brecht's attempt to depict the complex interaction between individual creativity and a specific historical context was no doubt inspired by the notion of constellation developed by Benjamin, drawing attention to the sometimes uncertain role of the individual scientist in such an endeavor. In his formulation of constellation as a concept, Benjamin was clearly also in a direct dialogue with Brecht's notion of the *Gestus*, which focused more distinctly on the theatrical image as a nexus of gradually evolving meanings, with social and ideological implications, whereas the constellation more directly draws attention to the historical, philosophical dimension of the dialectics of images.

For Benjamin the notion of constellation combined the sense of observing a historical development at a distance with the immediate state of emergency (or state of exception: the *Ausnahmezustand*) created by the present. While spending his days in the Bibliothèque Nationale in Paris, where he was simultaneously both close to and distant from the surrounding events—which I exemplify in more detail later—he penned his extensive notes and quotations for *The Arcades Project* and also included his reflections on the notion of the constellation. The following passage, a theoretical and highly abstract meditation on how such image constellations are constituted, can be read as a meta-diary in which Benjamin reflected directly on his own time, emphasizing the historical embeddedness of images as well as the notion of "origin," which was crucial for Benjamin's understanding of the notion of the performative. According to Benjamin,

> The historical index of the images not only says that they belong to a particular time; it says, above all, that they attain to legibility only at a particular time. And indeed, this acceding "to legibility" constitutes a specific critical point in the movement of their interior. Every present day is determined by the images that are synchronic with it: each "now" is the now of a particular recognizability. In it, truth is charged to the bursting point with time. (This point of explosion, and nothing else, is the death of the *intentio*, which thus coincides with the birth of authentic historical time, the time of truth.) It is not that what is past casts its light on what is present, or what is present its light on what is past; rather, image is that wherein what has been comes together in a flash with the now to form a constellation. In other words: image is dialectics at a standstill. For while the relation of the present to the past is purely temporal, the relation of what-has-been to the now is dialectical: not temporal in nature but figural [*bildlich*].

Only dialectical images are genuinely historical—that is, not archaic—images. The image that is read—which is to say, the image in the now of its recognizability—bears to the highest degree the imprint of the perilous critical moment on which all reading is founded.[3] (italics in the original)

In addition to presenting the spatial dimension of image constellations, situating them in a visual mise-en-scène (as the celestial constellations also do), Benjamin introduced a temporal, historical dimension governed by images and their dialectical contextualizations.

Benjamin was certainly highly conscious of the role of the spectator in this spatio-temporal drama, because these constellations have been formed by "the perilous critical moment on which all reading is founded." At this moment of reading, Benjamin argued, time is arrested, transforming the image into a "dialectics at a standstill" in which "what has been comes together in a flash with the now to form a constellation." The constellation does not only bring the past and the present together, it also connects between the temporal and the spatial. And at the same time it is possible, I believe, to interpret Benjamin as saying that the image can actually only emerge when the temporal dialectics of history have come to such a standstill; or in his own formulation, "the image in the now of its recognizability—bears to the highest degree the imprint of the perilous critical moment on which all reading is founded." This is the image of the wagon of Mother Courage moving in one direction while the revolving stage is moving in the opposite direction.

Only in such a moment of danger, as Benjamin somewhat later formulated this idea in his fragments "On the Concept of History," does the image reach its full, inner clarity as a part of a more fully contextualized constellation. In his sixth thesis of this posthumously published collection of short, fragmentary texts Benjamin explained that:

Articulating the past historically does not mean recognizing it "the way it really was." It means appropriating a memory as it flashes up in a moment of danger. Historical materialism wishes to hold fast to that image of the past, which unexpectedly appears to the historical subject in a moment of danger. The danger threatens both the content of the tradition and those who inherit it. For both, it is one and the same thing: the danger of becoming a tool of the ruling classes. Every age must strive anew to wrest tradition away from the conformism that is working to overpower it. The Messiah comes not only as the redeemer; he comes as the victor over the Antichrist. The only historian capable of fanning the spark of hope in the past is the one who is firmly convinced that *even the dead* will not be safe from the enemy if he is victorious. And this enemy has never ceased to be victorious.[4]

The notion of constellation, if indeed this is what Benjamin is referring to here in a more extended sense than in *The Arcades Project*, also includes a metaphysical dimension in which the Messiah, according to Benjamin, is seen as a possible aspect of historical development, counteracting the constantly appearing dangers. It even seems that Benjamin intuitively relates to Nietzsche's final madness as a source of such danger.

At a time when the discursive practices of both philosophy and the theatre were confronting a deep crisis and their generally accepted assumptions could no longer be taken for granted, both Benjamin and Brecht raised issues and explored modes of expression systematically crossing the traditional borderlines between philosophy and performance. This contrasts with Hamlet, who was experimenting with theatre by staging a play to find out if Claudius had murdered his father; for Benjamin and Brecht there was no doubt what the sources of injustice and persecution were during their time. And to draw attention to the approaching catastrophe we now call the Second World War, when the traditional forms of making theatre by staging plays were not immediately available, Benjamin and Brecht (together with many others) recruited every possible rhetorical strategy to explore philosophical forms of performance and theatrical modes of philosophy. This was their outlet for experimenting with forms of writing intended to fully engage their potential readers. However, Benjamin would get the chance to engage an audience only after the catastrophic storm had receded (if that is what it in fact did).

The last two chapters of this book explore some of these strategies, in particular by accounting for the technological innovations that had enabled the extraordinary upgrading of the machineries of warfare that was taking place between the two world wars. These innovations, in tandem with the rise of fascism, are the main reason for the developing state of emergency Brecht and Benjamin had to confront. I contextualize this development by using the words "accidents" and "catastrophic" in the title of this chapter. In the first section I examine the notion of the street accident in a broader cultural context as well as its seminal importance to the theories of acting developed in particular by Brecht himself, but also by Constantin Stanislavski, the founder of the Moscow Art Theatre and a seminal theoretician of the modern theatre. Even if in many of his writings Brecht presented Stanislavski as the representative of the *k-typus* theatre, which he dismissed as being diametrically opposed to his own conceptions of the theatre, their respective views on the accident as a paradigm for the art of acting in particular, and their ideas about the theatre in general, are actually more closely aligned than previous research would suggest. The second section of this chapter explores Benjamin's notion of "constellation" in connection with the man-made catastrophes leading up to the Second World War. In particular, I focus on the bombings of Guernica (the Basque village bombed by the Nazis in April 1937) and the performative strategies employed to represent them by aesthetic means, in particular by Picasso's famous mural commemorating this event. I show how this painting, as well as Benjamin's famous meditation on Paul Klee's small painting *Angelus Novus*, is drawn into more comprehensive performative contexts that also express philosophical ideas, in the latter case through the genre of writing called *Denkbilder* (thought-images).

The last chapter then explores the performative aspects of some of Benjamin's *Denkbilder* more in depth. The *Denkbild* is a form of writing through which philosophical ideas become immersed in complex and sometimes quite enigmatic performative contexts. In these texts the direct competition between the two discursive practices, with which I set out my investigation—by examining Plato's *Symposium*—has been transformed into an intellectual and creative endeavor. Through this endeavor the philosopher becomes fully transformed into a thespian, not by trying to replace the thespian and therefore ousting him from the ideal state, but by integrating this form of writing within a much more comprehensive performative activity of thinking. Language becomes performative through a mode of creativity in which philosophy both thinks and performs at the same time. And this concomitant thinking and performing occurs not by limiting the performative functions of language to task-oriented situations, which are defined by the ability of words to achieve a certain clearly defined goal, but by creating an ongoing dialogical interaction with the reader.

Not surprisingly perhaps, I believe Walter Benjamin was able to make a full commitment to the Socratic method by incorporating within his philosophical discourse both tragedy—which for Benjamin is represented by history itself—and comedy, paradoxically articulated through his understanding of a messianic Utopia. Because a Utopian state will obviously never be realized, it has to be approached as an always receding possibility from which we have inevitably become alienated through history and its recurring catastrophes. At the same time as this form of performativity necessarily confronts the concrete historical circumstances of the utterance, it activates the questions to the transhistorical reader with which the first act of *Hamlet* opens: "Who's there?" and "Has this thing appeared again tonight?"

Accidents

The invention of the steam engine quickly improved the collective forms of transportation by ship, creating a whole new mode of transport—travel by train. Getting to the next village became both faster and more dangerous. And with the development of the combustion engine, "faster and more dangerous" applied to the more individual mode of travel by car as well. Since cars could be driven by almost anyone, they constituted a special kind of danger. Jeffrey Schnapp has made a useful distinction between "passenger-centered and driver-centered modes of transportation or, to state the matter otherwise, between modes of mass transit and individual transportation, whether in the experiences and fantasies to which they give rise or in the sorts of discourses that are elaborated in order to regulate and represent them"[5] Schnapp continues his argument explaining that with the new technologies, speed itself becomes "a kind of drug, an intensifier, an *excitant moderne* . . . where . . . the human subject of speed—typically the driver . . . finds himself caught in an addiction loop, threatened, on the one hand, by monotony, and, on the other, by the need for ever new stimuli in order to maintain the same level of intensity."[6] The dangers of such an addiction are obvious, even if the Italian futurists celebrated this form of intoxication and worshipped the new technologies of transportation, which according to their understanding had been quite successfully tested in the battlefields of the so-called Great War.

This newly achieved speed, and in particular the driver-centered modes of transportation, had a decisive influence on the sense of space, movement, and most of all danger. It informed the philosophical thinking as well as all the artistic practices at the time, including the theatre. The risks for accidents were steadily growing in the wake of the technological innovations, even if, as we have already seen, the dangers of the road apparently have much deeper roots than these modern technological "improvements," beginning already with Oedipus traveling from the oracle at Delphi and arriving at the place where the three roads meet and where he killed his father. In *Hamlet* this danger is ironically realized by the trip to England—Shakespeare's own home country—that Claudius forces on his nephew in order to kill him.

But by the nineteenth century, travel became more dangerous. In his book *The Railway Journey: The Industrialization of Time and Space in the Nineteenth Century*, Wolfgang Schivelbusch has argued:

> The pre-industrial catastrophes were natural events, natural accidents. They attacked the objects they destroyed from the outside, as storms, floods, thunderbolts, and hailstones. After the Industrial Revolution, destruction by technological accident came from the inside. The technical apparatuses destroyed themselves by means of their own power. The energies tamed by the steam engine and delivered by it as regulated mechanical performance destroyed that engine itself in the case of an accident. The increasingly rapid vehicles of transportation tended to destroy themselves and each other totally, whenever they collided. The higher the degree of technical intensification (pressure, tension, velocity, etc.) of a piece of machinery, the more thorough-going was its destruction in the case of dysfunction. The breaking of a coach axle in the eighteenth century merely interrupted a slow and exceedingly bumpy trip on the highway; the breaking of a locomotive axle between Paris and Versailles in 1842 led to the first railroad catastrophe that caused a panic in Europe.[7]

Accidents caused by transportation came to represent the contingency and randomness caused by the interactions between the recent technological inventions and the human individual. Accidents were in some cases even perceived as a link between the creativity endemic to artistic practices and the philosophical assumptions governing these practices.

For Kafka, Brecht, and Benjamin, as well as for many of their contemporaries, the notion of the accident—in particular the street accident—together with other man-made catastrophes, especially war, quickly became incorporated within the modernist aesthetic sensibility as one of the archetypal templates for the notion of modernity itself. The accident became a *topos* for exploring and experimenting with new forms of representation. These forms were seemingly freed from the deterministic laws of causality that had dominated the late nineteenth century avant-garde movements (including Nietzsche), which had been operating under the spell of Hegelian and Darwinian modes of thinking. The accident was ruled by another form of causality. And the newly developed and constantly improved technologies demanded new forms of expression, while at the same time—partly on the basis of the accident as a paradigm, like in Kafka's "The Next Village"—the basic aesthetic principles for artistic creativity in general, and in the theatre in particular, were radically reexamined and reformulated.

Kafka, who was employed by an insurance firm that used photographs to understand traffic accidents and, it would seem, prevent them, was as we have already seen, expressing this budding modernist sensibility, which was drawing its "inspiration" from the street accident. Reminiscent of the short story about the rider is Kafka's quite remarkable diary entry from December 15, 1910. He was visiting Paris for the first time:

> When I sit down at the desk I feel no better than someone who falls and breaks both legs in the middle of the traffic of the Place de l'Opéra. All the carriages, despite their noise, press silently from all directions in all directions, but that man's pain keeps better order than the police, it closes his eyes and empties the Place and the streets without carriages having to turn about. The great commotion hurts him, for he is really an obstruction to traffic, but the emptiness is no less sad, for it unshackles his real pain.[8]

Here Kafka depicts how he is suddenly drawn into the middle of one of the busiest places in Paris, the Place de l'Opéra. It is the act of writing itself, while sitting at his desk, that makes Kafka imagine and even directly experience the violent onslaught of the traffic, surrounded by the carriages and their noise, pressing in from all directions. However, at the moment he believes that he will be run over by these carriages, something like a miracle takes place. The pain he feels causes him to close his eyes, and the Place de l'Opéra is completely empty of traffic. However, the ensuing "emptiness is no less sad, for it unshackles his real pain." For Kafka, creativity and the dangers of the traffic, even if these are an unexpected collocation, are intimately connected with each other, giving expression to the inner life of despair and pain experienced by the individual in the technological age of modernity. In Benjamin's diary entry from the same day that he discussed "The Next Village" with Brecht (August 31, 1934), he also reflected: "Kafka's perspective: that of a man who has fallen under the wheels." And, he adds, it "is a Kafkaesque irony that the man was an insurance agent who appeared to be convinced of nothing more surely than the invalidity of all guarantees."[9]

The life of the city and of Paris in particular, but also of Berlin and Moscow, had a vital effect on Benjamin's thinking as it did on Kafka's. He obsessively devoted *The Arcades Project* to tracing the primal scene of modernity to the street life of nineteenth-century Paris. While sitting in the Bibliothèque Nationale, he became a *flâneur*, that is, "one who strolls"—rather than an exilic wanderer—strolling through the city streets in his imagination. And only on very rare occasions did he let his direct experiences of the city come into view in his own writing. This contrasts with Kafka, who, while sitting at his writing desk, imagined himself an integral, if suffering, participant in the life of the city. Less than a year after his first visit, Kafka returned to Paris, and in a long diary entry from this second visit, he gives a detailed description of a traffic accident he has witnessed.[10] Benjamin on the other hand, even if he minutely documented Paris's past, is much more frugal in sharing his own direct experiences of the city. However, one such rare instance, when Benjamin enabled his reader to hear the sounds of contemporary Paris, occurred in a letter to his close friend and mentor, the philosopher and cultural critic Theodor Adorno, from November 2, 1937. When writing this letter, Benjamin had just found temporary, and very uncomfortable, lodgings. He had been thrown out of his apartment when a prospective tenant gave the owner—what Benjamin in an earlier letter to Adorno had called—"an unmatchable offer."[11] In the letter describing his new lodgings Benjamin observed:

I can see myself sitting here, wide awake since six o'clock in the morning, listening away to the oceanic rather than intelligible rhythms of the Paris traffic, which rumbles in through the narrow asphalt aperture right in front of my bed. In front of my bed—for the bed stands right there where the window is. If I lift the shutters the street itself is a witness to my literary labours, and if I close them, I am immediately exposed to the monstrous climatic extremes which the (uncontrollable) central heating creates in this spring-like October.[12]

One of Benjamin's intentions with this letter was obviously to draw Adorno's attention to the physical and psychological hardships he suffered, indirectly asking for help and compassion. The interesting point in this context, however, is that instead of imagining himself being drawn out from his writing desk into the middle of the Paris traffic, as Kafka had done in his diary, Benjamin "lets" the traffic enter his room so that it becomes "a witness to my literary labours." Had it not been for the unbearable heat, Benjamin would probably have kept the windows closed all the time, completely shutting out the city from his small room.

In his book *Berlin Childhood around 1900*, as he does in his letter, Benjamin recalls how he was listening to the distant sounds of the city from a protected, interior space. He observes:

Nothing has fortified my own memory so profoundly as gazing into courtyards, one of whose dark loggias, shaded by blinds in the summer, was for me the cradle in which the city laid its new citizen. The caryatids that supported the loggia on the floor above ours may have slipped away from their post for a moment to sing a lullaby beside that cradle—a song containing little of what later awaited me, but nonetheless sounding the theme through which the air of courtyards has forever remained intoxicating to me. . . . The rhythm of the metropolitan railway and of carpet-beating rocked me to sleep. It was the mold in which my dreams took shape—first the unformed ones, traversed perhaps by the sound of running water or the smell of milk, then the long-spun ones; travel dreams and dreams of rain.[13]

This kind of meditative recollection of a general, recurring experience from a long time ago, indirectly leads Benjamin to the arcades of Paris. These arcades are liminally situated between the bustle of the city and the intimate places where Benjamin's dreams of the past have taken shape, reflexively interacting with the outside world from what seems to be an intentionally introverted point of view. In his recollection of the outside world as a child in Berlin, beginning with the loggia and the caryatids, he gradually becomes connected with the more distant sounds of the metropolitan railway, which just like the noise of the traffic in the letter to Adorno, take on a richer meaning for the child gazing into the courtyard, enabling his dreams of travel gradually to take shape. In *The Arcades Project* the constellations created by simultaneously moving backward in time and to distant vistas gradually become transformed into a meditation on history as catastrophic accident.

Ludwig Wittgenstein approached the dangers of traffic much more pragmatically. In his diaries written during the First World War, Wittgenstein presented a completely different perspective on this modern, paradigmatic approach to the street accident. The picture theory of statements he later developed in the *Tractatus Logico-Philosophicus* (*Logische-Philosophische Abhandlung*), published in 1921, originated from his reading of a magazine during the First World War. This experience led to the first seeds of Wittgenstein's picture theory, which was to become one of the constantly recurring ideas of his philosophy of language. On September 9, 1914, in his *Notebooks 1914–1916*, Wittgenstein wrote, "The general concept of a proposition carries with it a quite general concept of the co-ordination of proposition and situation: The solution to all my questions must be *extremely* simple. In the proposition a world is as it were put together experimentally" (italics in the original), adding in parentheses: "As when in the law-court in Paris a motor-car accident is represented by means of dolls, etc."[14]

Georg Henrik von Wright, one of Wittgenstein's students, later an influential philosopher in his own right, draws attention to Wittgenstein's picture-theory discovery in his memoirs, although it has been debated whether the theory was actually hatched on the Eastern front. If it happened there, the obvious connections between accident and war would no doubt have been even more clearly emphasized. According to von Wright,

It was in the autumn of 1914, on the Eastern Front. Wittgenstein was reading in a magazine about a lawsuit in Paris concerning an automobile accident. At the trial, a miniature model of the accident was presented before the court. The model here served as a proposition, that is, as a description of a possible state of affairs. It had its function owing to a correspondence between the parts of the model (the miniature houses, cars, people) and things (houses, cars, people) in reality. It now occurred to Wittgenstein that one might reverse the analogy and say that a *proposition* serves as a model or a *picture*, by virtue of a similar correspondence between *its* parts and the world.[15] (italics in the original)

Wittgenstein universalizes the traffic accident to suit his gradually budding theory of language as a form of expression for all languages.

The first sentence of Wittgenstein's *Tractatus Logico-Philosophicus*, to which I refer in connection with Hamlet's silence in Chapter 2, states that "*Die Welt ist alles, was der Fall ist*" (The world is everything that is the case).[16] In this sentence, the German word *Fall* means much more than just what "is the case." Besides referring to the notion of a grammatical "case," it is closely related to coincidence (*Zufall*) and accident (*Unfall*), both of which contain *Fall* in the sense of "falling," implying failure and collapse. The world, as all that which is "*der Fall,*" is immersed in tragedy and loss. Wittgenstein apparently also echoes something of Kafka's ideas when in the *Tractatus* he states, "The exploration of logic means the exploration of *everything that is subject to law*. And outside logic everything is accidental" (line 6.30; italics in the original). This could even refer to Kafka's *The Trial*. And Benjamin and Brecht even seem to be in dialogue with Wittgenstein, providing what could be seen as an additional reading of Kafka's "The Next Village":

> The sense of the world must lie outside the world. In the world everything is as it is, and everything happens as it does happen: in it no value exists—and if it did exist, it would have no value. If there is any value that does have value, it must lie outside the whole sphere of what happens and is the case. For all that happens and is the case is accidental. What makes it non-accidental cannot lie within the world, since if it did it would itself be accidental. It must lie outside the world. (6.41)

The German words that Wittgenstein uses are *Zufall* and *zufällig,* the same terms Kafka used in his short story to indicate the accidentally unexpected, regardless of which, in Kafka's world, it is impossible to reach the next village, to reach outside the closed and limited world. It is conceivable that Wittgenstein had read Kafka's story, and he could certainly have been a good partner in the discussion between Benjamin and Brecht.

There is a growing awareness that the accident is culturally significant. In his (in)famous 1910 essay "*Heine und die Folgen*" ("Heine and the Consequences"), Karl Kraus traces the degeneration of the German language to Heine's poetry at the same time as he makes some sarcastic side remarks, like the following one, with a clear reference to *Oedipus Tyrannus* and the riddle of the Sphinx:

> In Berlin things haven't gotten so bad yet, despite the nastiness of ambition. If a trolley crash has taken place, then Berlin reporters describe the crash. They pick out whatever is singular to this trolley crash and spare the reader everything that all trolley crashes have in common. If a trolley accident takes place in Vienna, then the gentlemen write about the nature of trolleys, the nature of accidents involving trolleys, and the nature of accidents in general, from the viewpoint: What is man? . . . Concerning the number of dead, which would perhaps interest us as well, opinions differ, if a letter doesn't take a stand on the matter. But

the mood, they all capture the mood; and the reporter, who could make himself useful as the rubbish collector in the world of facts, always comes running with a scrap of poetry that he has snatched up somewhere in the throng. One of them sees green, the other yellow—all of them see colours.[17] (translated by Russell Bucher)

Street Scenes

> If a crowd of men were brought out into the street by some catastrophe and were suddenly to unleash, each in his own way, their natural sensibility, quite independently of each other, they will create a wonderful spectacle, a thousand precious models for sculpture, painting, music and poetry.
> —Denis Diderot, *The Paradox of the Actor*[18]

The street accident became paradigmatic not only for an important aspect of modernity but also for the theories of acting formulated during the years before the war. The similarities between the city street and the stage are obvious, and were already evident for Diderot. The public executions during the French Revolution no doubt further strengthened this collocation between violence and theatricality. But I have not found any clear answer for why, during the 1930s, the act of witnessing a street accident became such a powerful paradigm for the art of acting and in particular for how the actor develops his unique skills. During this decade, the two most important director-theoreticians who were active at the time, Stanislavski and Brecht, both used the street accident as a foundation for the unique and very specialized knowledge an actor supposedly possesses: playing fictional characters on the theatrical stage in front of an audience.

In *An Actor Prepares*—first published in the United States in 1936, two years prior to its first Soviet edition—Kostya, Stanislavski's fictional narrator-student, relates that one day on his way home from an acting class he saw a large crowd on one of the boulevards. "I like street scenes," he continues, "so I pushed into the centre of it, and there my eyes fell on a horrible picture."[19] Kostya goes on to describe how an old man had been killed by a streetcar. As the wife and children towered over the victim, the conductor showed what was wrong with the machinery of the street car and "the rest of the crowd looked on with indifference and curiosity" (160). A few weeks later Kostya's memory transforms the scene of the accident and its participants into something stern and majestic. But mulling over its components, he was also reminded of another accident he had once witnessed.

Looking back, this earlier accident, in which a monkey belonging to an Italian beggar had been killed, had for some reason made a much deeper impression on him. He concludes as follows:

> It would seem that this scene had affected my feelings more than the death of the beggar. It was buried more deeply in my memory. I think that if I had to stage the street accident I would search for emotional material for my part in my memory of the scene of the Italian with the dead monkey rather than the tragedy itself. (161)

And when Kostya takes up this problem in one of his acting classes, Tortsov, the director-teacher—obviously Stanislavski's own alter ego—draws the following conclusion:

> Each one of us has seen many accidents. We retain the memories of them, but only outstanding characteristics that impressed us and not their details. Out of these impressions one large, condensed, deeper and broader sensation memory of related experience is formed. It is a kind of synthesis of memory on a larger scale. It is purer, more condensed, compact, substantial and sharper than the actual happenings. Time . . . not only purifies, it also transmutes even painfully realistic memories into poetry. (161)

The actor is able to transform his encounters with death into art through the synthesis of memory in a manner that is almost diametrically opposed to how Freud perceived trauma and obsessive behavior. The actor is seemingly able, without making any special effort, to move from one accident to another—there is apparently no repression leading to trauma. The different accidents are gradually superimposed until they become one composite memory image, making it possible for the actor to reenact, even relive, on stage the emotional memories relevant to a particular performance, translating them into art. According to Stanislavski, the actor should be able to separate these efforts at synthesizing memory from the art of acting itself. Acting is based on the actor's creatively projecting emotions from his or her composite memory onto a particular character. Acting employs a psychic mechanism that prevents the creation of an obsession based on the similarities between events, which can lead to trauma, even if the events are nothing but a dramatic fiction. This form of revisiting the past through emotional memory is Stanislavski's method for satisfying his own requirement of the actor's simultaneous awareness of emotion and theatricality.

Stanislavski's depiction is very closely related to Brecht's essay "The Street Scene," subtitled "A Basic Model for an Epic Theatre" and apparently written in 1938. In this essay the street accident serves as the paradigmatic example for Brecht's own Epic Theatre and witnessing an accident as the primary trigger for the art of acting. Instead of building up a composite emotional memory from several accidents, the epic actor, Brecht argues in his essay, is modeled on a witness who reports the occurrence of a very recent accident to some bystanders so that they, as Brecht claims, will be "able to form an opinion about the accident."[20] Brecht is not interested in the projection of the emotional materials onto a specific role, but in the ability of his witness-actor-demonstrator to show the bystanders—the third parties—positioned like the spectators in a theatre, how the different participants involved in the accident reacted by presenting "the behaviour of driver or victim."[21] Brecht is interested in behavior and reactions, or counter-behavior, not in emotion.

Instead of discussing Brecht's 1938 essay in greater detail, I will instead refer to the poem "On Everyday Theatre," which was composed several years before the essay—even before Stanislavski made public his ideas about the relationship between the art of acting and the street accident, possibly even as early as 1930. Even if a connection between acting and the street accident can be discerned already in Diderot's *The Paradox of the Actor*, it was probably Brecht who first systematically developed the idea that the actor can be defined as a witness. The actor, on different levels, gives a report about a street accident that he or she has witnessed, claiming that this is how the actor develops his or her unique form of performativity: this is what the actor knows. The fact that Brecht had written these ideas in a poem at this relatively early date is also important because of a car accident that he himself experienced in 1929 and which was reported in detail in a newspaper article. In his 1930 poem and 1938 essay, he is perhaps making the connection between his own experience of that accident and his theoretical reflections on the Epic Theatre.

It is difficult to say whether Stanislavski responded directly to these ideas in *An Actor Prepares*—if he was even aware of them—emphasizing the psychological interaction between a street accident and acting. Making comparisons between Brecht's and Stanislavski's respective integrations of the street accident within a more comprehensive performative context of acting theory, Brecht's 1930 poem, "On Everyday Theatre," is more overtly political than his own "Street Scene" article, written almost a decade later, and even more so when compared to Stanislavski's formulations from the mid-1930s. Regardless of who initiated the theorizations of these more systematic connections between the street accident and the art of acting, it is its persistent recurrence in the thinking of both Brecht and Stanislavski that is of interest in this context.

Brecht's "On Everyday Theatre" is a "lecture" that directly addresses the actors as a collective, asking them to step out from the stage, illuminated by electric suns, to the "theatre" of the streets:

> You artists who perform plays
> In great houses under electric suns
> Before the hushed crowd, pay a visit some time
> To that theatre whose setting is the street.
> The everyday, thousandfold, fameless
> But vivid, earthy theatre fed by the daily human contact
> Which takes place in the street.

This invocation, in the style of the Homeric epic ("Sing, oh Goddess"), establishes direct contact between the storyteller and the everyday events taking place in the streets, then draws attention to what takes place on the street corner where someone is "showing how / An accident took place." This, Brecht argues, is what the actor has to model his or her art from. But the actor, he continues, is not a divine judge of what has happened, as in the classic epic. Rather, the actor is like a newspaper reporter, a human who informs the people gathered around the victim what has happened, "delivering the driver to the verdict of the crowd." And at a certain point he begins to show, or according to the term Brecht himself preferred to use in this context, to "demonstrate," to the crowd:

>   The way he
> Sat behind the steering wheel, and now
> He imitates the man who was run over, apparently
> An old man. Of both he gives
> Only so much as to make the accident intelligible, and yet
> Enough to make you see them. But he shows neither
> As if the accident had been unavoidable. The accident

Accidents and Catastrophes

> Becomes in this way intelligible, yet not intelligible, for both
>   of them
> Could have moved quite otherwise; now he is showing what
> They might have done so that no accident
> Would have occurred. There is no superstition
> About this eyewitness, he
> Shows mortals as victims not of the stars, but
> Only of their errors.

Brecht emphasizes that the accident could have been avoided, that the driver and the old man who was hit by the car could have behaved differently because they are mortals who, even if they possess free will, can make mistakes. And the witness reporting about the accident is also human.

Different scenarios for what happened and could have happened are placed beside one another in the report; alternatives are presented. At this point the poem turns into an acting lesson, and not just a reflection on human error and its consequences. Brecht asks his readers: "Note also / His earnestness and the accuracy of his imitation," because the stakes are apparently quite high. The poem continues:

> [He] knows that much depends on his exactness; whether the
>   innocent man
> Escapes ruin, whether the injured man
> Is compensated. Watch him
> Repeat now what he did just before. Hesitantly
> Calling on his memory for help, uncertain
> Whether his demonstration is good, interrupting himself
> And asking someone else to
> Correct him on a detail.

Repeating specific details from the accident, even perhaps trying to clarify when the turning point from which there was no return occurred, the "imitator" becomes aware of not being just a witness whose testimony in a courtroom can make a difference. The witness also carries a civil responsibility as an artist. Now as Brecht is addressing the acting students, the lack of involvement and identification of the "imitator" with what he is doing when recounting the accident also becomes crucial:

> And with surprise
> Observe, if you will, one thing: that this imitator

> Never loses himself in his imitation. He never entirely
> Transforms himself into the man he is imitating. He always
> Remains the demonstrator, the one not involved. The man
> Did not open his heart to him, he
> Does not share his feelings

Brecht clearly disassociates himself from Stanislavski's view of acting by recommending an emotional distance. This can be seen in the disinterest and distance that exist between the "imitator" and the people involved in the accident. And this remove is at least implied in the disabusing of the "imitator" as one who is above or beyond the gathered crowd:

> Our demonstrator at the street corner
> Is no sleepwalker who must not be addressed. He is
> No high priest holding divine service. At any moment
> You can interrupt him; he will answer you
> Quite calmly and when you have spoken with him
> Go on with his performance.[22]

The testimony about the street accident has become Epic Theatre.

The year before writing this poem, on May 20, 1929, while driving his Steyr car to Saint Cyr in France, Brecht was involved in a car accident. He was on a road near Fulda, Germany, where he was going to have lunch with Kurt Weill. Ahead of him, a car had just passed a truck and was suddenly hurtling toward Brecht on his side of the road. To avoid a head-on collision, Brecht, who was driving at the speed of seventy kilometers per hour, swerved to the right, leaving the roadway and hitting a tree. He escaped from the accident with nothing but bruised knees, for which he was taken back to Berlin for treatment. Later that year, the November issue of the magazine *UHU* (*Owl*), edited by Kurt Tucholsky and Vicki Baum, published a photo-essay titled "*Rekonstruktion des Autounfalls des Dichters Brecht*" (a reconstruction of the car accident of the writer Brecht) with the headline "*Ein Lehrreicher Auto-Unfall*" (An Instructive/Educational Car Accident).[23]

The photo-essay, reproduced and translated here (on pp. 162–163), consists of four pages and is composed like a didactic *Lehrstück*, or "lesson," play, reconstructing the accident exactly as Brecht describes it in both his poem and essay. It is a storyboard narrative for teaching the reader that the road is a dangerous place—that Brecht did the right thing by quickly and forcefully using the brakes—but most important, that the car manufactured by the Austrian company Steyr was a safe vehicle, allowing Brecht to walk away with only a few bruises. The Steyr company, which was confronting economic difficulties at the time (this was 1929), supplied a brand-new car for the demonstration published in the newspaper. On March 22, 1933, Brecht's new car was confiscated by the Nazis, because it was, as they claimed, involved in Communist activities.[24]

In 1934 the Steyr company merged with Austro-Daimler-Puch to form Steyr-Daimler-Puch, which became an important manufacturer of both weapons and vehicles during the Second World War, using slave labor in their plants in the Mauthausen-Gusen concentration camps in Austria.

Catastrophes

> The concept of progress must be grounded in the idea of catastrophe. That things are "status quo" *is* the catastrophe.
> —Walter Benjamin, *The Arcades Project*[25]

In his essay "Commitment," Theodor Adorno tells an anecdote about Picasso, who was living in Paris during the Second World War. In this anecdote Adorno describes how

> an officer of the Nazi occupation forces visited the painter in his studio and, pointing to *Guernica*, asked: "Did you do that?" Picasso is said to have answered, "No you did."[26]

This anecdote deserves attention for several reasons. One is purely historical, because when the Nazis occupied Paris in 1941, Picasso's *Guernica* mural, commissioned for the Spanish Pavilion at the 1937 Paris Exposition (*Internationale des Arts et Techniques dans la Vie Moderne*), had already been shipped to the United States. Thus the Picasso mural was not in Paris when the officer allegedly came to pay his visit to Picasso. And apparently, since the anecdote was quite well known, in an interview in March 1945, little more than half a year after Paris had been liberated, Picasso said that he had just shown the Nazi officer a postcard of the painting. And to the question of whether he had actually said "No *you* did," he responded, laughing, "Yes, that's true, that's more or less true"[27] (italics added).

"An Instructive Automobile Accident: Reconstruction of an Automobile Accident Involving the Writer Brecht," in *UHU—das neue Ullsteinmagazin*,

November 2, 1929. Article with photos by A. Stöcker. Published courtesy of *Kunstbibliothek Berlin*.

An Instructive Automobile Accident
Translated by Russell Bucher

The wild* driver is the enemy of the motorist, of the pedestrian, and of traffic in general. The wild driver is, in almost all traffic accidents, the guilty party, no matter whether he is riding a motorcycle or driving a Hanomag, an Opel, or a Mercedes. One can say with some confidence that in the realm of automobile traffic, England is the most well-bred country. There, the passing of another vehicle takes place, for the most part, solely with the permission of the leading car. And for this maneuver, the leading car itself creates space to make it easier for the speedier trailing car to pass when the opportunity arises. In England, there is the addition of the boulevard stop,** not only within the cities but also on roads through the countryside. The boulevard stop cuts the number of auto accidents in half from the very outset. In England, no one would dare turn from a side street onto a main thoroughfare without first stopping and assuring himself of the safety of the turn. For this reason, every driver on a main thoroughfare is allowed to drive at a high speed. The wild driver's catchphrase is "I've got my car under control." Only every time, he forgets that the driver approaching him must have his car just as securely under control.

A short time ago, the writer Brecht was involved in an automobile accident typical of many others. He was driving in his Steyr at seventy kilometers per hour on the road to Fulda. The road was not very narrow at all, but a much more powerful car than his shot out onto his side, attempting to pass from behind a truck coming toward Brecht, without having ascertained that another car (Brecht's car) was in fact coming toward them. For Brecht, the situation was extraordinarily dangerous; because of the truck, also traveling at quite a clip, he couldn't veer left, on the right side there were trees, and behind the trees the road fell off in a five-meter embankment. Brecht had two possibilities: either to drive down the embankment and roll over several times in an open-top car, or to drive into a tree at seventy kilometers per hour and splinter into pieces. The distance between the car coming toward him and his own was very small for two vehicles approaching each other at seventy kilometers per hour from each side. Thus, Brecht's car was forced to veer

*The German *wild* also has the meaning of "illegal" or "unlawful."
**Whether this refers to the red octagonal sign or to the procedure of making a full and complete stop is not completely clear.

away, and Brecht was able, by several vigorous closings and immediate reopenings of the brakes, to drive into the first possible tree. He succeeded in bringing precisely the middle of the radiator into contact with the tree, thus catching the car in place. The radiator was shattered and the protruding front end of the chassis bent itself in a ring around the tree, but this at the same time held the car in place. In the end, there were only minor injuries to report.

Reconstruction of an Automobile Accident Involving the Writer Brecht (photo captions)

I. Page 62 (top): A car traveling toward Brecht tries to pass a truck without having made sure that the other side of the road, on which Brecht is approaching at seventy kilometers per hour, is free.

II. Pages 62–63 (center): Instead of stopping, the passing car attempts to come back onto its side of the road by splitting the gap between Brecht's car and the truck.

III. Page 63 (top): This was the position of the vehicles a few seconds from catastrophe. Car 3732, having passed with such a lack of caution, [caption and photograph upside-down] no longer had space to turn back in and, in the next instant, had to drive straight into Brecht's car.

IV. Page 64 (top): How Brecht managed to help himself: On Brecht's right the road inclined steeply downward. Brecht pulled his car strongly to the right and, in order not to plummet down the incline, intentionally drove the exact middle of his car's radiator (see photograph V) directly into the first reachable tree. The car and its engine were reduced to a rubble of wreckage; except for a few cuts and scrapes, the passengers were completely fine. (The reconstruction of the accident was carried out with the generous assistance of Steyer A.-G.*)

V. Page 64 (bottom left): The incline, from which Brecht managed to save himself by deliberately and decisively driving his car into a tree.

VI. Page 64 (bottom right): Brecht's car after the accident. The wreckage of the car shows how accurately Brecht acted to catch his car against the tree.

Page 65: How the two cars would have appeared had they run head-on into each other. Photo of one of the many daily smashups.

*Probably *Auto-Gemeinschaft* (automobile association).

The reason for bringing Picasso's *Guernica* and the versions of the anecdote into play with Benjamin's notion of constellation and the idea of the image as dialectics at a standstill—like Mother Courage's wagon analyzed in Chapter 4—is that the gesture of pointing (in this case at a work of art) creates an interaction between the aesthetic field and a particular historical event at the same time as it activates the reader or viewer, inviting us to "participate" in the interaction: to think about it and to form an opinion. George Steiner has even compared the silent scream of Helene Weigel as Mother Courage—when her executed son, Schweizerkas, whom she cannot admit is her son, is carried off the stage—with the gesture of the screaming horse in Picasso's *Guernica*.[28]

The act of pointing at the painting, regardless of whether it was immediately present in the original or reproduced on a postcard, creates a performative situation involving Picasso and the officer, who look and point at *Guernica* as well as at each other, saying respectively: "Did *you* do that?" "No *you* did!" This form of interaction is paradigmatic for how aesthetic images build up a performative significance. And because it is integrated within political and even subversive activities, the act of pointing and commenting sometimes becomes even more complex and open-ended than the traditional forms of scripted embodiment presented on a theatrical stage. This form of interaction also expounds upon the issues I have dealt with in the previous chapters: the direct personal encounters between philosophers and thespians. Instead what the following examples show is how the interactions between the respective discursive practices function within a specific historical context. Looking back at the *Symposium* and *Hamlet* there are also harsh political realities looming in the background, represented by Alcibiades and Fortinbras respectively. The presence of these political realities no doubt influences the understanding of the performative.

The question I want to raise is how narratives like the Picasso anecdote—involving human agents and visual images of catastrophe and affliction—give rise to performative image constellations. The bombings of Guernica in April 1937 generated clusters of meaning through meta-narrative contextualizations, involving the painting itself, in particular by pointing at it, as exemplified by the two versions of the Picasso anecdote. And this form of constellation, reacting to the ideological and political developments gradually leading up to the Second World War, is further amplified by Benjamin's well-known text about Paul Klee's *Angelus Novus*, which Benjamin points at, calling this figure the angel of history.

In retrospect the years between the two world wars can be viewed as a desperate and finally failed attempt to retrieve order and rationality in the turbulence and frenzy brought about by the newly developing technologies, which in tandem with the Fascist ideologies of that time had made the bombings of Guernica possible. The Paris exhibition—devoted to technological achievements—where Picasso's *Guernica* was first exhibited, opened less than three months after these bombings. The presentation of the mural at this exhibition somewhat ironically implied that *Guernica* was a celebration of art and technology in modern life. Even if Picasso produced a huge painted canvas as a response to these bombings, the speed with which it was created clearly reflected the technological innovations for disseminating and reproducing images that had begun during the latter half of the nineteenth century. These technologies had already created the basis for new modes of presenting large scale catastrophes as well as for reporting on more local calamities. The speed with which images were now created and "exposed" (in the two senses of this term: in photographic terms, as the exposure time, as well as in terms of being presented publicly in an exhibition space) was complemented by the constantly accelerating velocity with which people were able to move from one place to another. This speed enabled the bombings to be carried out on a grand scale, as well as more locally, with the use of private vehicles, which as we have seen, could lead to fatal accidents.

Walter Benjamin's essay "The Work of Art in the Age of Its Technological Reproducibility" is probably one of the best-known and critically acclaimed formulations of the new modes of "image thinking" emerging during this period. In the last section of his essay, toward which Benjamin steers his argument about the complex dialectics between the aura and technological reproducibility, he directs the attention of the reader to the close relationship between war and aesthetics. There is a third and final version of this essay, most likely finished in March or April 1939, which is much more explicit in its formulations of these matters than the second one which Benjamin had published in 1936.[29] In this third version, he was perhaps reacting directly to the bombings of Guernica and to Picasso's painting, even if he never says that this was the case. Benjamin does however mention Picasso in relation to Charlie Chaplin's films in this essay. Whereas films have mass audiences, paintings intrinsically do not, Benjamin argues, pointing at "the special conflict in which painting has become enmeshed by the technological reproducibility of the image."[30] Saying this Benjamin must no doubt have been aware of the attention Picasso's *Guernica* was receiving not far away from where he was working in the Bibliothèque Nationale.

In the final section of his essay, after quoting the Italian futurist Filippo Marinetti, who had made the point that "war is beautiful because it enriches a flowering meadow with fiery orchids of machine guns,"[31] Benjamin comments that this statement has "the merit of clarity,"[32] saying:

Imperialist war is an uprising on the part of technology, which demands repayment in "human material" for the natural material society has denied it. Instead of draining rivers, society directs a human stream into a bed of trenches; instead of dropping seeds from airplanes, it drops incendiary bombs over cities; and in gas warfare it has found new ways of abolishing the aura.

"Fiat ars—pereat mundus" [Let art flourish—and the world pass away], says fascism, expecting from war, as Marinetti admits, the artistic gratification of a sense perception altered by technology. This is evidently the consummation of *l'art pour l'art*. Humankind, which once in Homer was an object of contemplation for the Olympian gods, has now become one for itself. Its self-alienation has reached the point where it can experience its own annihilation as a surprise aesthetic pleasure. *Such is the aestheticizing of politics as practiced by fascists. Communism replies by politicizing art.*[33] (italics in the original)

This conclusion perhaps sounds somewhat naive to our ears today, but I have quoted the whole final passage to draw attention to how the presentation of images creates constellations as exemplified by the Picasso anecdote. Fascist ideologies aestheticize politics by asking the supposedly subversive artist "Did *you* do that?" Picasso politicized art by answering, "No *you* did!" And from the broader perspective developed in this book, Benjamin's distinction enables us to explore the performative dimensions of the philosophical, aesthetic issues and the performativity of thinking, not only in the performing of drama, but in the interactions between these constantly revolving perspectives.

The ways in which visual images were contextualized through written texts during this period of upheaval and crisis were of course not unique. They were already discerned in the multilayered forms of emblematic thinking developed during the Baroque period that Benjamin had explored in depth in his *Trauerspiel* book written between 1924 and 1925. In this book Benjamin argues that "the present age reflects certain aspects of the spiritual constitution of the baroque, even down to the details of its artistic practice."[34] Early-twentieth-century modernism of thinking *in*, *through*, and *about* images was gradually rediscovering, even reinventing, these modes of relating to such visual images more directly as catastrophic constellations. Even if they had lost some of their previous more exclusive and direct theological foundation, they continued to draw attention to their own theatricality, negotiating between visual, often figurative, allegorical images in interaction with a human agent, first witnessing them and then in different ways delivering a testimony. But at the same time the new modes of emblematic thinking, in particular for Benjamin, reintroduced a theological-metaphysical dimension, situating historical events—catastrophes—as the nexus of the immediately present materialist dialectics and a messianic scheme of time.

Picasso's *Guernica* was first exhibited in the Spanish Pavilion, located just behind the German Pavilion designed by Hitler's architect Albert Speer on the Trocadéro, connecting the Eiffel Tower and the Palais de Chaillot. Speer's building was topped with an eagle. The Soviet Pavilion, located on the opposite side of the Trocadéro, had on its rooftop a giant statue of a young couple holding a sickle in their outstretched hands as they ran toward a Utopian future. All these locations created a map of images giving rise to a complex dramaturgy in which art and technology interacted with ideology on several levels.[35] It is worth noting that more or less simultaneously with the Paris fair, the exhibition of *Entartete Kunst* (*Degenerate Art*) opened in Munich, on July 19, 1937, one day after the first "Great German Art Exhibition" had been launched there as well. This was just a week after the Spanish Pavilion had opened in Paris, on July 12, 1937. All of Europe had become included in a performative mapping of images intersecting politics and art.[36]

The day before the opening of the Spanish Pavilion with Picasso's *Guernica* as its most prominent image, the French-born writer and critic Max Aub addressed the assembled construction workers who had built the pavilion, pointing at the painting as he was speaking:

At the entrance, on the right Picasso's great painting leaps into view. It will be spoken of for a long time. Picasso has represented here the tragedy of

Gernika[sic]. It is possible that this art will be accused of being too abstract or difficult for a pavilion like ours which seeks to be above all, and before everything else, a popular manifestation. This is not the moment to justify ourselves, but I am certain that with a little good will, everybody will perceive the rage, the desperation, and the terrible protest that this canvas signifies . . . To those who protest saying that things are not thus, one must answer asking if they do not have two eyes to see the terrible reality of Spain. If the picture by Picasso has any defect it is that it is too real, too terribly true, atrociously true.[37]

It is hardly an exaggeration to claim that this speech already contained the seeds for the narrative and dramatic structure of the Picasso anecdote: "Did *you* do that?" "No *you* did!"

At more or less the same time, but in a more secluded, less public context, not very far from the exhibition grounds in Paris, Walter Benjamin—as can be seen in the famous photograph of Benjamin sitting at a table in the Bibliothèque Nationale—was collecting materials for his *Arcades Project* as well as making the final revisions to the third version of "The Work of Art in the Age of Its Technological Reproducibility." In writing about being in the library, however, Benjamin seems to have been quite oblivious to the larger events surrounding him at that time, creating a very different image constellation under the ceiling of the library:

These notes devoted to the Paris Arcades were begun under an open sky of cloudless blue that arched above the foliage; and yet—owing to the millions of leaves that were visited by the breeze of diligence, the stertorous breath of the researcher, the storm of youthful zeal, and the idle wind of curiosity—they've been covered with the dust of centuries. For the painted sky of summer that looks down from the arcades in the reading room of the Bibliothèque Nationale in Paris has spread out over them its dreamy, unlit ceiling.[38]

Benjamin, as he frequently does in his writing, positions himself in a closed interior space as he mentally reconstructs the image constellations of the public Parisian arcades.

In 1935, a few years before the opening of the Paris Exhibition, Benjamin sent to Adorno the preliminary exposé to his *Arcades Project*. Benjamin addresses the World Exhibition as an institution, already formulating his negative opinion of these "global" events. In a passage about the 1867 World Exhibition, he refers directly to the complex relationships between image and ideology, arguing that the imminent demise of the idea of such supposedly "universal" expositions is an expression of the illusions created by the emerging forms of mass culture. These exhibitions are "places of pilgrimage to the commodity fetish," and "open a phantasmagoria which a person enters in order to be distracted. The entertainment industry makes this easier by elevating the person to the level of the commodity. He surrenders to its manipulations while enjoying his alienation from himself and others."[39]

If Picasso's *Guernica* immediately became an expression for protest against violence as it was expressed in the public sphere (even a fetish), Benjamin developed a very personal relationship to an image that he owned privately, the Klee painting *Angelus Novus*. Benjamin purchased this watercolor for approximately fourteen dollars at an exhibition in Munich in 1921, and it became one of his most valued possessions. After he had fled the Nazis, it was brought to him in Paris, and before fleeing to the Spanish border, where he committed suicide, Benjamin deposited the painting together with the manuscripts that became *The Arcades Project* in one of the two suitcases that Georges Bataille hid from the Nazis in the Bibliothèque Nationale. Following the war, the painting made its way to Theodor Adorno in New York and he brought it back to Frankfurt before passing it over to one of Benjamin's oldest and closest friends, the Kabbalah scholar Gershom Scholem, in Jerusalem. After the death of Scholem's widow, Fania Scholem, the painting was given to the Israel Museum in Jerusalem.

Klee's *Angelus Novus* has become most known through Benjamin's often-quoted and much-discussed interpretation of the painting in "On the Concept of History" from 1940.

There is a painting by Klee called *Angelus Novus*. It shows an angel who seems about to move away from something he stares at. His eyes are wide, his mouth is open, his wings are spread. This is how the angel of history must look. His face is turned toward the past. Where a chain of events appears before *us*, *he* sees one single catastrophe, which keeps piling wreckage upon wreckage and hurls it at his feet. The angel would like to stay, awaken the dead, and make whole what has been smashed. But a storm is blowing from Paradise and has got caught in his wings; it is so strong that the angel can no longer close them. This storm drives him irresistibly into the future to which his back is turned, while the pile of debris before him grows toward the sky. What we call progress is *this* storm.[40] (italics in the original)

In his meditation on the Klee watercolor, Benjamin dramatized and contextualized the mysterious figure in a way that was diametrically opposed to the ways in which the Picasso painting became contextualized through the different narratives it triggered. Benjamin's short text pointing to the Klee painting, an almost whispering meditation, is a *Denkbild*—a "thought-image"—a genre of writing briefly touched upon earlier that I discuss in greater detail in Chapter 6. According to Sigrid Weigel, a *Denkbild* is an image "in written form . . . in which the dialectic of image and thought is unfolded and becomes visible." Weigel, for whom the Benjamin text about *Angelus Novus* is a prime example of such a *Denkbild*, draws attention to the visual concreteness of the image presented through this form of writing, creating what she has termed a philosophical counterpart, not a comparison.[41] The *Denkbild* performs a thought through an image that has come to a muted, silenced standstill.

Looking more closely at Benjamin's text, we see how he creates a theatrical staging, an *Inszenierung*, of the small painting that gradually involves not only Benjamin himself, but the readers of the text as well. After briefly drawing attention to the figure, who has his mouth open and his wings spread, and who "seems to move away from something he stares at,"[42] Benjamin declares, "*This* is how the angel of history *must* look"[43] (italics added). The opposition between the "seems" of the first sentence and the "must" of the second creates a strong dynamic tension. On the one hand, Benjamin uses the subjunctive mood of potentiality, whereas on the other, he conveys necessity because he does not say this "could" be the angel of history or even that he "looks like" such an image in the painting. *This* is rather how the angel of history *must* look, creating some form of necessary connection between the image on the canvas and a more general, abstract notion of history. After establishing this tension between possibility and necessity, Benjamin widens the circles of performative contextualizations by saying that the face of the angel is turned toward the past, to Paradise, whereas the future is situated behind his back.

This means that as we are looking at the picture we are turned with our faces toward the future, whereas Paradise must be behind our backs. And at the same time, "while a chain of events appears before *us,* *he* sees only one single catastrophe, which keeps piling wreckage upon wreckage and hurls it as his feet."[44] This points to the catastrophes of history in a more general sense, indicating that the physical distance between the painting and the onlooker has received a temporal dimension. This brings out the difference between the history that for us is a chain of discrete events, but for the angel is "one single wreckage." This is the same rhetorical strategy Benjamin employs in the general explanation of the constellation. Here too the moment we accept that what we see is how the angel of history *must* look as he peers back at us, creating an encounter of our gazes, the meditative, dialectical mise-en-scène Benjamin has activated from its standstill presents the "thought-image" of the progression of history. Benjamin's short meditation on the angel has given rise to a "theatrical" performance, in which the reader is invited to take an active part in the cosmic historical drama involving Paradise and a messianic futurity.

As we've seen, what Benjamin points out in *The Arcades Project* (see extract on p. 144 of this chapter) is that the "image is that wherein what has been comes together in a flash with the now to form a constellation." The wreckages and the catastrophes of history that the angel sees have been piled up and are reflected back to us when we are looking at him, creating a performative constellation of contemplation, understanding, and even insight. The angel serves as a witness to the full flow of history—the "single catastrophe." The gaze of the angel reflects this cosmic drama back to us, the viewers of the painting, making us see the chain of events, partly situated behind our backs (therefore we do not see them directly), and to a certain extent also situated in the space between us and the painting. The moment we look at the picture, Benjamin claims, it becomes dynamically activated by the simultaneous gaze, directed by the angel toward the past, allowing us to interact, dynamically, with the future toward which we are looking. We are witnesses of the angelic messenger-witness. Or as Benjamin wrote in the notes to the *Arcades*: "The image that is read—which is to say, the image in the now of its recognizability—bears to the highest degree the imprint of the perilous critical moment on which all reading is founded," signaling that the present moment of danger and violence is the foundational moment in which the text becomes a mentally staged performance. In this performance, two witnesses, one metaphysical and one human, are exchanging a double gaze. Or in the words of Rainer Maria Rilke, as quoted in the epigraph at the start of this book: "*Engel und Puppe: dann ist endlich Schauspiel*" (Angel and puppet, a real play finally) (translated by Stephen Mitchell).[45]

Benjamin's text on Klee's *Angelus Novus* created an almost diametrically opposed constellation to Picasso's *Guernica*. Benjamin composed a *Denkbild* text about the small, privately owned watercolor, dramatizing the moment of viewing by pointing at the painting and saying: "There is a painting by Klee called *Angelus Novus*." The debris, the wreckage, or the ruins, of history—Benjamin used the term *Trümmerhaufen*, a composite word in which both parts mean "rubble" or "heap"—can only be seen directly by the angel, whereas the onlooker has to imagine the wreckage as being situated in the space between us and the figure in the painting, but also behind our backs. Picasso's mural painting, on the other hand, because it is massive in scale, presenting a group of larger-than-human-sized figures—some animal, some mythological, some human—forces us to look directly at the debris, in particular the human suffering, created by the bombings of Guernica. This is a depiction of human suffering that enabled Picasso to tell the Nazi officer, "*You* have done this." Picasso has made us the direct witnesses of this particular catastrophe, whereas Benjamin asks us to transform the already known chain of events into a universal, 'abstract' catastrophe: history itself. We see only what Benjamin says the angel sees in our "mind's eye" (1.2.185), to quote Hamlet's reflection in his first meeting with Horatio before he has actually encountered the ghost.

Guernica and *Angelus Novus* exemplify two radically different forms of performative contextualization. Benjamin's slowly emerging meditative text, relating to his privately owned Klee picture, composed almost twenty years after he bought the artwork, stands in sharp contrast to the immediate, high-profile nature of Picasso's huge canvas. *Guernica* was exhibited as a protest that was quite public—presented in the Spanish Pavilion at the Paris Exposition—and based on a very recent event. Picasso's mural was not only finished a few months after the bombings, it was also very quickly contextualized through the public discourses it triggered: for example, in the speech before the opening of the Spanish Pavilion as well as in the anecdote about the painter himself and the Nazi officer, but in many other contexts as well. *Guernica* was immediately received as a public antiwar manifesto, whereas Benjamin's text remained unpublished until after his death. His short meditation on Klee's painting was not yet known as he was approaching the Spanish border and his own death.

At the 2007 *Dokumenta* exhibition in Kassel, Germany, despite

Benjamin's warnings against the loss of the aura in the age of technological reproducibility, a reproduction of Klee's *Angelus Novus* was presented as one of the central opening images of the exhibition. It could be seen in the narrow staircase in the Museum Fridericianum, the main building of the exhibition (the original remained in Jerusalem). One of the visitors to the exhibition made this comment:

> Over the *Documenta* hovers an angel, Paul Klee's "Angelus Novus." The angel is uneasily positioned; here is the triangle in which three sets of stairs run together. If one took a step back while gazing, one would tumble backwards down the stairs. What's more: the angel is a fake; over the greatest and most renowned German art exhibit hovers the replica of the "Angelus Novus." The little angel is an apt synonym for the splitting apart of assertion and reality in this *Documenta*.[46]

As the visitor indicated, the painting was hanging at the place where three stairs meet. This recalls Oedipus's vague memories of having reached the place where three roads come together. Benjamin's text has transformed the *Angelus Novus* into an icon of the catastrophic intersection of modernity and history.

Since 1992, Picasso's *Guernica* has been exhibited at Spain's national museum of twentieth-century art, the Museo Nacional Centro de Arte Reina Sofía, in Madrid. It was brought from the Prado when the Reina Sofía opened. Picasso stipulated that the mural was to be returned to Spain when the country became a democracy, which happened with the death of Francisco Franco in 1975. The Museum of Modern Art in New York City, where it was deposited already before the Second World War, did not give in to the pressures of ceding the painting to the Spanish people until 1981.

There also is a copy of *Guernica* at the United Nations, and further exemplifying the catastrophic intersection of modernity and history, Wikipedia has this to say about what happened at the UN:

> A tapestry copy of Picasso's *Guernica* is displayed on the wall of the United Nations building in New York City, at the entrance to the Security Council room. It was placed there as a reminder of the horrors of war. Commissioned and donated by Nelson Rockefeller, it is not quite as monochromatic as the original, using several shades of brown. On February 5, 2003 a large blue curtain was placed to cover this work, so that it would not be visible in the background when Colin Powell and John Negroponte gave press conferences at the United

Nations. On the following day, it was claimed that the curtain was placed there at the request of television news crews, who had complained that the wild lines and screaming figures made for a bad backdrop, and that a horse's hindquarters appeared just above the faces of any speakers. Diplomats, however, told journalists that the Bush Administration pressured UN officials to cover the tapestry, rather than have it in the background while Powell or other U.S. diplomats argued for war on Iraq.[47]

We are still confronting complex catastrophic constellations raising the question, "Did *you* do that?"

6

Wishes, Promises, and Threats

THE PERFORMATIVE STORYTELLING
OF WALTER BENJAMIN

> When you look for beginnings, you become a crab. Historians look backwards; and they end up *believing* in beginnings too.
> —Friedrich Nietzsche, *Twilight of the Idols*
>
> True literary activity cannot aspire to take place within a literary framework; this is, rather, the habitual expression of its sterility. Significant literary effectiveness can come into being only in strict alternation between action and writing.
> —Walter Benjamin, *One-Way Street*

With *One-Way Street* (*Einbahnstrasse*), published in 1928, one of Benjamin's early experiments applying the techniques of literary studies to real life, he lays the foundation for a performativity in the philosophical mode. The short quote from this work—appearing in this chapter's epigraph—claiming that only through the "strict alternation between action and writing" is it possible to achieve what Benjamin terms a "significant literary effectiveness," is indeed a form of performative writing, presenting an added dimension—what I have previously termed "scripted embodiment." By constantly alternating between action and writing, the discursive practices of theatre and philosophy are in effect woven together, creating a discursive formation that incorporates (in the literal sense of embodiment) a performative modality. The *Denkbild*—"thought-image" or "thought-picture" mentioned previously—is the term used for this type of writing. It was practiced by a vaguely defined group of writers and philosophers, among them, besides Benjamin himself, Franz Kafka, Bertolt Brecht, Ernst Bloch, Siegfried Kracauer, Robert Musil, and after the Second World War, Theodor Adorno.[1] *One-Way Street* is such a collection of *Denkbilder*.

Even if there are important differences among its many practitioners, the *Denkbild* typically brings out an abstract, philosophical idea through a short narrative or description that has a distinct emblematic quality. This is closely related to the tradition of the Baroque emblem but generally does not include the visual image itself. In this respect Benjamin's text about the Klee painting is an exceptional *Denkbild*, which even if it technically does not "include" a visual image, points to one: "There is a painting by Klee called *Angelus Novus*. . . ."

However, instead of striving toward a harmonization between its different parts, which the Baroque emblem generally does, the *Denkbild* draws attention to the need to rethink and reconsider the situation and the images. As a rule these images are depicted in very concrete and exact terms. And as a result, they are comprehensive in such a way that demands the reader's participation, not only as a "passive" observer, but as an active participant in the performative situation the text stages. The *Denkbild* can even present a moral, like Rilke's "Archaischer Torso Apollos," which despite its being a poem and focusing on a statue, has *Denkbild* characteristics. After describing the beauty of a statue, the poem abruptly concludes: *"Du mußt dein Leben ändern"* (You must change your life). The beauty of the statue makes it necessary for "you," the reader, to change your life. It presents an imperative concerning "your" future.

The *Denkbild*—the thought-image—thus implicitly asks the reader not only to visualize the concrete situation presented by the narrative and to "stage" its sometimes enigmatic state of affairs in his or her mind or thinking, but frequently also to confront the practical consequences of this contemplative activity. The performative scenario through which the reader allows himself or herself to be included in the situation and to become "staged" is actually equivalent to the interpretation of the text itself. The *Denkbild*, at least as practiced by Benjamin, initially reverses the opening sentence of *The Origin of German Tragic Drama* (which as I have mentioned before is deeply immersed in the baroque traditions): "It is characteristic of philosophical writing that it must continually confront the question of representation."[2] Rather than setting out to confront the question of representation philosophically, the concrete narrative of the *Denkbild* compels the reader to activate its representational dimensions by the reader's entering the complex dramatic situation that gradually emerges. Benjamin's *Denkbilder* contains an invitation and by closely adhering to its implicit stage directions the reader is inevitably directed to confront philosophical issues. However, no matter where we begin—with philosophy or with representation—Benjamin shows that the intricate ways in which they interact and are woven together is what matters most.

"Chinese Curios" is a section in *One-Way Street* that contains the following short text:

> The power of a country road when one is walking along it is different from the power it has when one is flying over it by airplane. In the same way, the power of a text when it is read is different from the power it has when it is copied out. The airplane passenger sees only how the road pushes through the landscape, how it unfolds according to the same laws as the terrain surrounding it. Only he who walks the road on foot learns of the power it commands, and how from the very scenery that for the flier is only unfurled plain, it calls forth distances, belvederes, clearings, prospects at each of its turns like a commander deploying soldiers at a front. Only the copied text thus commands the soul of him who is occupied with it, whereas the mere reader never discovers the new aspects of his inner self that are opened by the text, that road cut through the interior jungle forever closing behind it: because the reader follows the movement of his mind in the free flight of daydreaming, whereas the copier submits to its command. The Chinese practice of copying books was thus an incomparable guarantee of literary culture, and the transcript a key to China's enigmas.[3]

This short text begins with a comparison between two different modes of travel: walking along a country road and flying over a landscape in an airplane. Sustained throughout is the *figura* of traveling, which is central to the notion of performativity I explore in this book, beginning with Oedipus and leading up to the Kafka story. Benjamin goes on, in the next sentence, to apply this basic comparison to distinguish the act of reading, which is like flying, from copying text, whereby the traveler "journeying" slowly and meticulously through the text learns about the details of the road. From having figuratively walked on the road, like a countryside *flâneur*, carefully taking notice of the minute details of the textual landscape, the copier suddenly becomes transformed into a military commander who has complete control over the surrounding scenery.[4]

This military imagery may seem an inapt analogy, but I think Benjamin is referring to the struggle involved in taking complete possession of the textual terrain and overseeing all its details. As we shall see later, he frequently turned to images of war in connection with his *Denkbild* storytelling. In "Chinese Curios," upon deploying the soldiers, Benjamin goes on to draw conclusions on two levels, activating a dynamic relationship between the text and the "traveler." And at the end of this short text, he reaches a more general conclusion, claiming that the Chinese custom of copying books reveals something central about the sophistication of that culture, even serving as a key to its hidden enigmas. But before reaching this somewhat impersonal conclusion, Benjamin compares the effects that reading and copying have on the soul. The latter activity "commands the soul," as the military commander does his soldiers, enabling the copier to discover "new aspects of his inner self that are opened up by the text," prior to, as Benjamin characterizes it, finally submitting "to its command." The copier is able to enter the "interior jungle" of his or her soul. The reader, on the other hand, "follows the movement of his mind in the free flight of daydreaming." The reader is therefore unable to track the details of the text.

This is quite a remarkable text, first of all because at the same time as Benjamin valorizes his own practice as a researcher, in particular during the 1930s, while spending his days in the Bibliothèque Nationale in Paris, taking notes and making meticulous preparations for what was to remain his unfinished collection of quotations, *The Arcades Project* (*Das Passagen-Werk*), it indirectly describes this activity as a form of surrender, as opposed to "the free flight of daydreaming" found in reading. Benjamin obviously sees himself as captive to his own scholarly activity. Moreover, Hannah Arendt claimed that Benjamin posed an "ideal of producing a work consisting entirely of quotations, one that was mounted so masterfully that it could dispense with any accompanying text."[5] Before quoting, it was first necessary for him to copy. And today, *The Arcades Project* in its published form consists of the passages Benjamin copied from the books in the Bibliothèque Nationale. The quotations, interspersed with his own thoughts, were classified into categories, creating the densely textured constellation of quotations and reflections through which, he argued, the emergence of the culture of modernity could be distinguished. It is even possible to claim that modernity itself, and this is certainly true of postmodernism, consisted of salvaging the traces of the past, the "pile of debris" from history, by copying, or recording, the past.

Another interesting feature of Benjamin's text, which is also a salient feature of many of his *Denkbilder*, is directly connected to the idea of traveling. I intentionally call it the "idea" of traveling, because even if the road Benjamin depicted is concrete, the journey itself is of a much more abstract nature. It is more often imagined, remembered, or reconstructed, and presented as a possible existential projection directed toward a vaguely described past rather than presented as direct experience. Kafka's short text "The Next Village," which was the subject of the discussion between Benjamin and Brecht, presents such an idea in the exilic journey. This "idea" of traveling can also be seen in Klee's *Angelus Novus*, who is propelled into the future by the wind blowing from Paradise. Because the angel is flying he is not able to discern the individual historical details: "*he* sees one single catastrophe, which keeps piling wreckage upon wreckage and hurls it at his feet." By contrast, we, who are copiers, see a chain of individual, distinct catastrophes. And as we shall see later, this is also the beggar's situation in the story Benjamin has "copied" in his Kafka essay.

In his essay "The Storyteller," published in 1936, Benjamin refers directly to the relationship between storytelling and traveling, arguing that there are two kinds of storytellers:

And the figure of the storyteller takes on its full corporeality only for one who can picture them both. "When someone makes a journey, he has a story to tell," goes the German saying, and people imagine the storyteller as someone who has come from afar. But they enjoy no less listening to the man who has stayed at home, making an honest living, and who knows the local tales and traditions.[6]

The ideal, "complete" storyteller, Benjamin claims, has to integrate both the traveler and the person who stays at home. This double perspective constitutes an important aspect of Benjamin's performative storytelling, in which the concrete state of the storyteller, when telling the story, is a being at "rest" (at a standstill), though not actually "at home," but rather making a pause on the journey, that is, making a temporary home. Whereas for Hamlet "the rest is silence," with "reckoning closed and story ended,"[7] as Hamm—a combination of a maimed, aged *Ham*let and Hummel (from Strindberg's *Ghost Sonata*)—says in Beckett's

Endgame, Benjamin (until committing suicide) takes on the role of Horatio, continuing to tell the story as the angels are singing Hamlet to his rest, again.

Seen from this perspective, the journey of the storyteller to a temporary point of rest becomes integrated within the story itself and is highly charged with meaning. It is only through this double perspective of movement and rest that we can achieve what Benjamin terms a "dialectics at a standstill," the dynamic stasis through which the *Denkbild* as an image of thought is shaped by the journey of the storyteller that becomes transformed into the movement of the narrative itself. The dynamics of the narrative lead us back from the point of rest to a place in the distant past where the journey began. This basic structure can also be found in Benjamin's meditation on the Klee watercolor and in the story of the beggar and the shirt to which I return shortly. Likewise this structure can be seen in Benjamin's interpretation of Kafka's "The Next Village," drawing attention to the double perspective through which "memory flies from the next village back to the place from which the rider decided to leave."[8]

In the text from *One-Way Street*, Benjamin is simultaneously activating narratives on several levels that interact metaphorically with one another, stressing the importance of the relationship between the two forms of travel—walking and flying—but also, indirectly, emphasizing the notion of being at home, at a point of rest. Copying, which is carried out while seated at a table (like Benjamin sitting in the Bibliothèque Nationale in Paris, working on *The Arcades Project*), is similar to walking along a country road (as a *flâneur*). The "traveler," in the form of the copier or the walker, is able to discover new aspects of the "inner self that are opened by the text."

Returning to our original example of copying and reading, this double activity is partly real (copying) and partly imagined (reading). A juxtaposition is created between the copier and the text, leading to a complexity of thought that the reader (including the person currently reading this text), who merely "follows the movement of his mind in the free flight of daydreaming," is, according to Benjamin, unable to experience. While reading, it is as if we are in flight, relegated to daydreaming and that alone. This is another mental activity of being at home, reminding us of Benjamin himself as a boy, looking out of the window of his own home in the recollected childhood experience discussed in the previous chapter.

In the passage from *One-Way Street*, two forms of traveling—walking and flying—are paired with two distinct expressions: reflection, of truly experiencing one's inner self, and daydreaming. And these expressions—in both their mental and physical forms—are constantly interacting with "us" as we in turn are either reading or copying this book right *now*.

I took it upon myself to physically copy the passage from the first volume of Benjamin's *Selected Writings*. Reproducing and reenacting the central idea that Benjamin himself had developed in his text was a very special experience. Copying, Benjamin argues, creates an interactive relationship with the text that the "copy-paste" approach to writing, on computers for example—like traveling by airplane or even by satellite—cannot activate. According to Benjamin, copying the text allows the copier to become directly involved, integrating him or her within its own performative fantasy. And as we begin to look more closely at the details of the "Chinese Curios" text, we gradually become more and more involved and even encouraged by the possibility of finding ourselves participating in and actually finding ourselves inside the text. The act of copying thus creates a performative self-reflexivity, a "staging" (*Inszenierung*) that involves the person who is copying the text. This is not just a form of identification or empathy with something "in" the text, an event or a character, but a form of self-enactment that the text encourages—even demands—the copier to perform, and to which I think we gradually, but quite willingly, submit.

The act of quoting, a variation of copying, just as the narrator in Kafka's "The Next Village" does, citing what his grandfather has repeatedly said about the rider setting out to the next village, is another aspect of this characteristic feature of Benjamin's own practice as a storyteller. Benjamin frequently emphasizes that he is quoting the idea or the narrative for a *Denkbild* from another source, usually without supplying the exact reference as he meticulously did while working on his collection of quotes for *The Arcades Project*. He even took some pride in "not" having invented the images and the stories that he tells. In "The Storyteller," Benjamin claims that "storytelling is always the art of repeating stories, and this art is lost when the stories are no longer retained."[9] Thus in 1930 Benjamin published a story in the Berlin-based magazine *Uhu* (*Owl*)—the same publication that a year earlier ran the piece about Brecht's car accident. In "Myslowitz-Braunschweig-Marseilles: The Story of a Hashish

Rausch," Benjamin tells about the tragic consequences smoking hashish has for the bank affairs of a young and rather wealthy man, and how he loses a million. Benjamin begins this story by emphatically insisting that he is not speaking from personal experience. He then continues by referring directly to the telling of someone else's stories as an expression of what Benjamin calls "this age of plagiarism."

Benjamin's ideas about retelling, quoting, and copying stories are variations on the subject of reproducibility that he examines in his essay "The Work of Art in the Age of Its Technological Reproducibility." He argues that because of new technological inventions, the work of art has lost its aura. The art of storytelling, as his essay "The Storyteller" argues, has also lost its aura. However as a storyteller in his own right—and the wealth of stories in his essays is a poignant expression of this—Benjamin strives to re-create the aura that he claims storytelling and the arts of his own time have lost. Paradoxically, as we shall see in greater detail later, and this is the case in the hashish narrative as well as in the story about the beggar, by telling a story about the loss (of a million or a shirt and a kingdom, respectively), Benjamin wishes to retrieve and re-create the artistic, aesthetic, and metaphysical auras. The loss of material wealth or of an object serves as the source—the origin of the attempt to salvage something more inclusive and important.

Before presenting Benjamin's opening to his story about losing a million, it is important to mention that Scherlinger, the painter-storyteller mentioned in the first sentence, is an invented figure. His name is based on the German word *Schierling*, which in English means "hemlock," the poison that Socrates drank and that killed him. In 1930, that same year, the philosopher Ernst Bloch, Benjamin's close friend, published *Spuren* (*Traces*), his own collection of *Denkbilder*. As I show later, there was a hidden competition between them about who had been the source of the stories they were telling. Benjamin apparently had good reason for being critical of Bloch, although he clearly also admired him.[10] Benjamin's story begins as follows:

This story is not one of mine. Whether Edward Scherlinger, the painter who I saw only that one evening when he told it, was a great storyteller or not, I won't say, for in this age of plagiarism, there are always a few listeners ready to credit a story to somebody else as soon as a person merely mentions that it was rendered faithfully. Be that as it may, I heard it one evening at one of Berlin's only classical spots for storytelling and listening, Lutter & Wegener's. Though it was pleasant enough sitting amongst our group at the round table, the conversation had for some time become scattered, taking on a muffled, marginal existence in groups of two or three who seemed unaware of one another. Then, in some context or other which has never been clear to me, my friend, the philosopher Ernst Bloch, tossed out the sentence that there was no one who had not already come within a hair of becoming a millionaire once in his life. There was laughter. The sentence was taken for one of his paradoxes. But then a peculiar thing happened. The longer we were occupied with debating this assertion, the more contemplative each of us became, reflecting back to such a point in our own lives when we had come the closest to touching the million. The story told by Scherlinger, who was never heard from again, belongs among the peculiar stories that came to light that evening, and I shall retell it as much as possible in his own words.[11]

After this introductory paragraph, depicting the storytelling situation of friends seated around a table in one of the well-known restaurants in Berlin, in the same square, the Gendarmenmarkt, to which Kierkegaard returned, Benjamin presents the story told by Scherlinger himself of how he had lost the possibility of earning a million because of a hashish *rausch*, that is, a hash "rush," or "high." The idea of retelling a story that someone else has told points toward another important performative characteristic of Benjamin's version of the *Denkbild* genre, repeating an important aspect of Plato's *Symposium*.

In his study of the *Denkbild*, Gerhard Richter has argued that this genre of writing "both illuminates and explodes the conventional distinctions among literature, philosophy, journalistic intervention and cultural critique."[12] And he continues, claiming that "the Denkbild always operates as a double performative," through which

it enacts the relationship between the universal and the singular: each Denkbild thematizes a singular content—in other words it is "about" something, and its "aboutness" opens into larger questions of writing to the extent that each Denkbild is itself the singular instantiation, regardless of its specific theme, of a larger, universal idea of literature.[13]

This aspect of the *Denkbild*, reminiscent of Hamlet's instructions to the actors, asking of them to "suit the action to the word, the word to the action" (3.15), combines thought and doing through a self-reflexive performative gesture, constantly moving between the act of "performing" a particular *Denkbild* and reflecting over "the universal idea of literature." This self-reflexivity is according to Richter not just based on the fact that someone quotes an already existing story, but that the *Denkbild* quotes all of literature. And this in turn, Richter continues,

> [h]elps us to ask if there can be . . . political potential in the literary, that is, if there can be a promise in literature that goes beyond the pleasure principle and, if so, what it would mean for such a promise to unfold on the far side of mimesis and realist criticism.[14]

Claiming that a literary work contains a promise, that it is a "speech-act" in the public, political arena, is both a guarantee and a hope for such an ongoing performativity, showing the way to an experience that actually lies beyond the traditionally accepted functions of literature.

This train of thought, examining the promise encapsulated in the text, a promise that the reader, according to Richter, will finally be able to transform into action, even political action—making the text performative in a much broader sense than generally recognized—has to be carefully examined. The promise expressed in the text about copying and reading that I have quoted is not primarily political, but it does contain a promise. It implies that, "if" we copy this text, "then" we will not only be able to grasp its hidden meanings, but also discover new aspects of our inner selves that this action of copying opens to us. This promise, which even if it is not expressed in the form of a sentence beginning with the words "I promise that . . . ," contains a dimension of language that has been referred to by linguists like J. L. Austin and John Searle as a "speech-act," in the general sense that verbal expressions can be understood as forms of action; language performs. And in particular it raises the question of how such speech-acts relate to the future, because by making a promise we defer a certain action—fulfilling the promise that we make at a certain point in time—to the future when certain conditions will be fulfilled.

Together with the promise, which is the most prominent speech-act dimension revealed by Benjamin's text about reading and copying, I explore two additional forms of speech-acts in Benjamin's *Denkbilder* that contain such a deferment to the future: wishes and threats. Benjamin's performative employment of promises, wishes, and threats, and possibly other kinds of speech-acts as well, represents an added dimension in the complex forms of performativity the text activates. And it is on this dimension that the reader is "invited" to take part and become an active participant. This is quite an ambitious claim, which ideally would involve both a discussion of the traditionally more well-known categories of speech-acts introduced by Austin and Searle, and an attempt to counterbalance their deeply rooted hostility to fictional discourses in general and to the theatre in particular, which I have mentioned. I have already expanded the notion of performativity far beyond these linguistic dimensions in my previous discussion. In particular, as I have taken into consideration contextual components like the competition (the *agon*), the confrontation with the supernatural (Hamlet), and the fear of being overtaken by insanity (Nietzsche and Strindberg), let it suffice to mention that the forms of performativity introduced by Benjamin were mainly based on modes of communication related directly to the ritual aspects of speech and storytelling. These modes of communication were not related to the formal (and limiting) linguistic analysis employed by Austin and Searle. I hope my final examples are sufficient for making these claims.][15]

The primary forms of speech-acts activated by Benjamin's *Denkbilder* are promises, threats (which can sometimes also be seen as warnings), and wishes. Their common feature is that they formulate something that can have future consequences for speaker and listener alike; at the same time, these speech-acts can often evoke a distant past. Among these speech-acts, promises and threats are what Douglas Walton termed "commissive speech acts," a category of speech-act committing the speaker to a future course of action, which in the case of threats can also have the implied effect of a grammatical imperative.[16]

The wish, on the other hand, is an almost tautological form of expression, and therefore its ritual function becomes foregrounded—"If my wish comes true, then I will have my desire fulfilled, and I will have that which I wished for"—containing clear implications for the future, but also for the notion of origin, because the wish, at least in Benjamin's case, relates to something that has been lost. The wish can even be compared to a prayer that is ritually repeated to appease some form of metaphysical being, asking for something that is lacking or has been irretrievably lost. And as Sigmund Freud had already shown, most systematically in *The Interpretation of Dreams*, "a dream can represent a wish as fulfilled."[17] The wish is a very powerful trope. It expresses desire, referring us directly to Eros and the metaphysical yearnings of the *Symposium*, as well as to the

188 CONSTELLATIONS

worlds of fantasy, imagination, and creativity that originate in the dreams of the individual.

The last section of Benjamin's essay on Kafka, called "Sancho Panza," opens with a story that is not by Kafka himself and that I already mentioned (and quoted) in connection with the discussion between Benjamin and Brecht of Kafka's "The Next Village." Benjamin tells this story because, as he claimed, it "takes us deep into the household that is Kafka's world":

In a Hassidic village, so the story goes, Jews were sitting together in a shabby inn one Sabbath evening. They were all local people, with the exception of one person no one knew, a very poor, ragged man who was squatting in a dark corner at the back of the room. All sorts of things were discussed, and then it was suggested that everyone should tell what wish he would make if one were granted him. One man wanted money; another wished for a son-in-law; a third dreamed of a new carpenter's bench; and so each spoke in turn. After they had finished, only the beggar in his dark corner was left. Reluctantly and hesitantly he answered the question. "I wish I were [*Ich wollte, ich wäre*] a powerful king reigning over a big country. Then, some night while I was asleep in my palace, an enemy would invade my country, and by dawn his horsemen would penetrate to my castle and meet with no resistance. Roused from my sleep, I wouldn't have time even to dress and I would have to flee in my shirt. Rushing over hill and dale and through forests day and night, I would finally arrive safely right here at the bench in this corner. This is my wish." The others exchanged uncomprehending glances. "And what good would this wish have done you?" someone asked. "I'd have a shirt," was the answer. ["*Und was hättest du von diesem Wunsch?*" *fragte einer. "Ein Hemd,*" *war die Antwort.*]¹⁸

The opening, "so the story goes," again emphasizes that Benjamin has "copied" this story from another source. In the German original of this story, what has been translated as "Sabbath evening" in the first sentence actually says, *Sabbath-Ausgang*, "the ending of the Sabbath." At this time, after the so-called *Seudah shlishit* (the "third meal," in Hebrew), while waiting for the three stars to appear in the firmament signaling the end of the Sabbath, the participants traditionally sing songs and tell stories. This is yet another aspect of the self-reflective performativity of Benjamin's art of storytelling, telling a story about a storytelling event.

According to the note in the English translation, this story was "current in books on Jewish humor around 1900,"¹⁹ whereas Liliane Weissberg has argued, but without giving any exact source, that this story came from one of Buber's collections of Hassidic stories.[20] I have however not yet been able to trace this short, enigmatic tale to these or to any other specific source. Benjamin's close friend Ernst Bloch had already included another version of this story (see appendix to this chapter for the text) in his *Spuren*.

It seems likely that Bloch had actually heard this story from Benjamin himself. And as we have already seen, Benjamin and Bloch apparently met at storytelling sessions in restaurants, just as this Hassidic story is about a storytelling event in an inn, after finishing a meal together. The exchange of letters during the summer of 1934 between Benjamin and his close friend the Kabbalah scholar Gershom Scholem, in Jerusalem, contains a direct reference to the fact that two stories (I return to the other one shortly) appear in Bloch's *Spuren* as well as in Benjamin's Kafka essay. While he was visiting Brecht in Denmark, Benjamin had sent the manuscript of his Kafka essay to Scholem. In the last paragraph of his letter from July 9, 1934, Scholem suddenly asks Benjamin: "And one question: Who is actually the source of these stories? Does Ernst Bloch have them from you or you from him? The great rabbi with the profound dictum on the messianic kingdom who appears in Bloch is none other than *I* myself; what a way to achieve fame!! It was one of my first ideas about the Kabbalah"[21] (italics in the original). And Benjamin, in his response to Scholem, laconically answers: "The origin of the stories in 'Kafka' remains my secret—one you would only succeed in unravelling by being present in person, in which case I would promise you a whole series of even more exquisite ones."[22] It is uncertain if Benjamin ever revealed the origin of the story to Scholem. In any case, it is obviously an issue with which they were deeply concerned.

The personal, sometimes tense relationships between Benjamin, Scholem, and Bloch are however not the main focus of the present discussion. Regardless of their biographical-historical importance, these letters point to a central issue with regard to the performativity of the story of the beggar, at least in Benjamin's version, which is directly connected to the notion of origin, the *Ursprung*. Therefore, besides the obvious factual question about the actual source of the story about the beggar, the question of origin is connected to a profound meta-narrative or meta-performative dimension related to the origin of the beggar: where he comes from, what kind of kingdom he wishes to have overseen before his palace was invaded by the enemy—an additional expression of the military aspect of Benjamin's *Denkbilder* that I mentioned before—and finally, what kind of journey the beggar has made to end up at the table in the inn. This is a story about a lost messianic kingdom, situated in the past, and the wish for a shirt constitutes the first step toward reestablishing this kingdom and imagining it as a possibility. The question Benjamin so poignantly asks and which is completely missing in Bloch's version of the story is how to find the way back to the origin where the imagined messianic kingdom is located. This is the function of the wish.

When Benjamin composed his Kafka essay, he had already written a "scholarly" book on the notion of origin, his *Habilitationsschrift Ursprung des deutschen Trauerspiels*, in English titled *The Origin of German Tragic Drama*. It was published in 1928, and in its "Epistemo-Critical Prologue" he had formulated in theoretical, abstract terms what the story about the beggar and the shirt so effectively concretizes:

Origin [*Ursprung*], although an entirely historical category, has, nevertheless, nothing to do with genesis [*Entstehung*]. The term origin is not intended to describe the process by which the existent came into being, but rather to describe that which emerges from the process of becoming and disappearance. Origin is an eddy [*Strudel*] in the stream of becoming [*im Fluß des Werdens*], and in its current it swallows the material involved in the process of genesis. That which is original [*das Ursprüngliche*] is never revealed in the naked and manifest existence of the factual; its rhythm is apparent only to a dual insight. On the one hand it needs to be recognized as a process of restoration and reestablishment, but, on the other hand, and precisely because of this, as something imperfect [actually "unfinished," *Unvollendetes, Unabgeschlossenes*] and incomplete. There takes place in every original phenomenon a determination of the form in which an idea will constantly confront the historical world, until it is revealed fulfilled, in the totality of its history.[23]

This is no doubt a very complex text, but the narrative of how the beggar has reached the inn where his story can be told is a concrete exemplification of the abstract notion of *Ursprung*—origin—which in German literally means "a first leap," by setting his own body in motion, which the beggar was forced to do when his imagined palace was invaded and he had to flee. This leap into exile is the *Ursprung*. Here the profound differences between Benjamin and Nietzsche also become obvious.

Through his story of having made a real or an imagined journey, finally reaching the destination where the story about the journey can be told, the beggar's wish becomes a performance of origins—"that which emerges from the process of becoming and disappearance"—made possible by his temporal rest and the telling of the story at the inn. The image of the imagined shirt becomes a "dialectics at a standstill," a point in time of danger with an uncertain future, but also a time of potentialities that need "to be recognized as a process of restoration and reestablishment." Therefore, Benjamin continues his theoretical deliberations; "precisely because of this" it must also be acknowledged "as something imperfect." The imagined shirt enables Benjamin to imagine and perform the notion of origin situated at a juncture where not only restoration and imperfection but also philosophy and the theatrical meet. The gestures of pointing backward to the uncertain and hidden origin of the story itself as well as to the imagined kingdom, from which the beggar had to flee, at the same time reveal and conceal these complex points of origin / departure for thinking as well as for "performing" this thought through the story.

The beggar's wish to have a shirt also contains an implied promise—should the wish be fulfilled to have such a shirt, regardless if it has been lost or is imagined—of regaining his lost kingdom. From the perspective of such a messianic temporal modality, Benjamin's story about the beggar is in itself simultaneously a wish and a promise, and beyond that actually wishing for a promise—the shirt—which will enable both him and the readers to imagine the reclamation of the lost "and" imagined kingdom. This radical ambiguity, of what it means to wish for a promise of this kind, constitutes another aspect of the performative thought—the *Denkbild*—expressed by Benjamin's version of the story.

Actually to have a shirt—which is obviously not the case for the beggar—will be the first visible sign that it is possible to regain this kingdom, a sign that it actually exists. This nonexisting shirt becomes the physical object that connects the beggar to his lost kingdom, implicitly pointing out to the eager listeners in the inn and to us, that on some level it has actually existed, and not only as the wish to have been a king mediated by a nonexisting shirt. Having a shirt will not just bring him back to the time and place where his imagined journey began, when the enemy entered his royal castle, it will "prove" that it is possible to find this lost kingdom, again. The interaction between the imagined past of the beggar and the possibility that one day he will actually have a shirt gives rise to a complex apocalyptic dimension in Benjamin's story. And the possibility that this will not happen, that the beggar will also arrive at the next inn without a shirt, becomes an extended threat which we, as readers of Benjamin's short narrative find difficult and even cruel, but apparently necessary to finally accept. Here the wish, the promise, and the threat become compressed into one poignant and powerful concrete image: the nonexisting shirt, which at different times in the process of thinking about it undergoes transformations of actuality: as a wish, a promise, or a threat.

In "The Storyteller," in conjunction with his argument that "the art of storytelling is coming to an end," Benjamin raised the question if it wasn't noticeable that "at the end of the [First World] war . . . the men who returned from the battlefield had grown silent—not richer but poorer in communicable experience." From this observation, a local observation about the wreckage that the angel of history observed or about the place from which the beggar had really come, vividly returning to the image of the journey as well, Benjamin draws this conclusion: "A generation that had gone to school on horse-drawn streetcars now stood under the open sky in a landscape where nothing remained unchanged but the clouds and, beneath those clouds, in a force field of destructive torrents and explosions, the tiny, fragile human body."[24] This is the locus where Benjamin constantly positioned himself as storyteller, and through the complex forms of performativity that he developed in his texts, also his readers, each one of us, as a "tiny, fragile human body." From the initial triad of wishes, promises, and threats, only the threat continues to be tangible and real.

*

> This process of assimilation [integrating the story in the life of the listener], which takes place in the depths, requires a state of relaxation which is becoming rarer and rarer. If sleep is the apogee of physical relaxation, boredom is the apogee of mental relaxation. Boredom is the dream bird that hatches the egg of experience. A rustle in the leaves drives him away.
> —Walter Benjamin, "The Storyteller"[25]

The silence of the men returning from the battlefield is of a different kind from Hamlet's silence. But they all lack voice. I set out by trying to account for the dialectics between the one voice and the many legs in the riddle of the Sphinx. I have explored how the originary voice of the Delphic oracle and of the sphinx was split into two discursive practices: the philosophical and the thespian. In Beckett's *Waiting for Godot*, Estragon draws Vladimir's attention to "All the dead voices." Apparently, they have angelic qualities, because Vladimir responds, "They make a noise like wings," to which Estragon replies, "Like leaves . . . They rustle." And after a moment of silence they continue:

> VLADIMIR: What do they say?
> ESTRAGON: They talk about their lives.
> VLADIMIR: To have lived is not enough for them.
> ESTRAGON: They have to talk about it.
> VLADIMIR: To be dead is not enough for them.[26]

The philosophers and the thespians I have been listening to here have spoken with their dead voices. What remains is the rustle of the leaves.

The story of the beggar's wish/promise/threat, with which Benjamin opens the last section of his Kafka essay, brings us back to the notion of origin (*Ursprung*), on several levels simultaneously, performing the primary leap (the *ur-Sprung*) to which we have to go back in order to continue forward. The story with which Benjamin begins this essay, about Potemkin's signature—which apparently originated in a collection of anecdotes and stories by Pushkin published in a German translation in 1924 and also appears in Bloch's *Spuren*—no less enigmatically tackles the notion of closure, and it is significant that Benjamin opens his essay with this story. It tells about a young civil servant in the Russian court—named Shuvalkin in Benjamin's version—who, when the depressed Chancellor Potemkin refuses to sign the important decrees that had to be published, declares he will attempt to get Potemkin to sign. It serves as the closure to this book.

I quote Benjamin's version of this story here. The other two versions are quoted in full in the appendix to this chapter.

It is said that Potemkin suffered from states of depression which recurred more or less regularly. At such times no one was allowed to go near him, and access to his room was strictly forbidden. This malady was never mentioned at court, and in particular it was known that any allusion to it would incur the disfavour of Empress Catherine. One of the chancellor's depressions lasted for an extraordinary length of time and caused serious difficulties; in the offices documents piled up that required Potemkin's signature, and the empress pressed for their completion. The high officials were at their wit's end. One day, an unimportant little clerk named Shuvalkin happened to enter the anteroom of the chancellor's palace and found the councillors of state assembled there, moaning and groaning as usual. "What is the matter, Your Excellencies?" asked the obliging Shuvalkin. They explained things to him and regretted that they could not use his services. "If that's all it is," said Shuvalkin, "I beg you gentlemen to let me have those papers." Having nothing to lose, the councillors of state let themselves be persuaded to do so, and with the sheaf of documents under his arm, Shuvalkin set out, through galleries and corridors, for Potemkin's bedroom. Without knocking or even stopping, he turned the door handle; the room was not locked. In semidarkness Potemkin was sitting on his bed, in a threadbare nightshirt, biting his nails. Shuvalkin stepped up to the writing desk, dipped a pen in ink, and without saying a word pressed it into Potemkin's hand while putting one of the documents on his knees. Potemkin gave the intruder a vacant stare; then, as though in his sleep, he started to sign—first one paper, then a second, finally all of them. When the last signature had been affixed, Shuvalkin took the papers under his arm and left the room without further ado, just as he had entered it. Waving the papers triumphantly, he stepped into the anteroom. The councillors of state rushed toward him and tore the documents out of his hands. Breathlessly they bent over them. No one spoke a word; the whole group seemed paralyzed. Again Shuvalkin came closer and solicitously asked why the gentlemen seemed so upset. At that point he noticed the signatures. One document after the other was signed Shuvalkin . . . Shuvalkin . . . Shuvalkin . . .[27]

"This story," Benjamin immediately adds, "is like a herald of Kafka's work, storming two hundred years ahead of it. The enigma which beclouds this story is Kafka's enigma." But it is also closely tied to Benjamin's enigma, which he in turn passes on to his readers. What Benjamin wants to tell us is that what we finally discover in his complex performative texts is our own signature; and we can never be completely sure how it got there. Here, in any case, is mine . . .

Appendix: Variations on Two Themes

The Beggar's Wish According to Bloch

We can also happen onto the Here and Now in the strangest ways; it's never far from us. I know a little—almost a low—Eastern European Jewish story whose ending is of course remarkably disappointing. The ending is clearly meant to be a joke, a truly awkward and flat one, unfunny, but a joke meant only to fill up the hole we've fallen into. That hole is the now where we all are, and which the story does *not* narrate away from as usual; the little trap door thus needs to be built on.

They studied and debated till they were sleepy. Now the Jews in the prayer house of the village conversed about what they would wish for if an angel should come. The rabbi said he would be happy if he could just be rid of the cough. I wish, said another, that I had married off my daughter. Said a third, And I would wish that I had not had a daughter at all, but a son, who could take over my business. Finally the rabbi turned to a beggar who had wandered in the night before and now sat, ragged and miserable, on the last bench: what would you wish for, friend? God help you, alas, you don't look as though you could wish for nothing.

I would wish, said the beggar, that I were a great king, and had vast lands. In every city I would have a palace, and in the most beautiful a capital of onyx, sandalwood and marble. There I would sit on the throne, would be feared by my enemies, loved by my people, like King Salomon. But in battle I don't enjoy Salomon's good fortune; the enemy breaks through, my armies are defeated, and every city and forest goes up in flames. The enemy is already before my capital; I hear the uproar on the streets, and sit all alone in the throne room, with crown, scepter, royal purple, and ermine, deserted by my standard bearer, and I hear how the people scream for my blood. Then I strip down to my shirt and throw off all my finery; I jump out the window into the courtyard. I make it through the town, through the commotion, into the open and run, run for my life, through the plundered land. Ten days, to the border, where no one knows me, and I get across, to other people who know nothing of me, want nothing of me; I am saved, *and since last night I've sat here.*

Long pause, and shock as well; the beggar jumped up, the rabbi looked at him.

I must say, said the rabbi slowly, I really must say, you are a curious person. Why would you wish for everything again, if you will only lose it again? What good were your riches and your splendor?

Rabbi, spoke the beggar, sitting down again, I would have something, actually: a shirt.

Now the Jews laughed, and shook their heads, and granted the king a shirt; by a joke the shock was overcome. This remarkable Now as End, this End of the Now in the words: since last night I've sat here, this breakthrough of Being Here from right out of the dream. Mediated verbally, through the intricate detour that the beggar takes from the subjunctive from with which he begins, through the narrative present, suddenly to the actual present. Something comes over the listener when he lands just where he is; no son will take over this business.

From Ernst Bloch, *Traces*, translated by Anthony A. Nassar (Stanford University Press, Stanford, Calif., 2006), 72–73.

Potemkin's Signature According to Pushkin

Potjomkin often suffered from attacks of hypochondria. At such points he could sit alone in his room for days on end, letting no one in and busying himself with nothing. On one occasion, when he was again in such a state, there had piled up a heap of documents that needed to be dealt with promptly; no one was daring enough, however, to enter his room unbidden and report this to him. Hearing the discussions being held on the subject, a young clerk by the name of Petuschkow declared himself willing to bring the most important of the documents before the prince for signing. This task was readily given over to him and the others impatiently awaited what would come of this. Potjomkin was sitting barefoot and unkempt in his nightgown, pensively chewing his fingernails. Petuschkow brazenly informed him of how things stood and laid the documents out in front of him. Without a word, Potjomkin took up his pen and signed them in order. Petuschkow bowed and entered the outer office with a triumphant air. "Signed!" . . . Everyone rushed up to him and saw: the documents had in fact been signed. Petuschkow was congratulated. "Quite an efficient fellow! There's no arguing with that!" It suddenly occurred to one of them, however, to look at the signatures—and what was to be seen? On each and every document, instead of the signature: Prince Potjomkin—was written only: Petuschkow, Petuschkow, Petuschkow . . .

From A. Pushkin's *Anekdoten und Tischgespräche*, edited by Johannes von Guenther (Allgemeine Verlagsanstalt, Munich, 1924), 42 (translated by Russell Bucher).

Potemkin's Signature According to Bloch

Prince Potemkin had hours when he would admit no one. His room would be deathly quiet then; no one knew what he was up to. Affairs of state idled, and his councillors had a good time. No report took place; the peak was clouded. Once, however, as an attack lasted an unusually long time, the most urgent documents arrived. They could be handled without the president, but not without his signature. His councillors waited in the antechambers; no one dared to step before the prince for fear of losing his position or being exiled. Until a young scribe by the name of Petukov saw the great chance of his career. He fetched the sheaf of documents and went in to the president with one push, without knocking; Potemkin sat in a corner of the darkened room, hair unkempt, and utterly vacant, chewing his nails. Petukov set the documents wordlessly before him, handed the prince a pen, and the prince took his fingers from his mouth, undersigned decree after decree, with his eyes as though asleep, one after the other. The scribe burst from the room: Success! The prince had signed everything!—and held out the documents. Couriers hastened by to carry the decrees to Moscow, Kiev, Odessa, to the regional governors. Yet before the envelopes were sealed, an older official took out one of the documents that had come from his jurisdiction. Started, pulled out the remaining papers, showed them: they had certainly all been signed. At the bottom of every document, in Potemkin's hand, stood: *Petukov, Petukov, Petukov.* . . .

Pushkin, who tells more or less this story, thereby provides not only the most uncanny documentation of melancholy, of the relentless brooding that burrows through the fog, of the mind lost in a nameless twilight, who takes the name Petukov because there at least something stirs, to that mind lost under the false sun that can still make any name gray—Petukov or Potemkin, whichever. Instead, insofar as the story concerns Prince Potemkin, the luckiest of men, the favorite, insofar as the lucky ones generally (not only despots) easily become melancholy at the peak of their lives (the still ambitious or wistful more easily get manic), one can see how little peak there is above the fog that is man, how his name and character often lie like an island within it, one perhaps more solidly elevated than Potemkin's, but always prone to fog, Hebridean: indeed that this, which we already call heaven, even when painted to the dimensions of our happiest days, might in the long run (which is what matters), be really just a hothouse of images that are still never far above the fog of existence, the sorrow of fulfillment.

From Ernst Bloch, *Traces*, translated by Anthony A. Nassar (Stanford University Press, Stanford, Calif., 2006), 88–89.

Notes

Introduction

1. During the past few years, a gradually growing number of publications about the relationship between philosophy and the theatre have been published. I will only mention some of the more recent ones that have inspired my own work: Samuel Weber, *Theatricality as Medium*, Fordham University Press, New York, 2004; *Staging Philosophy: Intersections of Theater, Performance, and Philosophy*, edited by David Krasner and David Z. Saltz, University of Michigan Press, Ann Arbor, Mich., 2006; Martin Puchner, *Poetry of the Revolution: Marx, Manifestos and the Avant-Gardes*, Princeton University Press, Princeton, N.J., and Oxford, 2006; Helmar Schramm, Ludger Schwarte, and Jan Lazardzig, *Collection—Laboratory—Theater: Scenes of Knowledge in the 17th Century*, Walter de Gruyter, Berlin and New York, 2005; Alan Read, *Theatre, Intimacy & Engagement: The Last Human Venue*, Palgrave Macmillan, Basingstoke and New York, 2008; Paul A. Kottman, *A Politics of the Scene*, Stanford University Press, Stanford, Calif., 2008; Rikard Schönström, *En försmak av framtiden: Bertolt Brecht och det konkreta*, Brutus Östlings bokförlag Symposion, Stockholm/Stehag, 2003.

2. See for example: Thomas Gould, *The Ancient Quarrel between Poetry and Philosophy*, Princeton University Press, Princeton, N.J., 1990; Stanley Rosen, *The Quarrel between Philosophy and Poetry: Studies in Ancient Thought*, Routledge, New York and London, 1988; Susan B. Levin, *The Ancient Quarrel between Philosophy and Poetry Revisited: Plato and the Greek Literary Tradition*, Oxford University Press, Oxford, 2001.

3. Alexander Nehamas, *The Art of Living: Socratic Reflections from Plato to Foucault*, University of California Press, Berkeley/Los Angeles/London, 1998, 6.

4. Shannon Jackson, *Professing Performance: Theatre in the Academy from Philology to Performativity*, Cambridge University Press, Cambridge, 2004.

5. *Report of the Task Force on the Arts*, Harvard University, Cambridge, Mass., 2008, 1, http://www.news.harvard.edu/press/pressdoc/supplements/081210_Arts TaskForceReport.pdf.

6. Plato, *Symposium*, in *Complete Works*, edited by John M. Cooper and D. S. Hutchinson, translated by Alexander Nehamas and Paul Woodruff, Hackett Publishing Company, Indianapolis/Cambridge, 1977. All references are indicated in parentheses after the quotation.

7. J. L. Austin, *How to Do Things with Words*, Harvard University Press, Cambridge, Mass., second edition, 1975. See also Chapter 6, note 15.

8. Judith Butler, *Antigone's Claim: Kinship between Life and Death*, Columbia University Press, New York, 2000, 65.

9. Sue-Ellen Case, "Classical Drag: The Greek Creation of Female Parts," *Theatre Journal*, 37, 3, 1985, 317–327. Includes an interesting discussion of the theatrical *agon*.

10. *Aristotle's Poetics*, translated by S. H. Butcher, Hill and Wang, New York, 1999, chapter 9, 68.

11. Ibid., 69.

12. Gerald F. Else, *Aristotle's Poetics: The Argument*, Harvard University Press, Cambridge, Mass., 1963, 307; 313. See also G. E. M. de Ste. Croix, "Aristotle on History and Poetry" (*Poetics*, 9, 1451a36–b11), in Amélie Oksenberg Rorty, *Essays on Aristotle's "Poetics,"* Princeton University Press, Princeton, N.J., 1992, 23–32; and Nurit Yaari, "Greek Tragedy in Theory and Praxis: Aristotle's Theory of Tragedy in the Perspective of Aristophanes' Theatre Practice," *Maske und Kothurn*, 35, 1, 1989, 7–19.

13. Una Chaudhuri, *Staging Place: The Geography of Modern Drama*, University of Michigan Press, Ann Arbor, 1995, 11–12.

14. Walter Benjamin, "On the Concept of History," in *Selected Writings*, translated by Harry Zohn, volume 4, 1938–1949, Belknap Press of Harvard University Press, Cambridge, Mass., and London, 2003, 391.

Chapter 1

A portion of this chapter was originally published as "The Philosopher and the Two Playwrights: Socrates, Agathon and Aristophanes in Plato's *Symposium*" in *Theatre Survey*, 49, 2, November 2008, 239–252. © American Society for Theatre Research 2008. Reprinted with the permission of Cambridge University Press.

1. Diogenes Laërtius, *Lives of Eminent Philosophers*, book 3: Plato, translated by R. D. Hicks, Harvard University Press, Cambridge, Mass., 1966, 279–281.

2. Plato, *Symposium*, in *Complete Works*. All references are indicated in parentheses after the quotation.

3. *Brecht on Theatre*, edited by John Willet, Methuen, London, 1982, 121.

4. Ibid.

5. The ending of the dialogue has received ample critical attention from philologists and philosophers, as well as literary scholars, drawing attention to its enigmatic, unresolved ironies. In this context I want to mention the following in

particular: Diskin Clay, "The Tragic and Comic Poet of *The Symposium*," *Arion*, New Series, 2, 2, 1975, 238–261; C. Kahn, *Plato and the Socratic Dialogue: The Philosophical Use of a Literary Form*, Cambridge University Press, Cambridge, 1996; Frisbee C. C. Sheffield, *Plato's "Symposium": The Ethics of Desire*, Oxford University Press, Oxford, 2006. See also Ruby Blondell, *The Play of Character in Plato's Dialogues*, Cambridge University Press, Cambridge, 2002.

6. Our knowledge of Agathon is not very extensive, and none of his tragedies has survived. However, he also appears, together with Euripides, as a character in Aristophanes' play *Thesmophoriazusae*, whereas Socrates appears in *The Clouds*. For an extensive and illuminating analysis of Agathon's character in a theatrical context, see Anne Duncan, *Performance and Identity in the Classical World*, Cambridge University Press, Cambridge, 2006, chapter 1. See also Froma Zeitlin, "Travesties of Gender and Genre in Aristophanes' *Thesmophoriazusae*," *Critical Inquiry*, 8, 2, 1981, 301–327 (also published in *Playing the Other: Gender and Society in Classical Greek Literature*, University of Chicago Press, Chicago, 1996, 375–416). In this essay the relations between tragedy and comedy, though in a way that is not directly related to the *Symposium*, are discussed.

7. Plato, *Republic*, in *Complete Works*, revised edition, C. D. C. Reeve, Hackett Publishing Company, Indianapolis/Cambridge, 1977. All references from the *Republic* are indicated in parentheses after the quotation.

8. For a comprehensive historical overview of this position, see in particular Jonas Barish, *The Anti-theatrical Prejudice*, University of California Press, Berkeley, 1981.

9. "Art," "poetry," "drama," and "theatre" are frequently used synonymously by Plato. However, there is no doubt that "theatre" and "acting" are the two artistic expressions that Plato attacks most vehemently. In any case this is not the context in which to try and find an orderly pattern in Plato's use of terminology.

10. Andrea Wilson Nightingale, *Spectacles of Truth in Classical Greek Philosophy: Theoria in Its Cultural Context*, Cambridge University Press, Cambridge, 2004, 3.

11. Plato, *Laws*, in *Complete Works*, translated by Trevor J. Saunders, 1483, 816e.

12. See for example James Arieti, *Interpreting Plato: The Dialogues as Drama*, Rowman & Littlefield Publishers, Savage, Md., 1991; and Max Statkiewicz, "Platonic Theater: Rigor and Play in the *Republic*," *MLN*, 115, 2000, 1019–1051.

13. See P. W. Harsch, "Plato Symposium 194B and a Raised Position in the Theater," *Classical Philology*, 44, 2, 1949, 116–117; and Richard Hunter, *Plato's Symposium*, Oxford University Press, Oxford, 2004.

14. The Greek term used here is *agônizomai*, "to contend for a prize."

15. The Greek term used here is *agônotheteô*, "to direct the games," "to exhibit them."

16. My reading radically differs from that of K. J. Dover, who claims "that Plato means us to regard the theme and framework of Aristophanes' story as characteristic not of comedy but of unsophisticated, subliterate folklore" (45). K. J. Dover, "Aristophanes' Speech in Plato's *Symposium*," *Journal of Hellenic Studies*, 86, 1966, 41–50.

17. Claude Lévi-Strauss, "The Structural Study of Myth," in *Structural Anthropology*, Anchor, New York, 1983, 212.

18. Euripides, *Phoenician Women*, translated by Elizabeth Craik, Aris and Phillips, Wiltshire, England, 1988, 61. This is also the formulation quoted in the following: Sophocles, *The Plays and Fragments*, translated and edited by Richard C. Jebb, Cambridge University Press, Cambridge, 1914, 6; Charles Segal, *Tragedy and Civilization*, Harvard University Press, Cambridge, Mass., 1981, 214, 454, note 20 cf; Apollodorus, *The Library*, translated by James George Frazer, Heinemann, London, 1967 ("What is that which has one voice and yet becomes four-footed and two-footed and three-footed?"); and Athenaeus, *Deipnosophistae*, translated by Charles Burton Gallick, Harvard University Press, Cambridge, Mass., 1961, 4, 569 ("There walks on land a creature of two feet, of four feet, and of three; it has one voice, but sole among the animals that grow on land or in the sky or beneath the sea, it can change its nature; nay, when it walks propped on most feet, then is the speed in its limbs less than it has ever been before").

19. In a previous article I have speculated what these "wrong" answers to the riddle were: "One Voice and Many Legs: Oedipus and the Riddle of the Sphinx," edited by Galit Hasan-Rokem and David Shulman, in *Untying the Knot: On Riddles and Other Enigmatic Modes*, Oxford University Press, New York and Oxford, 1996, 255–270.

20. The Delphic oracle, as described in Plato's *Apology*, had a very different significance for Socrates, explicitly declaring him to be the wisest man on earth, whereas it declared Oedipus to be the most cursed one.

21. Adriana Cavarero, *Relating Narratives: Storytelling and Selfhood*, translated by Paul A. Kottman, Routledge, London, 2000, 7.

22. In Euripides' *Hippolytus*, Theseus says that "all men should have two voices, one of justice and one as it happens to be, so that the voice of unjust thoughts would be tested and refuted by the just voice, and so we would not be deceived." Charles Segal, who provides this quotation, sees this play as a reverse of *Oedipus Tyrannus*, with a hero falsely accused of incest with his stepmother. Charles Segal, *Oedipus Tyrannus, Tragic Heroism and the Limits of Knowledge*, Oxford University Press, New York and Oxford, second edition, 2001, 11.

23. Aristophanes also hints at the dialectics between one and many: when the two halves have become unified there are many legs, not just two.

24. This is the translation given by S. Goodhart in his article, "*Leistas ephaska*: Oedipus and Laius' Many Murderers," *Diacritics*, 8, 2, 1978, 56. Line 934 in Fagles's translation reads: "One can't equal many." The translation given

by Jebb is somewhat less pointed: "If then, he still speaks, as before, of several, I was not the slayer: a solitary man could not be held the same with that band" (844–845). In his notes, however, Jebb says that "one cannot be made to tally with (cannot be identified with) those many." Sophocles, *Plays and Fragments* Cambridge University Press, Cambridge, 1914.

25. Jean-Joseph Goux, *Oedipus, Philosopher*, Stanford University Press, Stanford, Calif., 1993, 132–133.

26. Segal, *Oedipus: Tragic Heroism*, 5.

27. Ibid., 11.

28. Friedrich Nietzsche, *The Birth of Tragedy [from the Spirit of Music]*, translated by Douglas Smith, Oxford World Classics, Oxford University Press, Oxford, 2000, #9, 55.

29. Ibid., 54–55.

30. Ibid., 55.

31. Aristotle, *The Works of Aristotle*, translated by G. R. G. Mure, Oxford University Press, Oxford, 1928, 1, 91b, 40–92a, 1–2. See also Plato's *The Statesman*:

> The Stranger: I say that we should have begun at first by dividing land animals into biped and quadruped; and since the winged herd, and that alone, comes out in the same class with man, should divide bipeds into those which have feathers and those which have not, and when they have been divided, and the art of the management of mankind is brought to light, the time will have come to produce our Statesman and ruler, and set him like a charioteer in his place, and hand over to him the reins of state, for that too is a vocation which belongs to him. (The Internet Classics Archive, "Statesman by Plato," http://classics.mit.edu/Plato/stateman.html)

32. Sophocles, *Oedipus the King*, in *The Three Theban Plays*, translated by Robert Fagles, Penguin Books, Harmondsworth, England, 1982, lines 1130–1136; pp. 219–220.

33. Aristotle, *Aristotle's Poetics*, translated by Leon Golden, Prentice Hall, N.J., 1968, 27–28.

34. See *Plato: Selected Myths*, edited and with an introduction by Catalin Partenie, Oxford University Press, Oxford, 2004. Partenie has also confirmed this in several conversations, and I thank him for his valuable comments and suggestions.

35. Austin, *How to Do Things with Words*, 9.

36. Ibid., 10.

37. Ibid., 22.

38. For an introduction to this complex debate, see Hent de Vries, "Must We (Not) Mean What We Say? Seriousness and Sincerity in the work of J. L. Austin and Stanley Cavell," in *The Rhetoric of Sincerity*, edited by Ernst van Alphen, Mieke Bal, and Carel Smits, Stanford University Press, Stanford, Calif., 2009,

90–118; and J. Hillis Miller, *Speech Acts in Literature*, Stanford University Press, Stanford, Calif., 2001.

39. Nietzsche, *Birth of Tragedy*, #13, 76.

40. Walter Benjamin, *The Origin of German Tragic Drama*, translated by John Osborne, Verso, London and New York, 1998, 30.

41. Ibid., 118.

Chapter 2

1. William Shakespeare, *Hamlet, Prince of Denmark*, in *The New Cambridge Shakespeare*, Cambridge University Press, Cambridge, 1989. All references are to this edition, and are given in parentheses in the text (act, scene, line).

2. Quoted in Benjamin, *The Origin*, 108.

3. Michel de Montaigne's possible influences on *Hamlet* have been discussed from a variety of perspectives, and they are no doubt important for an understanding of the philosophical subtexts of the play. But they are not directly relevant to the competition between the discursive practices of philosophy and theatre explored here.

4. T. S. Eliot, *The Sacred Wood: Essays on Poetry and Criticism*, published in 1922, "Hamlet and His Problems," http://www.bartleby.com/200/sw9.html.

5. There are some interesting echoes from *Hamlet* in *King Lear*, which was first performed in 1605. In the storm scene (3.4) Kent asks Gloucester, "Who's there?" (3.4, 113), and then Lear repeatedly calls Edgar "philosopher" (3.4, 137, 154, 159), drawing attention to the connections between madness and philosophy, a theme that is also prominent in *Hamlet*.

6. Shakespeare has also developed a dialectic between speaking and writing in *Hamlet*. Hamlet writes letters, and after the first encounter with the ghost, he uses his tables to write something. He has also written a dozen or so lines to be added to the performance that the players will perform for the king. However, the question that still needs to be explored is why Shakespeare makes Hamlet a clumsily juvenile writer and yet a superb oral poet.

7. Today the university is called Martin Luther University Halle-Wittenberg and is located in both of these German cities. There is also a Wittenberg University, a Lutheran college, in Springfield, Ohio.

8. Shakespeare's own religious convictions, most probably in sympathy and even identification with the Catholic faith, no doubt influenced the way Wittenberg figures in *Hamlet*. See Stephen Greenblatt, *Hamlet in Purgatory*, Princeton University Press, Princeton, N.J., 1991; and *Will in the World: How Shakespeare Became Shakespeare*, Norton, New York, 2004.

9. The story about Faust's life first appeared in Germany in 1587, and in 1592 it was translated into English as *The History of the Damnable Life and Deserved Death of Doctor John Faustus*. Scholars believe Marlowe heard or read the story of Johann Faust and composed *Doctor Faustus* sometime between 1588 and 1592.

It was first staged in 1594, and London's Stationer's Register entered the play into the official record in 1601.

10. For the figure of the Wandering Jew, which is marginal to *Hamlet* but clearly also belongs to the academic-creative milieu in which Hamlet studied, see *The Wandering Jew: Interpretations of a Christian Legend*, edited by Galit Hasan-Rokem and Alan Dundes, Indiana University Press, Bloomington 1986.

11. See Alfred R. Ferguson, "Politics and Man's Fate in Sophocles' *Antigone*," *The Classical Journal*, 70, 2, 1974–1975, 41–49, here 44.

12. Jerzy Limon has informed me that "there is evidence that there were actresses in the companies of players that went beyond the seas, although the evidence is of later date. George Jolly, for instance, boasted in the 1650s that his company included 'skilful women.' Some of the actors travelled with their families, and one may suspect that some of the wives and children could take part in the shows." E-mail, November 20, 2008.

13. Philip Edwards, Introduction, in *Hamlet, Prince of Denmark*, 5. This refers to E. A. J. Honigmann, "The Date of *Hamlet*," *Shakespeare Survey*, 9, 1956, 27–29.

14. See also Jaques's famous "All the world's a stage" speech in *As You Like It* (2.7), with the line: "And one man in his time plays many parts," which means that the same actor plays many different roles.

15. For a discussion of how the different roles an actor plays affect not only our appreciation of the actor's artistic ability but also the way in which we perceive every new role the actor plays, see Marvin Carlson, *The Haunted Stage*, University of Michigan Press, Ann Arbor, 2001.

16. Jacques Derrida, *Specters of Marx: The State of the Debt, the Work of Mourning, & the New International*, translated by Peggy Kamuf, Routledge, New York and London, 1994. Derrida bases a long philosophical meditation on this Hamlet quote.

17. Stephen Orgel, "Shakespeare and the Kinds of Drama," *Critical Inquiry*, 6, 1, 1979, 107–123, here 117. See also Ramie Targoff, "The Performance of Prayer: Sincerity and Theatricality in Early Modern England," *Representations*, 60, 1997, 49–69.

18. The question "Who's there?" appears in several of Shakespeare's plays, all in all more than forty times, but the best-known instance is of course the opening line of Hamlet.

19. Both F and Q1 give this line to Marcellus. Q2 gives it to Horatio.

20. We learn that they have the same name when Hamlet, during their first meeting, says, "I'll call thee Hamlet / King, father, royal Dane" (1.4.44–45). This formulation has something hypothetical about it. And it is only in the fifth act, in the grave-digger scene, that we hear about Old Hamlet's victory against Old Fortinbras.

21. For a recent discussion of this tradition, see for example Margreta de Grazia, "Teleology, Delay and the 'Old Mole,'" *Shakespeare Quarterly*, 50, 3, 1999, 251–267.

22. Derrida, *Specters of Marx*, 15. This book is based on a series of lectures from 1993.

23. For a general introduction of Levin's plays in English, see Freddie Rokem, "Introduction," in *The Labour of Life: An Anthology of Hanoch Levin's Plays*, Stanford University Press, Stanford, Calif., 2003, ix–xxxv.

24. Karl Marx and Friedrich Engels, *The Communist Manifesto*, W. W. Norton, New York and London, 1988, 54.

25. Karl Marx, "The Eighteenth Brumaire of Louis Bonaparte," 1852, Chapter 7, http://www.marxists.org/archive/marx/works/1852/18th-brumaire/ch07.htm.

26. Karl Marx, "Speech at the Anniversary of the *People's Paper*," 1856, http://www.marxists.org/archive/marx/works/1856/04/14.htm.

27. Quoted from David Farrel Krell, "The Mole: Philosophic Burrowings in Kant, Hegel and Nietzsche," *Boundary*, 2, 9, 3, 173.

28. Karl Marx, "Eighteenth Brumaire."

29. I am much indebted to Ned Lukacher. For a discussion of Hegel's misquoting, see Ned Lukacher, *Primal Scenes: Literature, Philosophy, Psychoanalysis*, Cornell University Press, Ithaca, N.Y., and London, 1986, chapter 6. For a discussion of the Marx reference, see Peter Stallybrass, "'Well Grubbed, Old Mole': Marx, *Hamlet*, and the (Un)fixing of Representation," *Cultural Studies*, 12, 1, 1998, 3–14.

30. Peter Stallybrass, "'Well Grubbed, Old Mole,'" 13.

31. For a biting critique of Austin's position showing that his *How to Do Things with Words* from 1962 is a piece of literature, see J. Hillis Miller, *Speech Acts in Literature*, Stanford University Press, Stanford, Calif., 2001.

32. Butler, *Antigone's Claim*.

33. Heiner Müller, *Hamletmachine and Other Texts for the Stage*, Performing Arts Journal Publications, New York, 1984, 53.

34. Nietzsche, *Birth of Tragedy*, 46–47.

35. Benjamin, *The Origin*, 139.

36. Ibid., 158.

37. Plato, *Phaedo*, translated by Hugh Tredennik, Penguin Books, Harmondsworth, England, 1987, 64a, 107. See also Nehamas, *Art of Living*, 115.

38. Ludwig Wittgenstein, *Tractatus Logico-Philosophicus, the Logische-Philosophische Abhandlung*, Routledge & Kegan Paul, London, 1961.

Chapter 3

1. The Nietzsche Channel, http://www.geocities.com/thenietzschechannel/nlett1888.htm. The German original appears in *Nietzsche Briefwechsel, Frie-*

drich Nietzsche Briefe, edited by Giorgio Colli and Mazzino Montinari, Walter Gruyter, Berlin and New York, 1984, 3, 5, 1036.

2. Listed as letter #1154a in http://ora-web.swkk.de/swk-db/niebrief/index.html. See also *Strindberg's Letters*, selected, edited, and translated by Michael Robinson, University of Chicago Press, Chicago, 1992, volume 1, 292 (letter to Brandes, December 1, 1888); and Walter A. Berendsohn, "Strindberg och Nietzsche," Samfundet Örebro Stads och Länsbiblioteks Vänner, *Meddelande*, 16, 1948, 18.

3. Pierre Klossowski, *Nietzsche and the Vicious Circle*, Continuum, London and New York, 1997, 173.

4. Ernst Behler, "Nietzsche in the Twentieth Century," *The Cambridge Companion to Nietzsche*, Cambridge University Press, Cambridge, 1996, 289.

5. Quoted from Harold H. Borland, *Nietzsche's Influence on Swedish Literature: With Special Reference to Strindberg, Ola Hanson, Heidenstam and Fröding*, Elanders Boktryckeri Aktiebolag, Göteborg, Sweden, 1956, 15.

6. The lectures were held on April 10, 17, 24, and May 1 and 8, 1888, and the reports were published on April 17, 18, 25, and May 2 and 9, 1888. They were later published in the periodical *Tilskueren*, in August 1889, and in Brandes's *Samlede Skrifter*, 7, Copenhagen, 1901, 596–664.

7. Von Giorgio Colli and Montinari, *Nietzsche Briefwechsel*, 3, 6, #533, 185–186. All of Nietzsche's letters have been translated by Russell Bucher.

8. Robinson, *Strindberg's Letters*, 277.

9. A. Strindberg, *Brev (Collected Letters)*, 8, #1632, Bonniers, Stockholm, 1961.

10. Von Giorgio Colli and Montinari, *Nietzsche Briefwechsel*, 3, 5, #1130, 450.

11. Ibid., #586, 320.

12. Ibid., #1134, 457. This letter shows that the first direct communication between Nietzsche and Strindberg, the dedication of *Götzen-Dämmerung*, took place during the last days of October 1888.

13. Von Giorgio Colli and Montinari, *Nietzsche Briefwechsel*, #1148, 479.

14. Ibid., #1151, 483.

15. Brandes probably already lent Strindberg this book during the summer, together with *Jenseits von Gut und Böse*.

16. This is most probably a slight exaggeration, because the Brandes lectures had been held in April that year.

17. Robinson, *Strindberg's Letters*, 291.

18. Ibid., 292.

19. Ibid. The year 1889 refers to the centennial of the French Revolution. There is no published letter from Brandes to Strindberg reacting to this letter.

20. Von Giorgio Colli and Montinari, *Nietzsche Briefwechsel*, #1160, 493.

21. Ibid.

22. Friedrich Nietzsche, *Götzen-Dämmerung*, "Streifzüge eines Unzeitgemässen," #51, http://www.gutenberg.org/dirs/etext05/8gtzn10.txt.
23. Robinson, *Strindberg's Letters*, 294–295.
24. Ibid., 295–296.
25. *Georg Brandes: Selected Letters*, edited and translated by W. Glyn Jones, Norvik Press, Norwich, England, 1990, 160–161.
26. Von Giorgio Colli and Montinari, *Nietzsche Briefwechsel*, #1176, 507–509.
27. Robinson, *Strindberg's Letters*, 296–297.
28. Von Giorgio Colli and Montinari, *Nietzsche Briefwechsel*, #1229, 567–568.
29. Quoting Horace: *Odes*, II, 10, 1–4, from *Selected Letters of Friedrich Nietzsche*, edited and translated by Christopher Middleton, Hackett Publishing Company, Indianapolis, Ind., 1966, 344, note 239.
30. Robinson, *Strindberg's Letters*, 299.
31. Ibid.
32. Jones, *Georg Brandes: Selected Letters*, 161–162.
33. Ibid.
34. Von Giorgio Colli and Montinari, *Nietzsche Briefwechsel*, #1238, 572.
35. Ibid., #1243, 573. Among the final letters there are also several signed "Nietzsche Dionysos" or just "Dionysos."
36. Robinson, *Strindberg's Letters*, 304.
37. Ibid., 327.
38. *Georg og Edv. Brandes Brevveksling Med Nordiske Forfattere og Videnskabsmænd*, Gyldendalske Boghandel, Nordisk Forlag, Copenhagen, 1939, volume 6, 299.
39. Robinson, *Strindberg's Letters*, 328.
40. August Strindberg, *Strindbergs Brev 1858–1876*, edited by Torsten Eklund, volume 1, Bonniers, Stockholm, 1948, 360–363.
41. Olof Lagerkrantz, *August Strindberg*, Wahlstrom & Widstrand, Stockholm, 1979, 67; and Michael Meyer, *Strindberg: A Biography*, Random House, New York, 1985, 82.
42. This is an aspect of both letter and play, which, as far as I know, has never been brought up in the extensive literature on *A Dream Play*. See Kerstin Dahlbäck, "*Ändå tycks allt vara osagt: August Strindberg som brevskrivare*," *Natur och Kultur*, Stockholm, 1994, 286–287. Dahlbäck mentions the seemingly invented nature of the letter, as noted also in the edition of Strindberg's collected letters, but she makes no connection to *A Dream Play*, which premiered with Harriet Bosse playing Indra's Daughter, but this was after she and Strindberg had separated. See also Freddie Rokem, *Strindberg's Secret Codes*, Norvik Press, Norwich, England, 2004.

43. Hans Lindström, *Strindberg och Böckerna II, Boklån och Läsning*, Förteckningar och Kommentarer, Svenska Litteratursällskapet, Uppsala, Sweden, 1990, 25.

44. The source for this information is an article by EBG in the Swedish daily newspaper *Dagens Nyheter*, "*När Strindberg fuskade*" (When Strindberg Cheated), published on April 2, 1939. This article contains an interview with the then owner of the mansion who drew attention to Strindberg's "mistake" in his dream. See also Michael Robinson, *Strindberg and Autobiography*, Norvik Press, Norwich, England, 1986, chapter 4. Robinson discusses the principles of composition of Strindberg's epistolary novel called *He and She (Han och Hon)*. This novel, which was not published during Strindberg's lifetime, despite his efforts, contains most of the letters Strindberg and Siri von Essen exchanged.

45. For a detailed analysis of the preservation of the metaphysical aspects of the theatre and their remodeling from a post-Nietzschean perspective, see my article "*Deus ex machina* in the Modern Theater: Theater, History and Theater History," in *Theorizing Practice: Redefining Theatre History*, edited by W. B. Worthen and Peter Holland, Palgrave Macmillan, Houndmills, England, 2003, 177–195.

46. Jürgen Habermas, "Ernst Bloch—A Marxist Romantic," *Salmagundi* 10–11, Fall 1969 to Winter 1970, 313.

47. August Strindberg, *Ett Drömspel*, in *Samlade Verk*, Norstedts, Stockholm, 1988, volume 46, 76. All quotations are from this edition and references are indicated in parentheses after the quotation.

48. Søren Kierkegaard, *Fear and Trembling & Repetition*, translated by Howard V. Hong and Edna H. Hong, Princeton University Press, Princeton, N.J., 1983, 149. All quotations are from this edition and references are indicated in parentheses after the quotation.

49. Nehamas, *Art of Living*, 154–155.

50. See, for example, Matthew Rampley, *Nietzsche, Aesthetics and Modernity*, Cambridge University Press, Cambridge, 2000; and Aron Ridley, *Nietzsche on Art*, Routledge, London and New York, 2007.

51. Nietzsche, *Birth of Tragedy*, 19. All quotations are from this edition and references are indicated in parentheses after the quotation.

52. Nehamas, *Art of Living*, 9.

Chapter 4

A portion of this chapter was originally published as "Philosophy and Performance: Walter Benjamin and Bertolt Brecht in Conversation about Franz Kafka," in *Assaph: Studies in the Theatre*, 2005, 19–20; and *Bertolt Brecht: Performance and Philosophy*, edited by Gad Kaynar and Linda Ben-Zvi, Tel Aviv, 2005, 1–22. Reprinted with permission.

1. Benjamin, "Notes from Svendborg, Summer 1934," in *Selected Writings*, volume 2, 1927–1934, translated by Harry Zohn, Belknap Press of Harvard University Press, Cambridge, Mass., 1999, 783–791. All quotations are from this edition and references are indicated in parentheses after the quotation.

2. Br 544 (from Werke 1988–1997, volumes 28–30)—quoted from Verner Hecht, *Brecht Chronik 1898–1956*, Suhrkamp, Frankfurt am Main, 1997, 398.

3. *The Correspondence of Walter Benjamin: 1910–1940*, edited and annotated by Gershom Scholem and Theodor W. Adorno, University of Chicago Press, Chicago and London, 1994, #235, 443.

4. Gilles Deleuze and Felix Guattari, *A Thousand Plateaus: Capitalism and Schizophrenia*, translated by Brian Massumi, University of Minnesota Press, Minneapolis and London, 1987, 352–353. See the comparison between chess and Go in Deleuze and Guattari, which corresponds exactly to Benjamin's description and can also be applied to the dramaturgy developed by Brecht. Also discussed at Larval Subjects, September 2006, http://larval-subjects.blogspot.com/2006/09/working-notes-for-appendix-on-deleuzes.html.

5. Benjamin, "Franz Kafka: On the Tenth Anniversary of His Death," in *Selected Writings*, volume 2, 812.

6. Ibid. Compare this formulation with a previous discussion that Benjamin had with Brecht, in June 1931, in Juan-les-Pins, in which the notion of "dwelling" (*das Wohnen*) is discussed. Benjamin, diary entry, 1931, in *Selected Writings*, volume 2, 479.

7. Kafka's story was first published in *Ein Landartzt: Kleine Erzählungen*, Kurt Wolff Verlag, Munich/Leipzig, 1919, 88–89. Here quoted from Benjamin, "Franz Kafka," in *Selected Writings*, volume 2, 812–813.

8. Ibid., 805–806.

9. Ibid., 805.

10. Bertolt Brecht, *Poems 1913–1956*, Theatre Arts Books, Routledge, New York, 1987, 572.

11. Ibid., 314–316.

12. Fredric Jameson, *Brecht and Method*, Verso, London and New York, 1998, 74–75.

13. Ibid., 75. Jameson also reads this notion of "distance" or "split" (*Trennung*) realized through the journey, in the context of Brecht's theory of acting, as the *Verfremdung* between actor and character, "that process of watching one's self act that Brecht so admired in the Chinese theatre."

14. Benjamin, "Svendborg," in *Selected Writings*, volume 2 (all references are indicated in parentheses after the quotation). In a letter to G. Scholem from October 2, 1931, Benjamin writes: "Brecht's thoroughly positive attitude to Kafka's work took me by surprise in some conversations we had during the weeks in question." Scholem and Adorno, *Correspondence of Benjamin*, 383–384.

15. Bertolt Brecht, *Mother Courage and Her Children*, translated by Ralph Mannheim, in *Collected Plays*, volume 5, Vintage Books, New York, 1972, 340.
16. *The Arcades Project*, translated by Howard Eiland and Kevin McLaughlin, Harvard University Press, Cambridge, Mass., and London, 1999 (N3, 1), 463. I develop this notion in detail in the next two chapters.
17. Willet, *Brecht on Theatre*, 1978, 233.
18. See Gösta Bergman, *Den Moderna Teaterns Genombrott*, Albert Bonniers Förlag, Stockholm, 1966, 125. It was Lautenschläger who, on the basis of the Japanese Kabuki stage, constructed the first revolving stage, controlled by an electrical mechanism, at the Residenztheater in Munich in 1896. And Max Reinhardt, during the first years of the twentieth century, demonstrated what some of the artistic potentials of the revolving stage were. In particular this can be seen in Reinhardt's production of *A Midsummer Night's Dream* at the Deutsches Theater in Berlin, in 1905, where the forest moved in front of the audience, no doubt contributing to the popularity of this device. According to Bergman, this was an unrealistic effect, emphasizing that theatre is finally theatre and in fact not an imitation of reality.
19. David Richard Jones, *Great Directors at Work: Stanislavsky, Brecht, Kazan, Brook*, University of California Press, Berkeley, 1986, 96.
20. John Fuegi, *Bertolt Brecht: Chaos, According to Plan*, Cambridge University Press, Cambridge, 1987, 116.
21. Bertolt Brecht, *Mother Courage and Her Children*, translated by Ralph Mannheim, in *Collected Plays*, volume 5, Vintage Books, New York, 1972, 136.
22. George Steiner, *The Death of Tragedy*, Alfred A. Knopf, New York, 1958, 348. See also Peter Thomson, *Brecht: Mother Courage and Her Children*, Cambridge University Press, Cambridge, 1997.
23. Elizabeth Wright, *Postmodern Brecht: A Re-Presentation*, Routledge, London and New York, 1989, 52.
24. Brecht, *Poems*, 415.
25. Bertolt Brecht, *Life of Galileo*, translated by John Willet, Methuen, London, 1980. All quotations are from this edition and references are indicated in parentheses after the quotation.
26. Bertolt Brecht, *Schriften*, 2, Suhrkamp Verlag, Frankfurt am Main, 1993. Also partly in English translation by John Willet, *The Messingkauf Dialogues*, Eyre Methuen, London, 1965.

Chapter 5

A section of this chapter was originally published as "Catastrophic Constellations: Picasso's Guernica and Klee's Angelus Novus," in *International Journal of Arts and Technology*, 1, 1, 2008, 34–42, http://www.inderscience.com/ijart. Reprinted with permission.

Notes to Chapter 5

1. See Michael Taussig, *Walter Benjamin's Grave*, University of Chicago Press, Chicago and London, 2006.

2. Frederic Jameson has used the term "constellation" quite idiosyncratically to discuss "the way in which significant writers assemble their own canon around them," which, according to Jameson, in Benjamin's case was expressed through "the way in which he is able (or unable) to coordinate two frames of reference normally thought to be incompatible." Frederic Jameson, "Benjamin's Readings," *Diacritics*, 22, 304, 19.

3. Eiland and McLaughlin, *Arcades Project* (N3, 1), 462–463. In his preceding note Benjamin had used the following, almost identical, but more compressed formulation:

> It is not that what is past casts its light at what is present, or what is present on what is past; rather, image is that wherein what has been comes together in a flash with the now to form a constellation. In other words, image is dialectics at a standstill. For while the relation of the present to the past is a purely temporal one, the relation of what-has-been to the now is dialectical: is not progression but image, suddenly emergent.—Only dialectical images are genuine images (that is, not archaic); and where one encounters them is language. (Ibid. (N2a, 3), 462)

4. Benjamin, "History," in *Selected Writings*, volume 4, 391.

5. Jeffrey T. Schnapp, "Crash (Speed as Engine of Individuation)," *Modernism/Modernity*, 6, 1, 1999, 2.

6. Ibid., 2–3.

7. Wolfgang Schivelbusch, *Railway Journey: The Industrialization of Time and Space in the 19th Century*, University of California Press, Berkeley, 1986, 131.

8. *The Diaries of Franz Kafka 1910–1913*, edited by Max Brod, Schocken Books, New York, 1948, 33 (December 15, 1910). See also Hartmut Binder, *Kafka in Paris: Historische Spaziergänge mit alten Photographien*, Langen Müller, Munich, 1999.

9. Benjamin, diary entry, 1934, in *Selected Writings*, volume 2, 787.

10. Printed in Franz Kafka, *Tagebücher*, S. Fischer, Frankfurt, 1990, 1012–1017; also available at Reise August/September 1911, The Kafka Project, Mauro Nervi, http://www.kafka.org/index.php?rtbas1911. John Zilcosky claims this passage shows that Kafka wanted to move to a more fluid style, and that here he "resembles the note-taking policeman who, through his writing about the accident achieves a final 'calm' or 'peace' (*Ruhe*)." *Kafka's Travels: Exoticism, Colonialism and the Traffic of Writing*, Palgrave Macmillan, New York, 2003, 12.

11. Theodor Adorno and Walter Benjamin, *The Complete Correspondence 1928–1940*, edited by Henri Lonitz, Harvard University Press, Cambridge, Mass., 1999, 215 (September 23, 1937).

12. Ibid., 222 (November 2, 1937). This exchange is directly connected to Benjamin's difficult financial situation, something that Adorno was trying to help improve—but perhaps not enough.

13. Walter Benjamin, *Berlin Childhood around 1900*, translated by Howard Eiland, Harvard University Press, Cambridge, Mass., and London, 2006, 38–39.

14. Ludwig Wittgenstein, *Notebooks 1914–1916*, Basil Blackwell, Oxford, 1961, 7. See also Anthony Kenny, *Wittgenstein*, Penguin Books, New York and London, 1973; and Ludger Schwarte, *Die Regeln der Intuition, Kunstphilosophie nach Adorno, Heidegger und Wittgenstein*, Wilhelm Fink Verlag, München, 2000. I want to thank Ludger Schwarte for drawing my attention to this passage and to Wittgenstein's preoccupation with accidents.

15. From G. H. von Wright, "A Biographical Sketch," quoted from David G. Stern, *Wittgenstein on Mind and Language*, Oxford University Press, New York and Oxford, 1995, 35.

16. All quotations from the *Tractatus Logico-Philosophicus* are from the translation of D. F. Pears and B. F. McGuinness, Routledge and Kegan Paul, London, 1961. Reference is indicated in parentheses after the quotation.

17. Heinrich-Heine.com, http://heinrich-heine.com/sche1.htm. See also Paul Reiter, *The Anti-Journalist: Karl Kraus and the Jewish Self-Fashioning in Fin-de-Siècle Europe*, University of Chicago Press, Chicago and London, 2008, 17; and Ritchie Robertson, *The "Jewish Question" in German Literature, 1749–1939: Emancipation and Its Discontents*, Oxford University Press, Oxford, 1999, 315–320.

18. *Selected Writings on Art and Literature*, translated by Geoffrey Bremner, Penguin Books, London, 1994, 113.

19. Constantin Stanislavski, *An Actor Prepares*, translated by Elizabeth R. Hapgood, Penguin Books, Harmondsworth, 1965, 159. All quotations are from this edition and references are indicated in parentheses after the quotation.

20. Willet, *Brecht on Theatre*, 121.

21. Ibid.

22. Bertolt Brecht, from "On Everyday Theatre," in *Poems 1913–1956*, edited by John Willet and Ralph Manheim with cooperation from Erich Fried, Routledge, New York, 1987, 176–179. "*Über alltägliches Theater*" has been preserved in Brecht's own typescript and has been dated by the Bertolt Brecht Archives to 1930 and was also, together with the "Street Scene" article, included in the *Messingkauf*. Brecht's critique of the Stanislavski system has become an important aspect of Brecht's own method, but it is unclear to what extent Stanislavski himself was aware of this criticism. This is not the central issue of this discussion, but rather the fact that the accident became paradigmatic for the art of acting. John White, *Bertolt Brecht's Dramatic Theory*, Camden House, Rochester, N.Y., 2004. John White claims that the poems "On Everyday Theater" and "An Address to Danish Worker Actors on the Art of Observation" were written in 1935 (160, note 21), which I find unlikely, and mentions an article called

"*Schauspieler in der Strasse*," published in *Berliner Illustrierter Woche* (May 29, 1930), as a possible source for the idea of an everyday theatre. In this article the words and behavior of a huckster tie salesman are analyzed. The poem "Danish Worker Actors" also refers to a tie salesman. White further claims, "Given that Stanislavski's "An Actor Prepares" also contains an everyday illustration from a street accident to show what this kind of apolitical actor could learn from the situation, it may well be that Brecht's *Straßenszene* model was written as a counterargument to the passage in the Emotion Memory chapter there" (164). When Brecht read Stanislavski's "An Actor Prepares," in 1937, he had already written the poem, but had not yet written "The Street Scene" essay. Stanislavski died in August 1938. See also Joachim Fiebach, "Brecht's *Staßenszene*: Versuch über die Reichweite eines Theatermodells," *Weimarer Beittrage*, 24, 1978, 123–147; Freddie Rokem, "Acting and Psychoanalysis: Street Scenes, Private Scenes and Transference," *Theatre Journal*, 39, 2, 1987, 175–184; Meg Mumford, "Brecht Studies Stanislavski: Just a Tactical Move," *New Theatre Quarterly*, 43, 1995, 241–258.

23. "*Ein lehrreicher Autounfall: Rekonstruktion eines Auto-Unfalls des Dichters Brecht*," in *Uhu—das neue Ullsteinmagazin*, November 2, 1929, 62–65. Article with photos by A. Stöcker / Courtesy Kunstbibliothek Berlin. No details about the photographer are available. *Uhu* was published by the Ullstein publishing company between 1924 and 1934. At its height in October 1929, it sold 211,000 copies, decreasing to 111,000 by April 1933. See Eva Noack-Mosse, "Uhu," in *Hundert Jahre Ullstein 1877–1977*, zweiter Band, Im Ullstein Verlag, Berlin, 1977, 177–207.

24. For additional information on Brecht's Steyr car and the accident, see Hans-Christian von Herrmann, *Sang det Maschinen: Brechts Medienästhetik*, Wilhelm Fink Verlag, Munich, 1996, 143ff and 170–172.

25. Eiland and McLaughlin, *Arcades Project* (N9a, 1), 473.

26. Theodor Adorno, "Commitment," *Aesthetics and Politics*, Verso, London, 1977, 189–190. Originally published in *Neue Rundschau*, 73, 1, 1962.

27. Quoted from Gijs Van Hensbergen, *Guernica: The Biography of a Twentieth-Century Icon*, Bloomsbury, London, 2004, 139. The interview was published in *Les Lettres Francais* on March 24, 1945.

28. George Steiner, *The Death of Tragedy*, Faber and Faber, London, 1961, 354.

29. A somewhat shortened form of the second version was published in French in *Zeitschrift für Sozialforschung*, in May 1936. After that Benjamin began working on the third version of his essay, which was not published during his lifetime.

30. Walter Benjamin, "The Work of Art in the Age of Its Technological Reproducibility," third version, in *Selected Writings*, volume 4, 264.

31. Ibid., 269.

32. Ibid., 270.

33. Ibid.
34. Benjamin, *The Origin*, 55.
35. See James D. Herbert, *Paris 1937: Worlds on Exhibition*, Cornell University Press, Ithaca and London, 1998. There are also several images from the exhibition at La Cucaracha, World Exhibition 1937 Paris, http://lacucaracha.info/scw/diary/1937/may/pavillon. See also Van Hensbergen, *Guernica*.
36. Olinda.com, Art We Don't Like: Entartete Kunst, http://www.olinda.com/ArtAndIdeas/lectures/ArtWeDontLike/entarteteKunst.htm. Georg Grosz's painting *Metropolis* was shown at the *Entartete Kunst* exhibition.
37. Quoted from Van Hensbergen, *Guernica*, 71.
38. Eiland and McLaughlin, *Arcades Project* (N1, 5), 457–458.
39. Benjamin, "Paris, Capital of the Nineteenth Century," *Selected Writings*, volume 3, 2002, 36–37.
40. Benjamin, "History," *Selected Writings*, volume 4, 392.
41. Sigrid Weigel, *Body- and Image-Space: Re-reading Walter Benjamin*, Routledge, London and New York, 1996, 51.
42. Benjamin, "History," *Selected Writings*, volume 4, 392. In the German original: "*Ein Engel ist darauf dargestellt, der aussieht, als wäre er im Begriff, sich von etwas zu entfernen, worauf er starrt. Seine Augen sind aufgerissen, sein Mund steht offen und seine Flügel sind ausgespannt.*" In Walter Benjamin: *Gesammelte Schriften*, Unter Mitwirk, von Theodor W. Adorno und Gershom Scholem hrsg, von Rolf Tiedemann und Hermann Schweppenhäuser, Frankfurt a.M., Suhrkamp, 1974ff, Band I, 197f.
43. Ibid. In the German original: "*Der Engel der Geschichte muß so aussehen.*"
44. Ibid. In the German original: "*Wo eine Kette von Begebenheiten vor uns erscheint, da sieht* er *eine einzige Katastrophe, die unablässig Trümmer auf Trümmer häuft und sie ihm vor die Füße schleudert*" (emphasis added).
45. Rainer Maria Rilke, "Duineser Elegien," in *The Selected Poetry of Rainer Maria Rilke*, edited and translated by Stephen Mitchell, Picador Classics, London, 1987, 170–171.
46. Visitor-comment published in "Gefangen im Palmenhain," Art das Kunstmagazin, July 27, 2007, http://www.art-magazin.de/kunst/491.html. The original painting was exhibited for five days and five nights in Bern, Switzerland, in May 2008, drawing six thousand visitors.
47. Wikipedia, *Guernica*, http://en.wikipedia.org/wiki/Guernica_(painting).

Chapter 6

1. According to Klaus L. Berghahn ("A View through the Red Window: Ernst Bloch's *Spuren*," in *Not Yet: Reconsidering Ernst Bloch*, edited by Jamie Owen Daniel and Tom Moylan, Verso, London/New York, 1997, 202–214),

this "genre" includes, among other texts, Walter Benjamin, *Einbahnstrasse* (*One-Way Street*, 1928), Siegfried Kracauer, *Die Angestellten* (*The Salaried Masses*, 1930), Ernst Bloch, *Spuren* (*Traces*, 1930), Bertolt Brecht, *Geschichten von Herrn Keuner* (*Stories of Mr. Keuner*, 1926–1934), Robert Musil, *Nachlass to Lebzeiten* (*Posthumous Papers of a Living Author*, 1936), and Theodor Adorno, *Minima Moralia: Reflexionen aus dem beschädigten Leben* (*Minima Moralia: Reflections from Damaged Life*, 1944). To my understanding, many of Kafka's shorter prose pieces, like "The Next Village," clearly belong on this list.

2. Benjamin, *The Origin*, 27.

3. Benjamin, "One-Way Street," in *Selected Writings*, volume 1, 447–448.

4. The German word Benjamin has used for "command" is *kommandieren*.

5. Hannah Arendt, introduction to *Illuminations*, by Walter Benjamin, Jonathan Cape, London, 1970, 47.

6. Walter Benjamin, "The Storyteller: Observations on the Works of Nikolai Leskov," in *Selected Writings*, volume 3, edited by Michael W. Jennings, Belknap Press of Harvard University Press, Cambridge, Mass., and London, 2002, 144.

7. Samuel Beckett, *Endgame*, in *The Complete Dramatic Works*, Faber and Faber, London/Boston, 1990, 133.

8. Benjamin, "Svendborg," in *Selected Writings*, volume 2, 788.

9. Benjamin, "The Storyteller," in *Selected Writings*, volume 3, 149.

10. I do not know if Benjamin had already read Bloch's *Denkbilder* collection when he published this story.

11. Walter Benjamin, "*Myslowitz-Braunschweig-Marseilles*: The Story of a Hashish Rausch," The Walter Benjamin Research Syndicate, http://www.wbenjamin.org/story.html.

12. Gerhard Richter, *Thought-Images: Frankfurt School Writers' Reflections from "Damaged Life,"* Stanford University Press, Stanford, Calif., 2007, 7.

13. Ibid., 26.

14. Ibid.

15. J. Hillis Miller, in *Speech Acts in Literature*, Stanford University Press, Stanford, Calif., 2001, has very convincingly shown the indispensable presence of theatre within J. L. Austin's *How to Do Things with Words*. See also Hent de Vries, "Must We (NOT) Mean What We Say? Seriousness and Sincerity in J. L. Austin and Stanley Cavell," in *The Rhetoric of Sincerity*, edited by Ernst van Alphen, Mieke Bal, and Carel Smits, Stanford University Press, Stanford, Calif., 2009, 90–118. De Vries examines the seminal debates around Austin's Euripides quote from *Hippolytus* ("my tongue swore to, but my heart did not"; l. 612). These discussions lie beyond the scope of the present study. It is worth noting however that Walter Benjamin and his extremely keen sense of the relationship between language and the performative have not figured prominently in these debates.

16. Douglas N. Walton, "Practical Reasoning and the Structure of Fear Appeal Arguments," *Philosophy and Rhetoric*, 29, 4, 1996.

17. Sigmund Freud, *The Interpretation of Dreams*, Pelican Freud Library, volume 4, Penguin Books, Harmondsworth, 1982, 201. See also Sarah Ley Roff, "Benjamin and Psychoanalysis," in *The Cambridge Companion to Walter Benjamin*, edited by David S. Ferris, Cambridge University Press, Cambridge, 2004, 115–133.

18. Benjamin, "Franz Kafka," in *Selected Writings*, volume 2, 812. Walter Benjamin, *Gesammelte Schriften*, II, 2, Suhrkamp Verlag, Frankfurt, 1977, 433.

19. Benjamin, "Franz Kafka," in *Selected Writings*, volume 2, 818. See also Benjamin's own essay *"Der Wunsch," Gesammelte Schriften*, II, 3, *Aufsätze, Essays, Vorträge*, Suhrkamp Verlag, Frankfurt, 1989, 1275.

20. Liliane Weissberg, "Philosophy and the Fairy Tale: Ernst Bloch as Narrator," *New German Critique*, 55, 1992, 21–44. See also Günther Oesterle, *"Vom Wünschen und Erzählen: Eine chassidische Geschichte und ihre Variationen bei Ernst Bloch und Walter Benjamin*," in *AufBrüche: Theaterarbeit zwischen Text und Situation*, hrsg. Patrik Primavesi und Olaf A. Schmitt, *Theater der Zeit*, 20, 2004, 183–186.

21. *The Correspondence of Walter Benjamin and Gershom Scholem, 1932–1940*, edited by Gershom Scholem, Schocken Books, New York, 1989, 123. In a note to this letter Scholem added, "In Ernst Bloch's *Spuren*, the same sentence ascribed by W.B. to a 'great rabbi' (GS 2, 423) is quoted from a 'truly kabbalistic rabbi.' But in 1932 W.B. had already borrowed the sentence verbatim in the version originating from me, in his text 'In der Sonne' (GS 4:419): 'Everything will be as it is here—only slightly different.' I learned from this what honors one can garner for oneself with an apocryphal sentence."

22. Scholem, *Correspondence of Benjamin and Scholem*, 130.

23. Benjamin, *The Origin*, 45–46. For an illuminating discussion of this passage, see also Beatrice Hanssen, "Philosophy at Its Origin: Walter Benjamin's Prologue to the *Ursprung des deutschen Trauerspiels*," *MLN*, 110, 4, 1995, 822, note 27.

24. Benjamin, "The Storyteller," 143–144.

25. Ibid., 149.

26. Samuel Beckett, *Waiting for Godot*, Faber and Faber, London, 1975, 62–63.

27. Benjamin, "Franz Kafka," in *Selected Writings*, volume 2, 794–795. Pushkin's and Bloch's versions of the Petuschkow-Shuvalkin story were both published prior to Benjamin's version.

Index

accidents. *See* street accidents
Actor Prepares, An (Stanislavski), 155–158
actors: and acting theory, 155–161; compared to accident witnesses, 155–160; drawing on composite memory, 156; emotional distance of, 71, 160; playing actors, 68–71, 76–77
Adorno, Theodor, 151–152, 161, 170–171
aesthetic Socratism, 116
Agathon, 21–24, 27–29, 33–36, 55–57
agon defined, 33
Alcibiades, 35–36, 55–56; Nietzsche as reincarnation of, 133; as representative of historical action, 13–14, 166
alienation from self, 128, 168, 171
anagnoresis, 52
Analytica Posteria (Aristotle), 50
"ancient quarrel between philosophy and poetry", 3, 12, 31, 38, 40
Andrea, 135–137
Angelus Novus (Klee painting), 82–83, 127, 167, 171–175
Antigone (Sophocles), 49, 67, 77
Antigone's Claim (Butler), 11, 82
Apollodorus, 23–29, 32, 53
Apollonian and Dionysian forces, 39, 50, 57, 83–84, 90, 112–117
"Apology for Actors" (Heywood), 75
Arcades Project, The (Benjamin), 121–122, 128, 143–146, 151, 170–173, 180–183
"Archaischer Torso Apollos" (Rilke), 178
Arendt, Hannah, 180

Aristodemus, 23–30, 56
Aristophanes: as playwright, 13–14; protest of, 53–56; speech on Eros, 34, 38–41
Aristotle, 12–14, 50–52
art, works of, 23, 115
"Attempt at Self-Criticism" (Nietzsche), 114–115
Aub, Max, 169–170
Ausnahmezustand (state of exception), 144
Austin, J. L., 11, 55, 81–82, 186–187

Baroque emblem, 178
Beckett, Samuel, 181–182, 192–193
Benjamin, Walter: childhood memories, 152; compared to *Hamlet*'s Horatio, 181–182; comparing Go (board game) to stage, 120–121; on copying vs. reading, 179; on exhibitions and mass culture, 170–171; on *Hamlet*, 84–86; on Klee's *Angelus Novus*, 14, 82–83, 127, 167, 171–174; life and death of, 118–120, 142–143, 151, 171; on origin (*Ursprung*), 190, 193; on Plato's *Symposium* as template, 26, 57–58; rhetorical strategies as war approached, 146–147; and role of spectators, 145–146; on stories as journeys, 127, 181–182; on technology and reproducibility, 167–168, 184; and thought images (*Denkbilder*), 167–168, 172, 177–182, 185–187; on war and aesthet-

ics, 167–168. Works: "Epistemo-Critical Prologue," 57–58; "Myslowitz-Braunschweig-Marseilles," 183–185; *Notes from Svendborg*, 118, 126–127; *One-Way Street*, 177–180, 182–183; "On the Concept of History," 122, 127, 145, 171–172; *The Arcades Project*, 121–122, 128, 143–146, 151, 170–173, 180–183; *The Origin of German Tragic Drama*, 26, 57–58, 84–85, 169, 178, 190; "The Storyteller," 181–184, 192; "The Work of Art in the Age of Its Technological Reproducibility," 167–168, 184. *See also* Benjamin/Brecht conversation on Kafka

Benjamin/Brecht conversation on Kafka: the actual conversation, 126–127, 137; beggar story, 122–123, 188–191, 194–197; Benjamin's interpretation of Kafka, 105–151, 121, 123–127, 182, 193–194; Brecht's initial reactions to Benjamin's essay, 126; Brecht's interpretation of Kafka, 127–128; common exile in Denmark, 118–120; on journey through memory, 127; messianic perspective, 126–127; reflections on exile, 121–122, 124–126, 142; Talmudic legend, 124

Birth of Tragedy from the Spirit of Music, The (Nietzsche), 115; as allegory for self, 90; dedicated to Richard Wagner, 89–90; on Hamlet, 83–84; on Oedipus as philosopher, 49–50; on philosophy containing theatricalized modality, 90; preface to second edition, 114–115; on Socrates, 56–57, 90; union of Dionysian and Apollonian forces, 39, 112–115; union of male gods, 16, 39, 99

Blau, Herbert, 77

Bloch, Ernst, 108, 184–185, 189–190, 193, 194–197

body: fragility of, 192; leg narratives, 38–47; Oedipus' lack of awareness of, 42, 44, 50–53; performance as scripted embodiment, 52–53; Socrates' care for his, 56; village as, 124

Bosse, Harriet, 105

Brandes, Edvard, 92–93

Brandes, Georg: correspondence with Strindberg, 96–98; on Nietzsche's megalomania, 101; role in Nietzsche-Strindberg correspondence, 88, 91–92, 96; warning to Strindberg, 103

Brecht, Bertolt: on actors as witnesses, 157–160; and car accident, 157, 160–165; and cars, passion for, 119–120; on chain of reports, 26, 158–159; and Copernican/Ptolemaic world pictures, 133–137, 143; and Epic Theatre, 124, 129, 136–137, 157; and focus on spectators, 129, 131, 136; *k-typus* and *p-typus* theatre models, 136–137; life of, 118–119, 121, 128, 131, 142–143, 160–165; and scientific notion of theatre, 132–133; unfinished work on philosophy and theatre, 121; use of revolving stage, 124, 129, 131–135, 142; writing substituting for theater, 146–147. Works: "For Helene Weigel," 131; *Mother Courage and Her Children*, 121, 128–132; "Observation," 142; "On Everyday Theatre," 157–160; *Roundheads and Peakheads*, 120; "Stage Design for the Epic Theatre," 129; *Svendborger Gedichte*, 125; *The Caucasian Chalk Circle*, 131–132; *The Good Person of Szechuan*, 121; *The Life of Galileo*, 132–137, 143; *The Messingkauf Dialogues*, 121, 129, 132, 136, 143–144; "The Street Scene," 26, 157. *See also* Benjamin/Brecht conversation on Kafka

Büchner, Georg, 83
Burbage, Richard, 70–71
Butler, Judith, 11, 81

Caucasian Chalk Circle, The (Brecht), 131–132
Caverero, Adriana, 45

chain of reports, 23–26, 78, 158–159
Chaudhuri, Una, 15
Chekhov, Anton, 15
"Chinese Curios," in *One-Way Street* (Benjamin), 179–180, 183
chronotopos, 127
circular stages, 128–133
Claudius, 62–63, 65–69, 146, 149
coincidence, 98, 153
comedy: Aristophanes' speech avoiding label as, 41; Aristotle on, 13; Polonius on, 69; and tragedy, unifying, 27–30, 32, 37, 41, 58, 147–148
"Commitment" (Adorno), 161
Communist Manifesto (Marx), 78, 80
competition, 3; between Hamlet and Polonius, 72; Hamlet's internal, 60; *agon*, 32–38, 60, 187; within *Denkbilder*, 147
Constantinus, Constantin (Kierkegaard pseudonym), 109–112
constellations: defined, 143–146; and history as catastrophic accident, 152; as performative image, 166–167; and thought-images, 173
continental philosophy, 5–6
copying: difference between reading and, 179–183, 186; Plato on art as, 23, 26

Danton's Death (Büchner), 83
Defence of a Madman (Strindberg), 89
Delphic oracle, 43–47, 192
Denkbilder (thought images), 167–168, 172, 177–182, 185–187
Derrida, Jacques, 78, 80
Diderot, Denis, 155, 157
Diogenes Laërtius, 21–22
Dionysian and Apollonian forces, 39, 50, 57, 83–84, 90, 112–117
Diotima, 24–25, 36–38, 52–54, 108. *See also* Nietzsche
drama. *See* stage; theatre
Dream Play, A (Strindberg), 104–108

Eighteenth Brumaire (Marx), 81
Eliot, T. S., 61–62
Else, Gerald F., 13
Endgame (Beckett), 181–182
Epic Theatre, 124, 129, 136–137, 157
"Epistemo-Critical Prologue" (Benjamin), 57–58
Eros: competition in praise of, 33–34, 38–41; Diotima as Socrates' authority on, 24, 37–38, 54–55; and reuniting of philosopher and thespian, 16; Socrates as philosophical, 36, 38
eroticism, 16; in *Hamlet*, 72; Socrates as true eroticist, 57; between Strindberg and Nietzsche, 93–99 passim; in *Symposium*, 35–38, 93
Eryximachus, 25, 34–35, 41
Essen, Siri von, 89, 101, 103–107
Euripides, 43, 55
exile, reflections on, 15, 121–122, 124, 142, 190

Father, The (Strindberg), 95, 98–99
Ferguson, Alfred, 67
"For Helene Weigel" (Brecht), 131
Fortinbras, 14, 60, 82–83, 166
Freud, Sigmund, 187

Galileo, The Life of (Brecht), 132–137, 144
Gertrude, 62–63, 65–66, 70, 72–73
Gestus, 144
ghost images: interpretations of *Hamlet*'s, 77–81; Socrates as, 113; "spectre haunting Europe," 80; theatre itself as, 77
Giftas (*Married*) (Strindberg), 94
Glaucon, 23, 25, 32, 47
Go (Chinese board game) as stage, 120–121, 126, 132
Good Person of Szechuan, The (Brecht), 121
Goux, Jean-Joseph, 48
Grusha, 132
Guernica (Picasso mural), 161, 166–171, 174–175

Habermas, Jürgen, 108
Hamlet: actor's emotion compared to his own, 71, 72; belief in power of theatre over spectator, 74–75; both philosopher and thespian, 59–61, 67–69, 72–73, 76–79; and competition with Polonius, 72; inner self as true self, 73; madness as role he plays, 72–73; Nietzsche on, 83–84
Hamlet (Shakespeare): commentary by Benjamin on, 84–86; commentary by Nietzsche on, 83–84; commentary by T. S. Eliot on, 61–62; complex multiple perspectives, 61–62; fusion between history and tragedy in, 83; interpretations of ghost, 77–81; juxtaposing philosophical/theatrical discursive practices, 59–60, 76; meta-dialogue of actors playing actors, 61, 69–71, 76–77; motif around Horatio's name, 64–65; motif around silence, 63–65, 77–79, 83, 86, 153, 192; motif around "to be," 63; motif around "to speak," 65; motif around "Who's there?", 60–61, 64, 70, 76, 86; motif around Wittenberg and Elsinore, 62–63, 65–67, 76; playing with theatrical sign systems, 68; repetition as structural feature, 62–64; shared elements with *Communist Manifesto*, 78, 80; shared elements with *Oedipus Tyrannus*, 85; shared elements with *Symposium*, 69. See also individual roles
"Hamlet and His Problems" (Eliot), 61–62
Hamletmachine (Müller), 83
Hansson, Ola, 102
Hegel, Georg W. F., 80–81
"Heine and the Consequences" (Kraus), 154–155
Hemmings, John, 70
Heraclites, 46
Heywood, Thomas, 75
Hippolytus (Euripides), 55
history: angel of, 82–83, 127, 167, 171–175, 181; as catastrophic accident, 152, 169, 172–175, 181; contrasted with poetry, 13; end of, 78, 81–83; fused with tragedy, 83; historical materialism, 145–146; representatives of, 13–14, 60, 82, 166
Homer, 52, 158, 168
homoeroticism. *See* eroticism
Horatio, 63–66, 77–84, 182
How to Do Things with Words (Austin), 55
hubris, 48–49, 60
humans as halved creatures, 38–40, 50–51

images: circle, 128–133; composite memory, 156; constellations as composite, 143–144, 166–170, 173; "dialectics at a standstill," 144–145, 166, 190–191; thought-images (*Denkbilder*), 167–168, 172, 177–182, 185–187
incest, 43–44, 50
Indra's Daughter, 105–110
Inferno crisis, Strindberg's, 91, 103
insanity, real and feigned, 72–73, 84, 87–91, 100–104, 146, 187
Interpretation of Dreams, The (Freud), 187

Jameson, Fredric, 125–126
Jocasta, 43–44, 47, 51
Jones, David Richard, 129
journey, 15; different traveler at end of, 127–128; double perspective of traveler and one at rest, 181–182; memory as backward, 127, 182, 191; of philosophers to attend performances, 31; rotating stage depicting, 128–132, 137; *theoria* and the, 31
Julius Caesar (Shakespeare), 70–71

Kafka, Franz: irony of insurance agent occupation, 150–151; on *unglücklichen Zufällen* (accidents), 123–124, 129, 141.

Works: *Das Schloss*, 124; "The Next Village," 15, 121–124, 131, 141, 182–183. See also Benjamin/Brecht conversation on Kafka
Kierkegaard, Søren, 109–112
Klee, Paul, 82–83, 127, 167, 171–175
Klossowski, Pierre, 91, 102
Köselitz, Heinrich, 93
Kraus, Karl, 154–155
k-typus stage model, 136–137

Laertes, 62, 67
Lao-tzu, 125–126
Laws (Plato), 32
"Lectures on the History of Philosophy" (Hegel), 80–81
"Legend of the Origin of the Book Tao Te Ching" in *Svendborger Gedichte* (Brecht), 125
leg narratives: humans as halved creatures, 38–40; Oedipus' riddle of self-knowledge, 42–47
Levin, Hanoch, 79
Lévi-Strauss, Claude, 42
Life of Galileo, The (Brecht), 132–137, 143

madness. See insanity
man: essential nature of, 50; as halved creature, 38–40; as work of art, 115
Marinetti, Filippo, 168
Married (Strindberg), 94
Marx, Karl, 78, 80–81
memory, 16–17; as backward journey, 127, 182, 191; and image, 145; synthesized composite, 155–157; transmuted into poetry, 156; unreliability of, 24, 28
merry-go-round (*k-typus*) theatre model, 136–137
Messianic themes, 123–124, 127, 145–146, 173, 189–191
Messingkauf Dialogues, The (Brecht), 121, 129, 132, 136, 143–144
missing halves: Aristophanes speech on humans as, 38–40; comedy and tragedy as, 37, 39; incestuous aspect of, 43–44; "one" and "many" in *Oedipus Tyrannus*, 45–47; philosopher and thespian as, 16–17
Miss Julie (Strindberg), 104, 107–108
modernism, 169, 180–181
Mother Courage and Her Children (Brecht), 121, 128–132
motion, portrayed on stage, 128–133
Müller, Heiner, 83
multidisciplinary dialogues, 5–6
"Myslowitz-Braunschweig-Marseilles" (Benjamin), 183–185

name(s): Aristotle on character, 13; of Hamlet shared by son and ghost/father, 77; motif around Horatio's, 64–65; riddle of Oedipus', 42, 51–53
narrator, use of, 23–24, 27, 31–32
Nehamas, Alexander, 3, 111–113
"Next Village, The" (Kafka), 15, 121–124, 131, 141, 182–183
Nietzsche, Friedrich: repeating Socrates, 84, 111–112; acting out Ophelia, 88; as Alcibiades, 113; as Caesar in *To Damascus*, 90, 105; on classical tragedy as ideal expression, 4; and coincidence, 98; *Der Gekreuzigte* (the crucified) signature, 87, 95, 102; on Hamlet, 83–84; and his birth as philosopher, 113–117; madness and playing at madness, 87–88, 91, 100–104; on Oedipus, 49–50; Oedipus as forerunner of, 48; and Richard Wagner, 89–90; and search for uniqueness, 111–112; and Socrates, 56–57, 84, 90, 111–113, 116–117. Works: "Attempt at Self-Criticism," 114–115. See also *Birth of Tragedy from the Spirit of Music, The* (Nietzsche); Nietzsche-Strindberg correspondence
Nietzsche-Strindberg correspondence: attitude toward religion in, 97; circumstances of, 87–92; crossed letters in, 98; as philosopher/playwright

dialogue, 91; erotic subtext of, 95, 97–99; Heinrich Köselitz role in, 93–94; lead-up to, 92–93; madness and playing at madness, 87–88, 91, 100–104; possibility of Strindberg as translator, 94, 98–99; "staging" in, 88; Strindberg-Brandes discussions on, 91–94, 101–103
Nightingale, Andrea Wilson, 31
Notebooks 1914–1916 (Wittgenstein), 153
Notes from Svendborg, Summer 1934 (Benjamin), 118, 126–127

"Observation" (Brecht), 118, 142
Odysseus, 52
Oedipus: as autochthonous creature, 42; hubris leads to downfall, 60; ignorance of own identity, 42–47; implied competition with Socrates, 40–41, 56; as philosopher, 16, 40–41, 45, 48–50; riddle of his name, 51–53
Oedipus at Colonus (Sophocles), 49
Oedipus Tyrannus (Sophocles): Aristotle on, 51–52; "one" and "many" in, 45–47; shared elements with *Hamlet*, 85; shared elements with *Symposium*, 40–41; spectators seeing what Oedipus cannot, 49
one and many, 44–47, 48, 50, 192
"On Everyday Theatre" (Brecht), 157–160
One-Way Street (Benjamin), 177–180, 182
"On the Concept of History" (Benjamin), 122, 127, 145, 171–172
Orgel, Stephen, 75
origin (*Ursprung*), 16, 189–190, 193
Origin of German Tragic Drama, The (Benjamin), 26, 57–58, 84–85, 169, 178, 190

Palitzsch, Peter, 130
panta rei, 46
Paradox of the Actor, The (Diderot), 157
Paris Exhibition, 167, 169–170

Parmenides, 46
Pausanias, 24, 37
performance: copying as self-enactment, 183; and performative functions of language, 147; *Guernica* and *Angelus Novus* as different forms of, 174–175; not science, 135; performative utterances as hollow, 55; of philosophy, 61; as scripted embodiment, 4, 12, 52–53; thought-images as, 173, 185–186
Phaedo (Plato), 21, 86
Phaedrus, 24, 34–35
philosophers, defined, 2
Phoenician Women (Euripides), 43
Picasso, Pablo, 161, 166, 174
picture theory, 153
pioneer, in *Hamlet*, 79–80, 82–84
planetarium (*p-typus*) theatre model, 136, 143
Plato: compared to Shakespeare, 60, 75–76; desire to ban arts from ideal society, 4–5; former writer of tragedies, 21; on purification from resolving philosopher/thespian difference, 47; and search for true knowledge, 47; theory of Ideas, 23–26 passim, 46. Works: *Laws*, 32; *Phaedo*, 21, 86; *Republic*, 23, 25, 30–32, 47. See also *Symposium* (Plato)
play within a play, 12, 69–70, 135–137
Poetics (Aristotle), 13–14, 51–52
poetry: accidents and, 154–156; and "ancient quarrel," 3, 12, 31, 38, 40; and history/philosophy, 12–14, 30–33, 57–58; loses competition, 34, 37–38; should be banned, 31–32, 76; transformed into spirit, 80. See also stage; theatre
pointing, the act of, 166–167, 191
Polonius, 61–62, 69–73
posture, 48
Potemkin's signature, 193–194, 196–197
Powell, Colin, 175–176
promises, as speech-acts, 55, 186, 191

p-typus model of stage, 136–137
purgatory, 79–80
Pushkin, Alexander, 196–197

quarrel, ancient, 3, 12, 31, 38, 40
quoting, act of, 183–186

Railway Journey, The (Schivelbusch), 149
reality, relation of words to, 49, 55
Repetition (Kierkegaard), 109–112
Report of the Task Force on the Arts (Harvard University), 6
reports, chain of, 23–26, 78, 158–159
representatives of history: Alcibiades, 13–14, 166; Fortinbras, 60, 82, 166
Republic (Plato), 23, 25, 30–32, 47
Richter, Gerhard, 185–186
riddle of the Sphinx, 42–43, 46–47, 50–51, 192
Rilke, Rainer Maria, 173, 178
Roundheads and Peakheads (Brecht), 120

scars, significance of, 42, 47, 50–53
Schivelbusch, Wolfgang, 149
Schloss, Das (Kafka), 124
Schnapp, Jeffrey, 148
Scholem, Gershom, 171, 189
scripted embodiment, 4, 12, 52–53
Searle, John, 81, 186–187
Segal, Charles, 49
self-alienation, 128, 168, 171
self-reflexivity, 113, 116, 183–188 passim
Shakespeare, William. *See Hamlet* (Shakespeare); *Julius Caesar* (Shakespeare)
Silenus, statues of, 55–56
sincerity criteria, 81–82
Socrates: ambivalent statements on poetry/drama, 30–31; as ghost, 113; his preparation for death, 56–58, 86, 116–117; implied competition with Oedipus, 40–41; missing comments/information from, 28–29, 37, 40, 53; Nietzsche on, 56–57, 84, 90, 111–113, 116–117; parallels with Nietzsche, 84, 111–113; as philosophical Eros, 36, 38; on philosophy unifying comedy and tragedy, 27–30; as trickster, 47; undermined in *Symposium*, 24–27, 29, 35, 53–56; as victor over playwrights, 30, 33–34, 37–38, 57, 91
Socratism, aesthetic, 116
Sophocles, 49, 67, 77
spectator(s): as active participants, 178, 186–187; Andrea as both actor and, 135; Brecht's utopian wish regarding, 131; freeing, 136; illusion of safety as, 72; and impossibility of repetition, 110–111; objective/subjective, 136; seeing what Oedipus cannot, 49; should be aware of stage, 129
Specters of Marx (Derrida), 78
speech-acts, 11, 81–82, 186–187
Sphinx, riddle of, 42–43, 46–47, 50–51, 192
stage: compared to board game, 120–121; *k-typus* and *p-typus* models, 136–137; "Mother Courage Model" of, 128–131; motion, portrayed on, 128–133; spatial conditions of, 128; thought-images forming a, 172–173, 178–179. *See also* theatre
"Stage Design for the Epic Theatre" (Brecht), 129
standstill, 129, 144–145, 166, 172–173, 182, 191
Stanislavski, Constantin, 146–147, 155–158
state of exception (*Ausnahmezustand*), 144
Steiner, George, 131, 166
stories about storytelling, 188
"Storyteller, The" (Benjamin), 181–184, 192
street accidents: Brecht's own, 157, 160–165; imagery in Kraus, 154–155; imagery in philosophy, 148–151; imagery in Wittgenstein, 152–153; witnesses of portrayed as actors, 155–160

"Street Scene, The" (Brecht), 26, 157
Strindberg, August: compared to Hamlet, 88, 104; compared to Socrates, 108; dream letter and *A Dream Play*, 89, 104–108; faked psychic powers, 107; on hatred between sexes, 93, 95, 97; letters to Ola Hansson, 102–103; as precursor or disciple of Nietzsche, 94–95, 97–98, 100, 103; psychological breakdowns (Inferno crisis), 91, 103; theme of insanity, 88, 96, 98, 103–104; transforming people into characters, 88–90. Works: *A Dream Play*, 104–108; *Defence of a Madman*, 89; *Giftas* (*Married*), 94; *Miss Julie*, 104, 107–108; *The Father*, 95, 98–99; *To Damascus*, 90, 105. *See also* Nietzsche-Strindberg correspondence
Svendborger Gedichte (Brecht), 125
Symposium (Plato): chain of unreliable reports in, 23–28; compared and contrasted with *Republic*, 23, 25, 30–32; discursive universe of, 22–23; as earliest encounter between philosopher/thespians, 21; humans as halved creatures in, 38–40; Platonic irony in, 27; plot of, 23–24, 27–28, 34–35, 38–39, 56; on poetry/philosophy and tragedy/comedy, 14; preoccupation with human body in, 52; shared elements with *A Dream Play*, 108; shared elements with *Hamlet*, 60, 76; shared elements with *Oedipus Tyrannus*, 40–41; shared elements with *The Birth of Tragedy*, 114. *See also* Socrates

technology, impact of: *Guernica* showing at Paris Exhibition, 167–170; Kafka and *unglücklichen Zufällen*, 123–124, 141, 154. *See also* street accidents
theatre: dead can appear in, 79; death of God and modern, 108–109; as ghost, 77; holding a "mirror up to nature," 69, 74; Horatio's staging of Hamlet's death as, 82; as model/conception, 137; Plato and Shakespeare on, 76; presence/awareness of body crucial to, 52; spectatorship in, 110, 116; of the streets, 158–160; as testing ground for philosophy, 112; as therapeutic and cathartic, 74–76. *See also* poetry; stage
theatricalizing of philosophy, 4, 9, 73
theoria and *theatron*, 31
theories of acting, 155–161
thespians, defined, 2
Thespis, 2
thought images (*Denkbilder*), 167–168, 172, 177–182, 185–187
threats, as speech-acts, 186–187, 191–192
Three Sisters (Chekhov), 15
Tiresias, 46
To Damascus (Strindberg), 90, 105
Traces (*Spuren*) (Bloch), 184, 189, 193, 194–197
Tractatus Logico-Philosophicus (Wittgenstein), 86, 153–154
tragedy: Aristotle on, 13; and comedy, 27–30, 32, 37, 41, 58, 147–148; formal components of, 115; as history itself, 147–148; transformed into philosophy, 39–40, 113; from union of Apollonian/Dionysian art, 114–115. *See also Birth of Tragedy from the Spirit of Music, The* (Nietzsche)
traveling, "idea" of, 181–182. *See also* journey

unity and multiplicity, 44–47, 48, 50, 192
Ursprung (origin), 16, 189–190, 193
Utopian future: and end of history, 78, 81–83; *Hamlet*'s ghost pointing toward, 77, 79–81; journey to, 137; and link to past, 78; as supernatural female presence, 108–109; theatre as blueprint for, 131, 137; Wittgenstein and, 86

Verfremdung (self-alienation), 128
victors: none in *Hamlet*, 60; Socrates in *Symposium*, 30, 33–34, 37–38, 57, 91

Waiting for Godot (Beckett), 192–193
Walton, Douglas, 187
Wandering Jew legend, 66–67
Weigel, Helene, 118, 119, 131, 166
Weigel, Sigrid, 172
Weissberg, Liliane, 188
Wekwerth, Manfred, 130
wishes, as speech-acts, 187, 190–191
witnessing: act of, 155–160, 173, 174; chain of, 26, 31–32, 169; goal of *theoria*, 31
Wittgenstein, Ludwig, 86, 152–154. Works: *Notebooks 1914–1916*, 153; *Tractatus Logico-Philosophicus*, 86, 153–154
"Work of Art in the Age of Its Technological Reproducibility, The" (Benjamin), 167–168, 184
Wright, Elizabeth, 131
Wright, Georg Henrik von, 153

Zola, Émile, 88, 98, 99

Cultural Memory | in the Present

Jacob Taubes, *From Cult to Culture*, edited by Charlotte Fonrobert and Amir Engel

Roberto Esposito, *Communitas: The Origin and Destiny of Community*

Peter Hitchcock, *The Long Space: Transnationalism and Postcolonial Form*

Vilashini Cooppan, *Worlds Within: National Narratives nd Global Connections in Postcolonial Writing*

Josef Früchtl, *The Impertinent Self: A Heroic History of Modernity*

Michael Rothberg, *Multidirectional Memory: Remembering the Holocaust in the Age of Decolonization*

Jacob Taubes, *Occidental Eschatology*

Jean-François Lyotard, *Enthusiasm: The Kantian Critique of History*

Frank Ankersmit, Ewa Domańska, and Hans Kellner, eds., *Re-Figuring Hayden White*

Stéphane Mosès, *The Angel of History: Rosenzweig, Benjamin, Scholem*

Ernst van Alphen, Mieke Bal, and Carel Smith, eds., *The Rhetoric of Sincerity*

Alexandre Lefebvre, *The Image of the Law: Deleuze, Bergson, Spinoza*

Samira Haj, *Reconfiguring Islamic Tradition: Reform, Rationality, and Modernity*

Diane Perpich, *The Ethics of Emmanuel Levinas*

Marcel Detienne, *Comparing the Incomparable*

François Delaporte, *Anatomy of the Passions*

René Girard, *Mimesis and Theory: Essays on Literature and Criticism, 1959–2005*

Richard Baxstrom, *Houses in Motion: The Experience of Place and the Problem of Belief in Urban Malaysia*

Jennifer L. Culbert, *Dead Certainty: The Death Penalty and the Problem of Judgment*

Samantha Frost, *Lessons from a Materialist Thinker: Hobbesian Reflections on Ethics and Politics*

Regina Mara Schwartz, *Sacramental Poetics at the Dawn of Secularism: When God Left the World*

Gil Anidjar, *Semites: Race, Religion, Literature*

Ranjana Khanna, *Algeria Cuts: Women and Representation, 1830 to the Present*

Esther Peeren, *Intersubjectivities and Popular Culture: Bakhtin and Beyond*

Eyal Peretz, *Becoming Visionary: Brian De Palma's Cinematic Education of the Senses*

Diana Sorensen, *A Turbulent Decade Remembered: Scenes from the Latin American Sixties*

Hubert Damisch, *A Childhood Memory by Piero della Francesca*

José van Dijck, *Mediated Memories in the Digital Age*

Dana Hollander, *Exemplarity and Chosenness: Rosenzweig and Derrida on the Nation of Philosophy*

Asja Szafraniec, *Beckett, Derrida, and the Event of Literature*

Sara Guyer, *Romanticism After Auschwitz*

Alison Ross, *The Aesthetic Paths of Philosophy: Presentation in Kant, Heidegger, Lacoue-Labarthe, and Nancy*

Gerhard Richter, *Thought-Images: Frankfurt School Writers' Reflections from Damaged Life*

Bella Brodzki, *Can These Bones Live? Translation, Survival, and Cultural Memory*

Rodolphe Gasché, *The Honor of Thinking: Critique, Theory, Philosophy*

Brigitte Peucker, *The Material Image: Art and the Real in Film*

Natalie Melas, *All the Difference in the World: Postcoloniality and the Ends of Comparison*

Jonathan Culler, *The Literary in Theory*

Michael G. Levine, *The Belated Witness: Literature, Testimony, and the Question of Holocaust Survival*

Jennifer A. Jordan, *Structures of Memory: Understanding German Change in Berlin and Beyond*

Christoph Menke, *Reflections of Equality*

Marlène Zarader, *The Unthought Debt: Heidegger and the Hebraic Heritage*

Jan Assmann, *Religion and Cultural Memory: Ten Studies*

David Scott and Charles Hirschkind, *Powers of the Secular Modern: Talal Asad and His Interlocutors*

Gyanendra Pandey, *Routine Violence: Nations, Fragments, Histories*

James Siegel, *Naming the Witch*

J. M. Bernstein, *Against Voluptuous Bodies: Late Modernism and the Meaning of Painting*

Theodore W. Jennings, Jr., *Reading Derrida / Thinking Paul: On Justice*

Richard Rorty and Eduardo Mendieta, *Take Care of Freedom and Truth Will Take Care of Itself: Interviews with Richard Rorty*

Jacques Derrida, *Paper Machine*

Renaud Barbaras, *Desire and Distance: Introduction to a Phenomenology of Perception*

Jill Bennett, *Empathic Vision: Affect, Trauma, and Contemporary Art*

Ban Wang, *Illuminations from the Past: Trauma, Memory, and History in Modern China*

James Phillips, *Heidegger's Volk: Between National Socialism and Poetry*

Frank Ankersmit, *Sublime Historical Experience*

István Rév, *Retroactive Justice: Prehistory of Post-Communism*

Paola Marrati, *Genesis and Trace: Derrida Reading Husserl and Heidegger*

Krzysztof Ziarek, *The Force of Art*

Marie-José Mondzain, *Image, Icon, Economy: The Byzantine Origins of the Contemporary Imaginary*

Cecilia Sjöholm, *The Antigone Complex: Ethics and the Invention of Feminine Desire*

Jacques Derrida and Elisabeth Roudinesco, *For What Tomorrow . . . : A Dialogue*

Elisabeth Weber, *Questioning Judaism: Interviews by Elisabeth Weber*

Jacques Derrida and Catherine Malabou, *Counterpath: Traveling with Jacques Derrida*

Martin Seel, *Aesthetics of Appearing*

Nanette Salomon, *Shifting Priorities: Gender and Genre in Seventeenth-Century Dutch Painting*

Jacob Taubes, *The Political Theology of Paul*

Jean-Luc Marion, *The Crossing of the Visible*

Eric Michaud, *The Cult of Art in Nazi Germany*

Anne Freadman, *The Machinery of Talk: Charles Peirce and the Sign Hypothesis*

Stanley Cavell, *Emerson's Transcendental Etudes*

Stuart McLean, *The Event and Its Terrors: Ireland, Famine, Modernity*

Beate Rössler, ed., *Privacies: Philosophical Evaluations*

Bernard Faure, *Double Exposure: Cutting Across Buddhist and Western Discourses*

Alessia Ricciardi, *The Ends of Mourning: Psychoanalysis, Literature, Film*

Alain Badiou, *Saint Paul: The Foundation of Universalism*

Gil Anidjar, *The Jew, the Arab: A History of the Enemy*

Jonathan Culler and Kevin Lamb, eds., *Just Being Difficult? Academic Writing in the Public Arena*
Jean-Luc Nancy, *A Finite Thinking*, edited by Simon Sparks
Theodor W. Adorno, *Can One Live After Auschwitz? A Philosophical Reader*, edited by Rolf Tiedemann
Patricia Pisters, *The Matrix of Visual Culture: Working with Deleuze in Film Theory*
Andreas Huyssen, *Present Pasts: Urban Palimpsests and the Politics of Memory*
Talal Asad, *Formations of the Secular: Christianity, Islam, Modernity*
Dorothea von Mücke, *The Rise of the Fantastic Tale*
Marc Redfield, *The Politics of Aesthetics: Nationalism, Gender, Romanticism*
Emmanuel Levinas, *On Escape*
Dan Zahavi, *Husserl's Phenomenology*
Rodolphe Gasché, *The Idea of Form: Rethinking Kant's Aesthetics*
Michael Naas, *Taking on the Tradition: Jacques Derrida and the Legacies of Deconstruction*
Herlinde Pauer-Studer, ed., *Constructions of Practical Reason: Interviews on Moral and Political Philosophy*
Jean-Luc Marion, *Being Given That: Toward a Phenomenology of Givenness*
Theodor W. Adorno and Max Horkheimer, *Dialectic of Enlightenment*
Ian Balfour, *The Rhetoric of Romantic Prophecy*
Martin Stokhof, *World and Life as One: Ethics and Ontology in Wittgenstein's Early Thought*
Gianni Vattimo, *Nietzsche: An Introduction*
Jacques Derrida, *Negotiations: Interventions and Interviews, 1971–1998*, ed. Elizabeth Rottenberg
Brett Levinson, *The Ends of Literature: The Latin American "Boom" in the Neoliberal Marketplace*
Timothy J. Reiss, *Against Autonomy: Cultural Instruments, Mutualities, and the Fictive Imagination*
Hent de Vries and Samuel Weber, eds., *Religion and Media*
Niklas Luhmann, *Theories of Distinction: Re-Describing the Descriptions of Modernity*, ed. and introd. William Rasch
Johannes Fabian, *Anthropology with an Attitude: Critical Essays*
Michel Henry, *I Am the Truth: Toward a Philosophy of Christianity*
Gil Anidjar, *"Our Place in Al-Andalus": Kabbalah, Philosophy, Literature in Arab-Jewish Letters*
Hélène Cixous and Jacques Derrida, *Veils*

F. R. Ankersmit, *Historical Representation*
F. R. Ankersmit, *Political Representation*
Elissa Marder, *Dead Time: Temporal Disorders in the Wake of Modernity (Baudelaire and Flaubert)*
Reinhart Koselleck, *The Practice of Conceptual History: Timing History, Spacing Concepts*
Niklas Luhmann, *The Reality of the Mass Media*
Hubert Damisch, *A Theory of /Cloud/: Toward a History of Painting*
Jean-Luc Nancy, *The Speculative Remark: (One of Hegel's bon mots)*
Jean-François Lyotard, *Soundproof Room: Malraux's Anti-Aesthetics*
Jan Patočka, *Plato and Europe*
Hubert Damisch, *Skyline: The Narcissistic City*
Isabel Hoving, *In Praise of New Travelers: Reading Caribbean Migrant Women Writers*
Richard Rand, ed., *Futures: Of Jacques Derrida*
William Rasch, *Niklas Luhmann's Modernity: The Paradoxes of Differentiation*
Jacques Derrida and Anne Dufourmantelle, *Of Hospitality*
Jean-François Lyotard, *The Confession of Augustine*
Kaja Silverman, *World Spectators*
Samuel Weber, *Institution and Interpretation: Expanded Edition*
Jeffrey S. Librett, *The Rhetoric of Cultural Dialogue: Jews and Germans in the Epoch of Emancipation*
Ulrich Baer, *Remnants of Song: Trauma and the Experience of Modernity in Charles Baudelaire and Paul Celan*
Samuel C. Wheeler III, *Deconstruction as Analytic Philosophy*
David S. Ferris, *Silent Urns: Romanticism, Hellenism, Modernity*
Rodolphe Gasché, *Of Minimal Things: Studies on the Notion of Relation*
Sarah Winter, *Freud and the Institution of Psychoanalytic Knowledge*
Samuel Weber, *The Legend of Freud: Expanded Edition*
Aris Fioretos, ed., *The Solid Letter: Readings of Friedrich Hölderlin*
J. Hillis Miller / Manuel Asensi, *Black Holes / J. Hillis Miller; or, Boustrophedonic Reading*
Miryam Sas, *Fault Lines: Cultural Memory and Japanese Surrealism*
Peter Schwenger, *Fantasm and Fiction: On Textual Envisioning*
Didier Maleuvre, *Museum Memories: History, Technology, Art*
Jacques Derrida, *Monolingualism of the Other; or, The Prosthesis of Origin*
Andrew Baruch Wachtel, *Making a Nation, Breaking a Nation: Literature and Cultural Politics in Yugoslavia*

Niklas Luhmann, *Love as Passion: The Codification of Intimacy*
Mieke Bal, ed., *The Practice of Cultural Analysis: Exposing Interdisciplinary Interpretation*
Jacques Derrida and Gianni Vattimo, eds., *Religion*

The authorized representative in the EU for product safety and compliance is:
Mare Nostrum Group
B.V Doelen 72
4831 GR Breda
The Netherlands

www.ingramcontent.com/pod-product-compliance
Lightning Source LLC
Chambersburg PA
CBHW030539230426
43665CB00010B/961